# Critical Moments in Executiv

*Critical Moments in Executive Coaching* examines the change process supported by workplace and executive coaching, making use of empirical evidence from the study of a range of real coaching conversations and coaching relationships. It is both a complete handbook that for the first time gives access to a global qualitative research base in the field of executive coaching, and a look behind the scenes into the practice of both inexperienced and experienced coaches, their clients and their commissioners.

Erik de Haan allows the reader access to the wealth of Ashridge empirical research in this field to date, alongside prominent research groups around the world. This book provides practitioners with a range of suggestions for their contracts, backed up by qualitative and narrative research. It looks at what research is already telling us about the value of coaching conversations and the impact of critical 'moments of change' in coaching, from the perspectives of coaches, clients, stakeholders and sponsors. The detailed research findings outlined in the book are supplemented throughout by case studies and snapshots of coaching moments as well as practical advice and insights for those working in the field. The book also brings forward innovative new models and concepts for coaches which have emerged from research.

*Critical Moments in Executive Coaching* offers an evidence and research-based approach that will be of great interest to coaches in practice and in training, students of both undergraduate and graduate coaching programmes and those who supervise and commission coaching.

**Erik de Haan** is Director of the Ashridge Centre for Coaching at Hult International Business School and Professor of Organization Development at the VU University in Amsterdam, the Netherlands. He is the programme leader of Ashridge's MSc in Executive Coaching and PG Diploma in Organisational Supervision. He has published more than 180 professional and research articles and 12 books, covering his expertise as an organisational consultant, psychotherapist and executive coach.

"Unraveling the coaching process is a major and ongoing challenge with regard to coaching professionalization and its empirical coverage. This is where Erik de Haan's brilliant new book makes an important contribution. It combines his personal experiences as Director of the Ashridge Centre for Coaching with results from recent process-oriented studies as well as his own qualitative research on critical moments in coaching. In a clear and careful way, de Haan describes overlaps and differences in the perspectives of coaches, clients and sponsors. All rounded up by impressive insights into actual coaching sessions and practical guidance for inexperienced as well as experienced coaches. I also highly recommend this book as groundwork for supervision in coaching."

– **Patrizia M. Ianiro-Dahm**, professor in Work, Organizational and
Health Psychology at the University of Applied Sciences,
Bonn-Rhein-Sieg, Germany

"In *Critical Moments in Executive Coaching* Erik de Haan offers a richly textured research-based examination of the entire coaching process including contracting, critical incidents that often signal a developmental shift for coachees and coaches alike and the dynamics of ending. In a discipline that can often be biased towards the application of simple tools and reductionism, this book serves as a powerful reminder of the inevitable subtleties and complexities in the coaching relationship. This major contribution to the coaching literature will appeal to coaches looking to develop their practice as well as learn about qualitative research methodology and how to apply this as a relational approach coaching."

– **Simon Cavicchia**, author of *The Theory and Practice
of Relational Coaching*

"This book draws insightful and genuine connections between personal experiences of the author, research results and tips for coaching practice. A must-read for executive coaches!"

– **Professor Yvonne Burger**, organisational consultant,
executive coach and supervisor

"Insightful, revealing, frank and honest. The handbook for professionals who want to continue learning."

– **Frans Hoek, MBA**, managing partner, Hoek Consultants

"I wanted this book for the title alone. 'Critical moments' is a striking concept that describes the fascinating variety of situations where something crucial happens in a coaching process."

– **Carine Metselaar, MCM**, coaching supervisor and executive coach

"A real behind-the-scenes glimpse into the practice of executive coaching. Surprising insights, thrilling conflicts, critical doubts, dramatic schisms – and everything neatly organised."

– **Dr Tim Theeboom**, coaching researcher

# Critical Moments in Executive Coaching

Understanding the Coaching Process through Research and Evidence-Based Theory

Erik de Haan

LONDON AND NEW YORK

First published 2019
by Routledge
2 Park Square, Milton Park, Abingdon, Oxon OX14 4RN

and by Routledge
52 Vanderbilt Avenue, New York, NY 10017

*Routledge is an imprint of the Taylor & Francis Group, an informa business*

*British Library Cataloguing-in-Publication Data*
A catalogue record for this book is available from the British Library

*Library of Congress Cataloging-in-Publication Data*
Names: Haan, Erik de, author.
Title: Critical moments in executive coaching: understanding the coaching process through research and evidence-based theory / Erik de Haan.
Description: Abingdon, Oxon; New York, NY: Routledge, 2019. | Includes bibliographical references and index.
Identifiers: LCCN 2018060682 (print) | LCCN 2019003443 (ebook) | ISBN 9781351180764 (Master) | ISBN 9781351180757 (Adobe) | ISBN 9781351180733 (Mobipocket) | ISBN 9781351180740 (ePub3) | ISBN 9780815396901 (hardback: alk. paper) | ISBN 9780815396918 (pbk.: alk. paper)
Subjects: LCSH: Executive coaching.
Classification: LCC HD30.4 (ebook) | LCC HD30.4 .H253 2019 (print) | DDC 658.4/07124—dc23
LC record available at https://lccn.loc.gov/2018060682


ISBN: 978-0-8153-9690-1 (hbk)
ISBN: 978-0-8153-9691-8 (pbk)
ISBN: 978-1-351-18076-4 (ebk)

Typeset in Sabon
by codeMantra

To David Gray, dear friend and eminent qualitative researcher in coaching who is leaving us too soon

*"Where love is concerned, too much is never enough"*
Pierre-Augustin Caron de Beaumarchais,
*The marriage of Figaro* (1778)

# Contents

# Introduction

This is unapologetically a book about qualitative coaching research. Executive coaching has now become a true profession and besides the many manuals I believe it is time for a book that gives a thorough overview of the main research results; two books in fact, because this book is about qualitative research results and it will be followed next year by a companion volume on quantitative research results.

So, this is a truly *evidence-based* coaching manual, an overview of discoveries made all around the world about coaching relationships and coaching conversations. I keep as open a mind as possible and allow myself to be influenced by every form of research in this field, from case studies and action research to analyses of tens of thousands of video fragments and hundreds of coaching-moment descriptions. However, the emphasis in the middle chapters does lie on our own Ashridge research into critical moments in coaching, the majority of which has not previously appeared in book form.

With its hundreds of examples of coaching moments and extensive case studies, this book offers a look behind the scenes of executive coaching practice and a glimpse into the experience of coachees and sponsors as well as coaches.

Each chapter has three parts:

A: an anecdote from coaching practice, using many examples of our own, to give a clear and readable introduction to the theme of the chapter. The structure of these stories runs from the very beginning before coaching sessions (Chapter 1), to my very first coaching experience (Chapter 2), to my experiences with different coachees in the same company (Chapter 3), to the highly ideosyncratic and fascinating influences of coachees' personalities (Chapter 4), to the "underbelly" of coaching processes (Chapter 5), to the organisational context of coaching (Chapter 6) and finally to saying goodbye and ending the coaching relationship (Chapter 7). I have done my very best to render case histories anonymous. I have asked permission for as many case examples as I could. Nevertheless, it is possible that the people in a case may recognise themselves, but I trust that they will also know that outsiders or colleagues will not be able to do so. I am well aware of the ethical implications of publishing such real-life case material. However, it is impossible for coaches to continue learning if they cannot do so on the basis of written case materials.

B: a brief summary of the main conclusions or themes of the relevant chapter. So to grasp the essence of the book quickly, you can read just this short part B, or only the summaries at the end of each chapter.

C: a more detailed discussion of the methodology, hypotheses, tentative conclusions and limitations of each study. This part of the chapter is largely based on published peer-reviewed articles, so the reader can see in sufficient detail how the research summarised in part B was conducted. Chapters 2 through 6 deal with research projects into "critical moments" in coaching relationships, as described by coaches, coachees and sponsors. Chapter 1 gives an extensive summary of the original, qualitative research I have been able to find in academic journals (as well as several PhD dissertations and coaching manuals). Chapter 7 features an original piece of research based on a recorded and transcribed short coaching session, accompanied by some of the many doubts and thoughts I had about it afterwards. This research gives an illustration of what qualitative research looks like. And it shows how easy it is to set up an interesting piece of research into your own coaching relationships. Moreover, this fragment provides an insight into the aspects that I consider important when looking at my own coaching. This type of research is not unique in itself, because the overview of research in Chapter 1 includes a similar study of a single short coaching conversation (conducted by Kauffman & Hodgetts, 2016).

Together, these three storylines give an intimate look behind the scenes with plenty of information about how all of the relevant parties (coachees, coaches and sponsors) experience coaching. Readers can empathise with coaches and coachees and their critical moments, and equally with the researchers who are attempting to generate defensible conclusions from a vast wealth of information by drawing general observations from the rich and varied material without losing the colourful and unique details.

My aim was to present the material as accessibly as possible. This is why you can glean the essence of the book just by reading the brief summaries at the end of the seven chapters and why you can familiarise yourself with the material just by reading part B of each chapter. If the material really catches your interest, there are also the more detailed parts C, the anecdotes in parts A and even the bulk of the raw data with many more coaching anecdotes from the studies reported in Chapters 2 through 6 in the extensive appendices at the end.

The use of "I" and "we" alternates because parts of this book were written with co-authors. Specifically, from the second half of Chapter 3 through to the end of Chapter 6, "we" is more prevalent because we worked in teams of researchers. I would once again like to thank my dear colleagues who were closely involved in this research at many different stages and in many different ways: Yvonne Burger, Eddie Blass, Colin Bertie, Andrew Day, Charlotte Sills, Pip Haydock, Christiane Nieß, Monica Stroink and Heather Reekie (as independent MSc students in Organisational Behaviour at Birkbeck University, Monica and Heather conducted all the interviews for Chapter 5) and the "coders" Andy Copeland, Myrna Jelman, Stefan Cousquer, Niraj Saraf, Tsheli Lujabe and Dorothee Stoffels.

I would also like to thank Sue Stewart for translating the originally Dutch chapters into English, specifically Chapters 1, 2 and 7 and the parts A of all other chapters; and Claire Shaw and Rachel Piper from the Ashridge library for sourcing manifold articles and dissertations.

This book will soon be followed by a companion volume summarising the quantitative research in the same field, provisionally entitled *Tenable outcomes of coaching: what are the essential findings of quantitative research?*

Erik de Haan, London, September 2018.

# Chapter 1

# Coaching is doing research

## A. Anecdote

Just before a coaching session begins, I often feel like I am about to sit a test, or an exam. I am hyper-focussed and keep looking at the clock. I want to be precisely on time, not too early, no more than 30 seconds late, and I want to be completely "ready". Often there are only a few minutes between one session and the next, yet I usually manage to sink into a strange kind of trance. I grab another coffee, visit the toilet, glance at my notes from the last time (or if it's a telephone session, set them ready beside the phone), all while keeping an eye on the clock and "clearing the decks" internally. Through all of these automatic actions, completed quickly and efficiently, I end up fully in the moment and become extremely aware of myself, as I am now, and of the coachee I am about to meet in a few seconds' time. Sometimes I make a silly mistake, such as opening my emails just before a session. That's so easy to do these days because we always carry them with us. But it can put me completely off balance: suddenly another relationship crops up and takes over my mind, and inevitably my thoughts shift to that person and to drafting an answer to the message I've just read. I need to be tough and determined to pull myself out of this and use the remaining seconds to settle back into my trance. Sometimes I am obstructed by forces beyond my control, such as when a colleague buttonholes me in the corridor, or traffic grinds to a standstill on the way to a session, making it hard for me to get there on time. Then I break out in a cold sweat, dismayed that I am letting someone down. And in a sense that's true, I am letting them down because my distraction or delay diverts my attention from those initial moments of our session that I myself believe are so important.

Something in me confirms time and again how significant those first few seconds of an encounter are, so I try to be completely open to this beginning of the work. First impressions in any coaching session are not to be taken lightly; they often hint at what the coachee really wants to bring in and what she or he wants to get out of the session. And I can often pick up on how the coachee relates to me as the coach, and to the coaching sessions. At that very beginning, both my coachee and I are more laid bare, more naked, as we have not clothed or distracted ourselves with the happenings in the session. In a sense, I've been musing about this first impression for some time even before the session begins. Ultimately, in those initial moments of an encounter, I often come across as passive, or as neutral, quiet, relaxed, distant – whatever you want to call my regression into my 'trance'. Whereas I feel anything but relaxed. 'Oh right, it's up to *me*, isn't it?' my coachees often say, and then work out for themselves the best way to start the session.

## B. Essences

### *The intimate relationship between coaching and research*

Executive coaching, workplace coaching, career coaching and individual coaching – different names for a form of work-related learning through dialogues. During these conversations, the focus is on the objectives of the "coachee". These objectives often concern problems to which it is not easy to find an answer, such as:

- How to improve certain working relationships or teams
- Achieving ambitious objectives
- Reorienting my actions as a leader

An example: coaching at a Milan fashion house. Last week I received an email from a colleague in Switzerland saying that the company is looking for a coach. We are already on the preferred supplier list and the fact that I speak some Italian has played a role in the selection. My colleague says that 'when I get it', I should definitely visit the head office as it's a beautiful, famous building in the city centre. A number of coach profiles (brief descriptions of the coaches' qualifications and backgrounds) have been sent to Italy and used to select two coaches for a video interview with a board member and the HR director. This interview is to be followed by a chemistry call with the coachee, the new Purchasing Director.

The first interview gets straight to the point. The coachee's leadership style is described using a metaphor from his favourite sport: rugby. 'Luca goes all out for his targets. He keeps pushing and pushing, and doesn't care if people get knocked over or end up trampled and bloodied. What matters is the try that he does usually score'. Two moments from this interview stay with me. First, I misunderstand the word "borderline" and interpret it as referring to a fit of anger. My heart sinks when the Chief Operating Officer (COO) makes clear that I have completely misunderstood. Second, a little later, my despondency gives way to euphoria when I say: 'That's all very clear and as I understand it you've discussed it with Luca as well. If it's so clear, why does he need a coach in addition to his line manager?' A long silence follows, and then the COO says, 'that is a good question and I have no answer to it'. After another silence, he says: 'it would be good for Luca if we could hold up a mirror to him a bit more and if he could discuss specific, recent examples'.

Based on the chemistry session or click interview, the coachee chooses a coach and a first coaching session is held, often accompanied by several interviews with those closest to the coachee. After the first session, the coach draws up a provisional contract in which she attempts to summarise the coachee's objectives. In my case, this contract usually consists of two or three paragraphs identifying areas in which the coachee wants to develop. After summarising, I usually write encouragingly that these are areas that lend themselves well to shared exploration in coaching: right away, this is the first occurrence of the concept of exploration, that is, "research", in connection with coaching. In my contract, I also try to mirror the coachee's own words as far as possible. Sometimes I intentionally add a summary in my own words, or even a cautious hypothesis, to see how my own initial understanding goes down with the coachee.

Coachees' responses to this first contract, sent to them personally in confidence, differ widely. Often there is no response, and it is up to me to raise it again in the second session, whereupon the coachee usually says 'fine' or 'I really recognised myself in it'. Other coachees reach for the red pen or the track changes option on their computer and set to work. Sometimes there are additions, possibly coming from managers. I regard this first written contract as very helpful because it gives direction. With a contract, you enter into a much more targeted relationship, one that will take responsibility for what you achieve. Often the first written contract quickly becomes outdated due to advancing insight or things that happen at the coachee's work. Sometimes, it's because the objectives are achieved much sooner than initially envisaged. Nevertheless, it is helpful to compare even an outdated contract with the final results later on, because this often shows that there is much to celebrate and that the "case" looks different after a few months have elapsed.

Coaching contracts are less SMART (specific, measurable, attainable, realistic, time bound) than most other professional contracts in organisations, although to some extent they are similar to employment contracts (Sills, 2012). We can also compare coaching contracts with research plans. The first objectives can then be seen as a few "hypotheses" to be tested by further research. Like academic research, coaching is both about achieving existing objectives and about founding out something new that is even more relevant or ambitious for the coachee.

Another similarity between coaching and research lies in the underlying ethical principles. Coaching, writing about coaching and conducting research with participants or test subjects are governed by very similar ethical standards and principles. Here is an overview of these moral foundations which support integrity in coaching and also in research:

1 Independence – guarding the client's autonomy. It is important for coaches and researchers alike to be able to pursue their work wholly independently of influence from financial backers, sponsors or funding providers. And a crucial degree of independence must be maintained with regard to clients themselves and their issues, and those of other stakeholders such as their line managers. This is why it is so important that coaches (or researchers) do not enter into any partnerships or relationships with their clients (or research participants) other than a pure coaching (or research) relationship.

2 Informed consent – from the outset, the client must have a reliable idea of what she is getting involved in and what will be asked of her. This is why a written contract containing defined agreements is important, as well as a first informal meeting to discuss potential cooperation. If traceable information is to be cited in other forums, consent must be sought in advance and the client must feel truly free to say no.

3 Confidentiality – all information obtained in connection with the work must be treated with absolute confidentiality. This is why all of the case studies in this book have been anonymised and rendered untraceable. There may be an option of publishing or conducting research jointly, in which case traceable attributions can be made, provided that the client has given her explicit consent and is free to say no.

4  <u>Respect and diversity</u> – coaching should allow for multiple voices and perspectives, and treat at-risk groups or vulnerable parties with respect and care. This applies equally to research. Good coaching and research strengthen diversity and show respect for even the softest dissenting voices and tiniest notes of discord, if only because a single counterexample can revive an entire research programme or even an entire professional field. Special attention should be paid to the fact that the coachee is an active and sometimes vulnerable participant in the coaching sessions. In participatory research, this applies likewise to the research subjects.

5  <u>Integrity and trust</u> – this covers various aspects such as compliance with legislation, such as personal data protection laws, as well as integrity in a broader sense in the areas of data handling, data analysis and the publishing process. Finally, it includes fairness towards clients and striving for a high quality of service, supported by regular supervision or (in the research field) independent peer review.

## C. Summary of qualitative research in coaching

Qualitative research in coaching starts with the coaching session itself. During all coaching sessions, the coach and the coachee investigate what the coachee puts forward and wants to accomplish. Together they explore what this session is about, what else might be relevant and how to achieve the objectives. Moreover, one could argue that this exploration (i.e. qualitative research) is all they do together; the implementation of findings thereafter is entirely left to the coachee. So, one can argue that executive coaching is essentially a form of (collaborative) qualitative research, which takes place in a privileged, confidential environment. The outside world will have no knowledge of it, nor does this research explicitly inform other coaching sessions, for example, by other coaches or coachees.

A next step for coaching-researchers is to conduct research into their own coaching, for example, during the preparation of case studies on the basis of reflective notes. *Qualitative* research stays as close as possible to the events in the sessions themselves. This form of research does not work in the same way as the contrasting *quantitative* method which uses a myriad of 'data points' (usually numbers, more broadly: discrete, quantifiable information reported retrospectively) to make statistically reliable statements. Qualitative research starts from 'rich data': emotions in the moment, stories, notes and recordings, and it tries to achieve a cohesive understanding of that underlying richness.

In this chapter, I give an overview of the qualitative research conducted to date in the field of executive coaching and what that research has shown.

Quantitative research, in essence, takes sequences of numbers originating from coaching assignments (such as rated coaching outcomes according to various parties involved) and generalises to produce statistically reliable statements applicable to all coaching assignments. For example, the usual 'discovery' in quantitative papers is that the coaching sessions showed an average client-perceived effectiveness of 7.6 on a 10-point scale and that the spread of these outcomes was less than 1.8, in which case we can be reasonably certain that the sessions were fairly effective in the view of most clients. Any statement that quantitative researchers can make – and such statements are thin on the ground due to the statistical requirements that need to be met – immediately raises follow-up questions that cannot be answered. Once quantitative research has established a significant degree of effectiveness, questions arise such as

- 'Exactly how is that effectiveness achieved?'
- 'What makes some coaching sessions more effective than others?'
- 'How does this effectiveness manifest itself in the coachee's organisation?'
- 'How can you tell within the organisation that coaching has been effective?' or
- 'What does this result mean for my own specific coaching assignment?'.

All of these logical follow-up questions require very extensive follow-up research. No matter how easy it is to ask such questions, the quantitative researcher is usually unable to answer them.

Qualitative research, on the other hand, starts with extensive descriptions (or recordings) of the events themselves and thus with a detailed picture of what happens within coaching. This material *can* supply an answer to follow-up questions, albeit a personal and provisional answer, with no confidence interval or generalisability. The difference from quantitative research is substantial: quantitative research has to reduce an entire coaching assignment to a single number (or a row of numbers), while qualitative research takes time to listen very carefully to a whole story flowing from, say, a single moment in a session. Qualitative research provides a detailed, nuanced, coherent answer, but with no idea of whether it can be generalised. Nevertheless, based on this detailed account and descriptive information, qualitative research can ultimately lead back to quantitative research, provided that sufficient corresponding "data points" can be generated. However, a condition is that we need to gather a large number of such data. In addition, qualitative research produces new suggestions for questions to be investigated by means of quantitative research, and can even yield new theoretical variables and verifiable coaching models, as we will see later in this book.

Coaching is still an emerging profession, so there are very few systematic overviews of qualitative research (one exception being Athanasopoulou & Dopson, 2018, which included both quantitative and qualitative research articles). Below I aim to present a thorough overview of all qualitative research conducted to date in the field of executive and workplace coaching, including brief summaries of what this research has shown.

A vast amount of qualitative research has already taken place within coaching, for example:

Case studies based on client or coach experiences (see, e.g., Levenson, 2009).

Process research conducted by studying reports or direct recordings of sessions (see, e.g., Gessnitzer & Kauffeld, 2015; Ianiro, Schermuly, & Kauffeld, 2012).

Process research via interviews and surveys (see, e.g., Wasylyshyn, 2003).

Action research (see Reason & Bradbury, 2001) as a deeper exploration of coaching practice and of new actions within the coaching relationship (see De Haan et al., 2013, for a book brimming with research articles on coaching based on action research methodology).

Field research, often a form of participatory research in practice, for example, research via evaluation forms, Q-sort techniques and one-to-one or panel interviews (see, e.g., Perkins, 2009).

Table 1.1 An overview of qualitative research methods; the main distinctions are between simultaneous (phenomenological) and retrospective, and between researcher involved in the material (self-research) and remote researcher (independent research)

| Qualitative research methodologies | Phenomenological | Retrospective |
|---|---|---|
| Self-research | 1. Action research | 2. Case-study analysis |
| Independent research | 3. Field research | 4. Process research |

Descriptive research into coaching interventions and coaching situations, as reflected in numerous manuals and practical studies on coaching (see, e.g., Liljenstrand and Nebeker, 2008).

Often it is the coaches themselves who conduct qualitative research, in the role of researchers studying their own practice or that of other coaches. The coach's perspective on coaching sessions is therefore over-represented in the literature, and some studies may suffer from partisanship or bias on the part of the researchers, as they may embrace or highlight their own ideas, concepts and theoretical influences in the "research material". With the exception of action research, which is a disciplined form of self-study, results are usually better when the research is more independent, that is, when the researchers themselves are not part of the coaching practice being studied.

Table 1.1 contains a classification of the different types of qualitative research.

Here is an overview of these research traditions in executive coaching, with a summary of the most important and original qualitative research articles I have been able to find:

1   **Action research studies**

Action research is an extremely rich and creative exploration of coaching in real time, working from session to session. The process asks coaches (or clients) to formulate a research question and to study (i.e. explore, respond to, refine or transform) this question in their own practice. It also allows experimentation with the research question because the coach can, for example, try out a different type of intervention and then see what the result is in practice. Action research further allows other parties to be involved, although, of course, they do need to be informed in advance and give their informed consent. For coachees, taking part in research can be problematic: coaching is about them and serves their issues, so coaching objectives can be undermined if the client is distracted by considering and answering action someone else's research questions. The emphasis can then be placed too much on the coach at the expense of benefits for the coachee. Nevertheless, action research can yield much that is positive for the coach's practice: both generalisable and testable observations, as well as a deep study of active ingredients and emotions during coaching, which other coaches can benefit from. Moreover, action research opens up a cycle of research and of influencing the coaching process itself (via the learning process of the action researcher, that is, usually the coach), so it can also benefit the coaching itself.

Here are some examples of action research in coaching, collected from final theses published by graduates of the Ashridge MSc in Executive Coaching: Jane Cox (2012) studied the importance of idiom in coaching and the experience of coaching in a second or third language. She concludes that the experience and results of coaching are less dependent on such language barriers than was previously thought, and that time lags due to working in a foreign language can even benefit the process as they allow more reflection before a response. David Skinner (2012) studied the political influences of various stakeholders in multiparty contracts at the top of large multinational organisations. Rob Watling (2012) studied his own learning process en route to a different style of coaching. The book *Behind Closed Doors* (De Haan et al., 2013) summarises research by 15 other coaches focussing on a wide range of subjects, such as their own identity as coaches, the influences of self-criticism, self-disclosure, humour, safety and trust, and somatic perceptions on coaching relationships.

## 2  Case-study analysis

Case studies also bring the researcher very close to the live practice of coaching and enable fresh observations, but this is usually done retrospectively. Case studies attempt to recount the whole story of a coaching assignment, or a single coaching session, usually in chronological order. Choices made by coach and client from moment to moment are subjected to retrospective investigation, and the long-term effects of interventions can be monitored.

Here are some examples of case-study research in coaching:

A  <u>A single case with depth:</u> Older studies such as those by Winum (1995), Diedrich (1996), Kiel, Rimmer, Williams and Doyle (1996) and Tobias (1996) describe cases as illustrations of a particular approach, as do Day (2010) and Kets de Vries (2013). The cases from the 1990s, that is, the early days of executive coaching, show how the profession has changed and has become less dependent now on psychometric instruments, regular feedback with management and colleagues, and long-term involvement of the executive coach. Orenstein (2002) explores three case descriptions from her own practice as an illustration of the psychological depth of coaching conversations. Mansi (2007) describes an individual case in which a psychometric instrument played an important role. Blattner (2005) describes a case of executive coaching that lasted for two years. Peterson and Millier (2005) describe their collaboration as coach and coachee in quite a lot of detail, as do Freedman and Perry (2010) who describe a critical, intensive and lengthy case from their own perspectives, namely that of both coach and client, as is also done by De Haan and Nieß (2012; see Chapter 6 of this book).

Schnell (2005), Fahy (2007), Lawrence (2015) and Nanduri (2018) present case studies showing how coaching can support organisational change and growth. Schnell (2005) reports on a five-year internal coaching assignment for two "co-leaders" in a university institute evolving from a pioneering organisation towards vigorous growth and professionalisation. Fahy (2007) describes a senior team of 12 executives, each coached by himself as part of a cultural shift in a technology company. Lawrence (2015) researches – through longitudinal interviewing – his own two-year struggle to further a 'coaching culture' in a small Australian multinational with little experience of coaching or reflective dialogue, involving 15 coaching relationships (nine different coaches). Nanduri (2018) coached six managers and an HR business partner over a period of three months (five sessions) during a radical reorganisation, and conducted a phenomenological analysis after the end of the assignment.

Kauffman and Hodgetts (2016) take the transcript of a single, short coaching session as the starting point for detailed analysis of the conceptual and practical choices made by a coach. By introducing several perspectives on the same case, they explore the benefits of multiple perspectives in coaching. The same approach is taken in Chapter 7 of this book, where research is also conducted on the basis of a transcript of a single brief session.

B   Comparison of multiple cases: Huggler (2007) interviews six CEOs recently coached by herself. Levenson (2009) provides detailed information on the positive effect of coaching within a company using 12 of his own successful case studies, and analyses factors contributing to successful outcomes; he concludes that transfer to the workplace is the most important factor. Ben-Hador (2016) conducts a multiple case study of 23 of her own coaching contracts between 2011 and 2013 in eight organisations in Israel, based on 79 interviews with all parties involved. She describes her struggle with a hidden agenda often present in the organisation: that of assessing and influencing the managers through their coach. Hurd (2009) also describes four short cases of his own. Foster and Lendl (1996) illustrate through four case studies how EMDR (eye movement desensitization and reprocessing) can help when coaching executives who are struggling with a traumatic experience such as a serious accident, the need to face high-level job interview panels after decades in a tenured position in a different sector or, in the case of a CEO, a humiliating lay-off. Similarly, Anderson (2002) shows how rational-emotive behavioural therapy can be used in coaching with the help of seven short cases, and Gray, Burls and Kogan (2014) do the same for positive psychology, with five.

More good case studies are described in coaching handbooks for specialised applications, such as coaching in education (e.g. Van Nieuwerburgh, 2012) or coaching in specific cultures (e.g. Gallo, 2015, regarding coaching in China).

### 3  Phenomenological field research

Real-time field studies involve surveying coaches and coachees in action, to find out more about the intervention and about their experiences with coaching. Researchers get close to the existing coaching practice and interview participants, while they are still mid-process. Sometimes the researcher plays a dual role, that is, including that of coach (e.g. in Perkins, 2009). There is a degree of overlap with action research, which often describes this form of research as "action research in the second or third person" (see Reason & Bradbury, 2001), but there it usually goes hand in hand with the much more introspective form of first-person action research as described above.

Here are some examples of field research in coaching: Alvey and Barclay (2007) studied the development of trust in coaching relationships by interviewing 27 senior managers who had received coaching. They rank their identified factors and show how trust can build up incrementally over time for many of these coachees. Gray and Goregaokar (2010) studied how SME (small and medium enterprise) coachees choose their coaches by interviewing them during coaching relationships. Their coaches were also interviewed in forum groups. The authors show that gender played a major role in the choice of coach and how sexism was invariably at play when male coachees chose their female coaches. Brauer (2005) used interviews to examine the effects of greater or lesser degrees of voluntariness on the part of coachees. Skinner (2014) studied executive coaching for female leaders and showed how coaching can help female leaders develop their own role identity independent from dominant and traditional male role models. Rohmert and Schmid (2003) interviewed coachees several times during their coaching processes. Peel (2008) compares the coaching in ten SMEs in Wales and highlights factors that may differ compared with coaching in larger organisations, such as the dominant role played by senior executives in such companies (where ownership and senior management coincide). During a three-year systematic field study, Gray, Gabriel and Goregaokar (2011) interviewed up to 46 coachees at the top of SMEs in Surrey each just after the end of ten hours of coaching, and then reflected on the interview transcripts with two focus groups of altogether nine coaches. They discovered that the coaching had been more 'personal development' than 'performance improvement', even though the coachees attached more importance to the latter. Gray, Gabriel and Goregaokar (2015) undertook a longitudinal field research during 24 months among 13 managers who had recently become unemployed, starting the interviews after the completion of ten hours of coaching. All but one of the managers remained unemployed during the period of study, and they generally reported strong negative feelings about their unemployment and very mixed feelings about their coaching. Gray et al. (2015) found a positive relationship between the managers' attitudes towards the coaching and their ability to learn from their trauma. Buckle (2012) looks specifically at the use of psychometric instruments by interviewing three coaches and coachees with relevant experience. Yedreshteyn (2009) examines an internal coaching programme for 18 coachees by conducting a progressive case study of the entire programme. Machin (2010) studies internal coaching programmes from the coach's and coachee's perspective. He discovered that, even during brief internal coaching, a great deal of (psychological) depth was observed and appreciated by both sides, so it seems crucial for coaches to be prepared for this in internal coaching programmes as well. O'Broin and Palmer (2010) conducted field research among six coachees and six coaches to identify the dimensions needed for a "good coaching relationship"; both groups turned out to share very similar ideas about that.

In a comprehensive article, Perkins (2009) describes a particular form of field research in which he first rated 21 of his own coachees on "team leadership" during meetings, then coached them for as many months as were deemed necessary; finally, he observed and scored them again on their leadership behaviour. This type of pre- and post-measurement clearly contributes to the coaching process itself, and to research in the field of coaching, and makes the study at the same time less convincing as "evidence" for some kind of overall effectiveness of coaching if only because of the coach doing the scoring.

There is also ample field research into coachee and coach factors for success in coaching, for example, Blackman (2006) uses surveys among 114 current and recent coachees to study factors within the coach, coachee, coaching process and organisation that seem important to coachees for successful coaching. Liljenstrand and Nebeker (2008) surveyed 2,231 coaches to detect differences in their practices and thinking about coaching when coming from different backgrounds, namely those emerging from psychological, clinical, educational or business-school training, or still "other" qualifications.

A thorough way to do field research is by rigorous application of multiple live case studies (Yin, 1994). Audet and Couteret (2012) demonstrated this by comparing six cases of intensive coaching (up to one day a week) by experienced entrepreneurs for the benefit of start-up entrepreneurs. The cases ranged from very successful to unsuccessful, and the authors showed that the main ("necessary") factors determining success belonged entirely to the coachee: receptiveness to coaching, commitment to the coaching and respect for the coaching contract. Styhre (2008) conducts another impressive longitudinal field study by (re-)interviewing six site managers in the construction industry as they receive individual and group coaching from the same coach. Styhre discovers a multilayered contribution of executive coaching in terms of reflection and self-observation.

## 4 Process research studies

Process research seeks to map out and investigate aspects of coaching, including perspectives on the dynamics between coach and coachees, interaction patterns and active ingredients according to various parties involved. This type of research can take many different forms, as we will see in this overview. Common methods of data collection are interviews or recordings of conversations, which are then documented and examined by means of image, audio or textual analysis. Researchers can break down texts with the help of "grounded research", to yield meaningful fragments which can be studied to find themes and categories that appear to be of interest to those involved in the coaching process. Once categories have been identified, interviews and other textual or recorded (audio, video) information can be coded, and then even quantitative analysis can take place in some cases.

Here are some examples of process research in coaching: Hall, Otazo and Hollenbeck (1999) interviewed 75 executives and 15 coaches asking about coach behaviours that they found most helpful in the coaching conversations. Both coaches and coachees emphasised listening, but coachees also mention the introduction of helpful ideas, feedback and challenge as being very important.

David, Clutterbuck and Megginson (2014) base their study of the effectiveness of coaches in different countries on interviews. Rekalde, Landeta and Albizu (2015) and Salomaa (2017) studied observations of success criteria (or factors in effectiveness) among coaches, coachees and sponsors – Salomaa more specifically among expatriate coaches. Burger (2013) talked to top executives of large organisations, executive coaches and non-executive directors, to compare experiences of executive coaching on the part of leaders, sponsors and coaches. Bickerich, Michel and O'Shea (2018) studied the views of 15 coachees and 18 coaches on the use of coaching during organisational change. They found clear overlaps in terms of perspectives, but also differences. Coachees seem more focussed on practical help in terms of leading the changes and overcoming resistance, while coaches focus more on the coachees themselves and the coaching conversations, including emotions during the conversations. Terblanche, Albertyn and Coller-Peter (2017) studied experiences of transition coaching among 16 recently promoted leaders who had been coached during their transition, as well as their coaches and sponsors (see Chapter 6 of this book, where these three perspectives are also analysed). Stevens (2005), Bush (2005), Gyllensten and Palmer (2007), MacKenzie (2007) and Timson (2015) analysed the coachee experience of the coaching relationship by means of retrospective interviews. In the first three studies of seven, ten and nine executives with positive memories of coaching, Bush (2005) asked about "effectiveness" and Gyllensten and Palmer (2007) about the "coaching relationship". The fourth study, by MacKenzie (2007), took place in the context of a major leadership programme at the Royal College of Nursing. It involved interviews with eight coaches and asked a very open question about "your experience with coaching as part of the programme". Timson (2015) asked six coachees about their experiences after a brief resilience coaching intervention in the same organisation. Motsoaledi and Cilliers (2012) conducted research based on psychodynamic role analysis and extensive notes after each session, during ten months of coaching with six culturally diverse executives in a South African context. They show how psychodynamic coaching can help in understanding and learning to deal with conscious and unconscious intercultural dynamics.

A particularly fruitful programme of process research via filmed or recorded sessions was pioneered by Greif (2010) and Graf (2012), and then continued by Adrian Myers (2014). In his PhD, Myers looked at the descriptions of video-recorded coaching sessions given by different coachees and coaches. He found that coachees focus mainly on their interpersonal needs and on the space and structure to develop new perspectives. Coaches, on the other hand, focus on the application of their expertise and on choices made during their interventions. Different coaches interpreted the six recorded sessions very differently. Factor analysis shows that all Q-sorts spanned only two factors: 'client-led' coaching and 'process-led' (directive) coaching (Myers & Bachkirova, 2018). Two sessions could be shown to be more client-centred and two more directive (with the other two in between).

Braunschweig University produced a fascinating series of quantitative studies based on such process research, including Ianiro, Schermuly and Kauffeld (2012), Ianiro and Kauffeld (2014), Gessnitzer and Kauffeld (2015), Ianiro, Lehmann-Willenbrock and Kauffeld (2015) and Will, Gessnitzer and Kauffeld (2016). Here is a summary of these researchers' findings, based on their analysis of thousands of consecutive moments in sessions:

A   Ianiro et al. (2012) coded and analysed the complete coaching interaction belonging to 33 initial coaching conversations, on the basis of video recordings. Trainee psychologists acted as coaches, with students from other faculties taking the role of the coachees. The authors observed how coachee and coach behaved towards each other, focussing specifically on two fundamental variables: affiliation and dominance (Leary, 1957). From their findings, they conclude that both (1) the dominant behaviour of the coach and (2) comparable (observers') scores for dominance and affiliation in coach and coachee predict that after five sessions, the coachee will award more positive scores for (a) achieving goals and (b) quality of the relationship with the coach.

B   Ianiro and Kauffeld (2014) coded and analysed video recordings of the first coaching session of 48 coaching dyads and, just before the session, asked all coaches and coachees to score their mood using the Multi-Dimensional Mood Questionnaire (MDMQ, with sub-scales: good/bad mood, awake/tired and calm/nervous). The coachees also scored the working alliance after the fifth session, that is, three months later. Regarding coach behaviour, once again coach and coachee dominant-friendly behaviours (as seen by the observers) were found to correlate clearly, and both also correlated with the working alliance as scored by the coachee; in fact, coach behaviour emerged as the best predictor. The authors further found that coach mood (and also coachee mood) correlated significantly with their own dominant-friendly behaviour and with the working alliance as ultimately scored by the coachee, but only on the "good mood" and "calm" sub-scales, not on that of "awakeness", although the latter was negatively correlated with dominant-friendly coachee behaviour.

C   Gessnitzer and Kauffeld (2015) this time coded the video recordings of the first, third and fifth (last) coaching sessions of 31 coaching dyads (i.e. 93 sessions in total) and showed that the working alliance aspects "agreement on goals and tasks" and "affective bond" coded by observers scarcely correlated with the same working alliance aspects measured by coach and coachee using a standard questionnaire. Only the observed working alliance behaviours with respect to "agreement on goals and tasks" *initiated by the coachee* turned out to correlate with coaching outcomes (as measured by coachees in terms of the progression towards own goals).

D   Ianiro et al. (2015) looked for the first time at sequences in the coding, that is, at the order of behaviours between coach and coachee. All five coaching sessions of 31 psychology students, who were again coaching students from other faculties, were this time recorded and coded per behavioural segment. Frequencies of behaviour sequences were measured and by comparing with random fluctuations Ianiro's team could demonstrate that friendly coaching behaviour significantly evoked friendly coachee behaviour and vice versa. Moreover, the degree of this "mutual affiliation behaviour" predicted a higher score on working alliance. In addition, dominant-friendly coaching behaviour was found to be the only behaviour that significantly evoked dominant coachee behaviour and vice versa (whereas other dominant coach behaviour, namely both neutral and hostile, in fact, evoked dependent coachee behaviour). Dominant coachee behaviour related, in turn, to positive outcomes from the third session onwards (outcomes in terms of self-scored effectiveness on goals). Moreover, the opposite also appears to be true: dependent coachee behaviour was significantly inversely proportional (negatively correlated) to the same outcomes.

E   Will et al. (2016) analysed 19 video recordings of one-off sessions between 19 coach-coachee pairs in the same university setting. They measured not only self-perceptions of coaches' (cognitive) empathy but also their coachees' perceptions and compared these with observed empathic interventions (consisting of paraphrasing and naming coachee feelings). The authors found no correlation between coaches' and coachees' assessments of the coach's empathy. They went on to demonstrate that in these coaching sessions only coach paraphrasing was correlated with the coachee's perception of coach empathy. However, sequential analysis showed that both aspects of empathy (paraphrasing and naming coachee feelings) in the behavioural analysis of the video images induced a positive response in coachees with a frequency that could be classed as significant.

In summary, these five articles show very convincingly that a coach's positive-friendly mood prior to the session can lead to measurable (dominant-friendly) coach behaviours, which, in turn, can evoke similar coachee behaviour, leading to demonstrably better results in later sessions. We also see that empathic behaviour makes a positive difference to outcomes, but that the coach's own assessment of both his own empathy and the quality of the coaching relationship shows no correlation with the much more influential empathy and working alliance that can be measured by observers in the behaviour itself. From that measurement, they conclude, in particular, that the coachee-initiated "agreement on tasks and goals" (as measured by observers) shows a significant correlation with outcomes.

All in all, this is a very insightful series of articles that shows how, with careful process research and a large volume of useful data from qualitative data collection, one can make powerful, defensible and verifiable predictions about *all* coaching assignments, just as in more traditional quantitative research. In principle, this applies to all qualitative research (including case studies and interviews): with sufficient "measurements" based on a representative "sample", you can turn any qualitative exploration into a sustainable and generalisable quantitative research result. However, in order to make statistically significant statements, the numbers of these measurements can run into the tens of thousands, as in each of the "Braunschweig Gruppe" articles cited above.

Quantitative research need not be the ideal "end phase" or "objective" of qualitative research. Much smaller collections of measurements can also yield surprising, innovative or even theory-confirming insights with a significant influence on researchers and professionals. Take, for example, the pioneering work of Sigmund Freud into helping conversations. The only research he undertook to test some of his many bold statements about the human mind and about therapy consisted of a small number of highly subjective (i.e. described and analysed by Freud himself) case studies, the most famous of which are those of Anna O. and Dora (see Breuer & Freud, 1895; Freud, 1905). These are only limited measurements ("N=1" for each case study, so by no means statistically generalisable). However, these two case studies have had a major impact on the field: Anna O. on the introduction of the psychoanalytical method, and Dora on the understanding of transference (and as a first example of the use of dream analysis). Many generations of psychoanalysts, therapists and even coaches have employed these ideas and anchored their work in them, so their influence has far exceeded any (generalisable) significance they might have. And this is still the case with original and influential qualitative studies.

The research described in the coming chapters is also largely process research, based on descriptions of critical moments as experienced during coaching (De Haan et al., 2008–2015). To be specific, the research reported in Chapters 2–4 is process research, namely retrospective; that in Chapter 5 is field research, namely data collection during coaching; and that in Chapter 6 is a form of field research using a mixed methods design, namely an open question combined with a large quantitative survey.

This work can be briefly summarised as follows:

1   Chapter 2 is a reflection of De Haan (2008c), based on 80 descriptions by relatively inexperienced internal and external coaches of critical moments they encountered in their work. Around 75% of the coaches participating in this study had recently completed a full year of studies in management consulting, while the other participants were inexperienced executive coaches. Content analysis showed that all of the critical moments could be interpreted as expressions of *doubt* on the part of the coach.

2   Chapter 3 is a reflection of De Haan (2008d) and Day, De Haan, Sills, Bertie and Blass (2008), containing 78 plus 49 descriptions of critical moments of coaches with at least eight years' practical coaching experience. Content analysis showed that all of these critical moments could be characterised as *anxieties* in the coach; in other words, these experienced coaches struggled with recurring anxieties and, to a lesser extent, doubts in their work with coachees. The second study, using in-depth telephone interviews to allow investigation of the temporal process around critical moments, showed that these coaches always cited a minor or major "rupture" in the relationship (e.g. incomprehension, anger, recontracting, referral, non-attendance or termination) around each critical moment, and that in almost every case, the presence or absence of ongoing, shared reflection determined whether or not the rupture in the relationship could be overcome.

3   Chapter 4 is a reflection of De Haan et al. (2010a) with 59 descriptions of critical moments of coaching clients. Content analysis showed that coachees considered new forms of awareness and *new insights* to be the most important experiences in their coaching process. This finding differed from De Haan's earlier findings (2008c, 2008d) with regard to executive coaches.

4   Chapter 5 is a reflection of De Haan et al. (2010b) and De Haan and Nieß (2012), who collected descriptions of 86 plus 32 critical moments of coachees and coaches that were recorded immediately after specific coaching sessions, that is, in this case, the input did not come from random coaching sessions selected by the respondent. In this research, all previous data sets were also recoded by four raters using a simple coding structure with 12 codes (see Table 5.1 for the codes). The coding confirmed that in the case of inexperienced coaches, the code for doubt in the coach was given most frequently; in the case of experienced coaches, the code given most frequently was that for anxiety in the coach. In the new research, *both* coaches and coachees cited new reflection and insight as being of primary importance in their direct coaching experiences. Based on these findings, the authors hypothesised that the six data sets so far largely fall into two different classes of descriptions. In the data sets of De Haan (2008c, 2008d) and Day et al. (2008), coaches cited critical moments from their coaching work in the previous year, and thus will mainly have contributed examples of "exceptional circumstances", such as ruptures in the coaching relationships. In De Haan et al. (2010a), coachees looked at a single coaching relationship, and in De Haan et al. (2010b) and

De Haan and Nieß (2012), coachees and coaches looked at a single coaching session; on average, therefore, they probably had in mind more "everyday" coaching sessions rather than the "coaching in extraordinary circumstances" of the other three data sets. This hypothesis could explain why the coach data over a longer period in the first three articles (Day et al., 2008 & De Haan, 2008c, 2008d) and the coach and coachee data over a much shorter period (De Haan et al., 2010a, 2010b & De Haan & Nieß, 2012) so consistently failed to correlate when they were coded using the 12 codes. In summary, comparing the findings for critical moments reported by coaches and/or coachees, De Haan et al. (2010b) and De Haan and Nieß (2012) found that (1) in 53% and 47% of cases, respectively, coachees and coaches cite the same moments when asked independently what they regarded as "critical" in their session, and (2) in "everyday" executive coaching, coachees and coaches tend to mention the same general patterns as being the most important, with new awareness and insight being cited most frequently as being part of the critical moments.

5    Chapter 6 is a reflection of De Haan and Nieß (2015) and contains 147 descriptions of critical moments from 49 coaching relationships as recorded by coachee, coach and sponsor, plus 30 other critical-moment descriptions from sponsors. The results of this research show that there is much more alignment between coachees and coaches on the critical moments in their coaching relationship than there is between them and the sponsors. In the main, coachees and coaches described as "critical" those moments in which new knowledge, perspectives and insights were gained. Sponsors, for their part, appear to attach more importance to *new initiatives* and behavioural changes initiated by the coaching client. For coaching sponsors, as much as a third of all critical moments appear to consist of new actions and behaviours on the part of the coachee. For coachees and coaches, the patterns found in earlier research were confirmed as follows. There were again indications that coachees and coaches holding normal coaching sessions mainly describe as "critical" the moments in which new knowledge, perspectives and insights are gained, and in doing so cite the same moments to an extent that goes beyond pure chance.

I have found two other process studies focussing on critical moments in coaching: (1) Fatien-Diochon and Nizet (2015) analyse 27 'moments of ethical challenge' from the practice of an equal number of French accredited coaches. They conclude that codes of conduct have very limited use in such challenges: such ethical codes are either irrelevant, insufficient or an obstacle when it comes to resolving the challenges. (2) Turner and McCarthy (2015) collect and analyse descriptions of 'coachable moments' of line managers, that is, examples of informal, unplanned opportunities to coach their direct reports.

Smith and Brummel (2013) recorded interviews with 30 executives about their coaching, and had these coded in terms of three proposed active ingredients of executive coaching: the coachees' involvement with coaching, their perceptions of improvability and their personal development plans, and also in terms of the coachees' self-reported competency development and the examples given. The statistical analysis of the codes showed significant relationships with the reported competency change, for all three active ingredients.

All in all, this broad range of process research provides a deep understanding of how coachees, coaches and their sponsors each experience the coaching contracts and their effects differently – although a surprisingly large correspondence can also be demonstrated within these different perspectives on coaching. More on this will follow in subsequent chapters.

Other than the qualitative research reviewed here, there is a large group of researchers who use "mixed methods" whereby a number of open questions and/or interviews are combined with an otherwise quantitative research design (see, e.g., De Haan, Culpin, & Curd, 2011; Grant, 2014; Kombarakan, Yang, Baker, & Fernandes, 2008; Peel, 2008; or Bachkirova, Arthur, & Reading, 2015). Like purely qualitative paradigms, such open questions can generate new variables for future quantitative research.

A helpful way to map out the different types of research is in the form of concentric spirals (see Figure 1.1). Action research and field research stay very close to the coaching sessions themselves, while case studies and process research are slightly further away, as is quantitative research that only works with quantifiable conclusions from the coaching sessions and cannot therefore develop or test a hypothesis about how coaching works in practice. Somewhere in between the unique, non-replicable reality of the sessions and the universally valid conclusions from sound quantitative research, new perspectives and models of coaching are born and important heuristics are abstracted from direct experience.

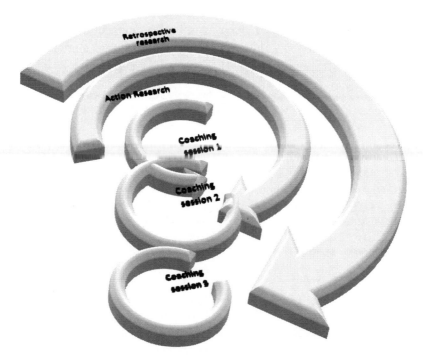

*Figure 1.1* A representation of how different forms of research are anchored in the coaching sessions, which, in turn, are themselves also a form of "doing live research".

This book reports mainly on process research via the analysis of "critical moments" selected by coach, coachee and sponsor from coaching experiences. However, in Chapter 5, we also take small excursions into field research, where critical moments are collected immediately after live coaching sessions, and into a "single case study" recorded by coach and coachee during the coaching contract.

---

### SUMMARY OF CHAPTER 1: "QUALITATIVE RESEARCH IN COACHING"

In qualitative coaching research, we can distinguish between:

1  **Action research**: personal research from inside coaching practice.
2  **Case studies**: retrospective, narrative research into existing coaching practice.
3  **Field research**: a participatory method of research using specific questions within coaching practice.
4  **Process research**: retrospective research into moments, processes, sessions and contracts.

So far, **qualitative** research within coaching has yielded the following:

* The approach to executive coaching has changed profoundly in the last 25 years.
* Coaching in a second language is entirely possible and has fewer disadvantages than expected for the coaching experience and its outcomes.
* We can learn from other coaches how to handle aspects such as psychometric instruments, internal coaching, coaching in SMEs, coaching for entrepreneurs, negative side effects of coaching and coach-coachee matching.
* A great deal of process research finds a set of success criteria in coaching (including specifically for expat, internal and SME coaching).
* The most important success criteria of coaching seem to be related to the coachee: the development of trust, acceptance of and commitment to coaching, and respect for the coaching contract.
* Another success criterion for both coaches and coachees seems to be the ability for both to achieve a deep level of psychological understanding.
* A long-running programme in Braunschweig shows how, for example, empathy and the working alliance are expressed in observable behaviour and which behaviour is related to the effectiveness of coaching (specifically, "friendly-dominant" behaviour).
* Coaches and coachees seem to have both overlapping and differing views on what is important in coaching, and sponsors have different expectations still. This has repercussions for managing expectations in triangular contracts.

The remainder of this book discusses a ten-year research programme in which **moments of coaching** were selected as research material. This is a form of (retrospective) process research involving analysis of moments selected as being "critical" ("exciting, tense or significant") within coaching relationships.

Chapter 2

# Critical moments in coaching
## What inexperienced coaches have to say

> The greater the doubt, the greater the awakening;
> The smaller the doubt, the smaller the awakening.
> No doubt, no awakening.
>
> —Chang Cheng Chi, *The Practice of Zen*

## A. Anecdote

When you are just starting out as a coach, the sensation of the new is very strong, even stronger than it is in any case when meeting prospective new coachees. I still remember my very first coachee quite clearly, even though it was nearly 25 years ago. He was a middle manager from the remote Dutch region of South-Beveland, and my strong sense of anticipation was reinforced by the two and a half hours it took to travel there. It meant that my whole day was devoted to a single coaching session. 'Who am I to be doing this?' was my strongest impression, one which I carefully concealed from my coachee. I do not believe I ever told him that he was "my first". Thanks to the coaching I got to know beautiful little towns such as Veere, Goes and Middelburg, where I spent hours walking around, processing the last session or fearfully anticipating the next. I still have that sensation of anticipation before each new session, as described in Chapter 1, but its sheer strength and the oppressive uncertainty about whether I am doing what is expected of me and how or whether it is of any help have happily diminished substantially.

Years later, when we began our research with inexperienced coaches, this all-encompassing impression of newness and self-doubt was confirmed by the material they contributed. I can now say with some evidence and conviction that coaching relationships are always oppressively new, and feel like great unknowns, and that at the start of coaching (and even of individual sessions) we as coaches are truly overwhelmed by the number of questions to which we have no answers and by the newness and freshness of the moment. And that we feel this most strongly in our first few years as coaches.

To an inexperienced coach, "everything" is still new. And because each coaching session is so different, this "newness" persists for many years. For that whole length of time, coaches hesitate about what to do and how to respond to things. And they often face this uncertainty entirely alone, because they cannot just ring up a more experienced colleague in the middle of a session. So they make decisions based on extreme doubt. This is what we discovered when we began collecting the most critical moments of inexperienced coaches. Here are two examples:

'My most critical moment was when I followed my coachee entirely in what she was saying in a coaching conversation, and kept "playing back her words". In the end, this left little scope for a solution to her problem. I always had the feeling, up to and including the next conversation, that I had forced something. And so I was afraid that my approach had disrupted the coaching process towards her longer-term goal. My "not quite knowing what to do" left me at a crossroads: giving back what she said or bringing the conversation back to her original question. The latter didn't seem like something a coach should do – I was afraid the conversation would get bogged down. This example shows that, even if I don't know what to do, I often decide just to do something. But perhaps I can still change that during the conversation and then ask for feedback about my approach.'

'The coachee in question was sent by his manager for coaching and for referral to a programme in the area of assertiveness. After a conversation with the coachee I told him that, on the basis of his story, I had a feeling that something else was the matter. The coachee started to shake all over and burst into tears, then it all came out about how he had been feeling in recent months. At that moment I didn't know what to do as the coach, apart from showing concern, and I asked the coachee if he was happy for me to refer him to the company doctor. In hindsight, that was a good decision. At the time, however, I was pretty nervous about it.'

## B. Essences

Our research question about "critical moments" came from a preparatory assignment in a five-day coaching module that I have been running since 2002. After some questions on the participants' strengths, weaknesses and learning goals, the final preparatory assignment was as follows:

> Describe briefly one <u>critical moment</u> (an exciting, tense or significant moment) with one of your coachees. Think about what was critical in the coaching journey, or a moment when you did not quite know what to do.[1]

This question generated so many interesting responses that I decided to investigate further. I collected the first 80 responses to the question and started a qualitative study, as described in Part C of this chapter. A brief summary of the outcomes of that study is given below.

As other research confirms (see, e.g., Miller, 1979), coaches are greatly impacted by the experiences of helping conversations gained early in life. In a sense, everyone has the experience of such conversations, so everyone is ready to coach other people and to become the client of a coach. But only if those experiences have made them receptive, sensitive and slightly suspicious (but not paranoid) do they stand a chance of becoming excellent coaches. The results of the extensive research into the content of the descriptions follow later in this chapter, and the descriptions of each critical moment can be found in Appendix A.

My analysis of 80 real-life critical moments of coaches led to the following conclusions:

- Critical moments go hand in hand with *doubts*;
- Those doubts usually come down to 'what is going on?' and 'do I have an answer to it?', or: 'what do I see?' and 'how do I respond?';

- Doubts and critical moments, provided they are used well and consciously, form a starting point for significant learning experiences ("breakthroughs") on the part of coachees;
- It helps when coaches have more critical moments, can sustain more doubts and remain open as well as suspicious, although it is probably better if they do not generate these critical moments themselves;
- Preparing oneself for critical moments implies coaching with "backbone and heart", being open and sensitive as well as robust and resilient.

The effectiveness of inexperienced coaches seems determined primarily by their ability to doubt, not to know what is coming next, and to greet what comes next with questions. Like Descartes in his famous *Meditations*, the coach experiences a significant turning point when she shifts her own attention from the many doubts and uncertainties that assail her during the coaching and towards the activity of doubting itself, which can be regarded as the starting point and *raison d'être* of her own professional behaviour. Descartes' famous saying *cogito ergo sum* can therefore be rephrased for coaches as "I doubt therefore I coach", so this research would encourage coaches to coach with that ongoing and deliberately maintained doubt as their only certainty.

## C. Research among inexperienced coaches: "I doubt therefore I coach"

### I. Introduction: research into critical moments among inexperienced coaches

Since November 2002, a colleague and I have been running a five-day *Coaching!* module for management consultants and executives who already have experience of conducting individual coaching conversations and want to develop their coaching skills further. The module invites participants to compare alternative coaching approaches, to gain a better understanding of their own preferred styles and to develop a more distinctive, unique coaching style. The final preparatory assignment for the module is:

> Describe briefly one critical moment (an exciting, tense or significant moment) with one of your coachees. Think about what was critical in the coaching journey, or a moment when you did not quite know what to do.

In the course of the module, participants learn on the basis of their own critical moments and coaching issues, by means of a variety of exercises, for example, in the form of observed coaching conversations.

Around three-quarters of the participants are professionals who have recently completed extensive training to become management consultants, while a quarter are independent coaches. None of them holds a diploma or is accredited as a coach or therapist and only a few have followed longer courses of training in this area. The module has now been run seven times and 72 of the 79 participants have sent in detailed preparatory assignments (a 91% response rate), leaving us with a treasure trove of accounts of "critical moments" as experienced by aspiring coaches, numbering 101 to be precise. Of the 101 moments, 21 were discarded at an early stage because they did not take place in a "pure" coaching relationship but within a hierarchical relationship or between immediate colleagues. The 80 remaining moments proved to be very recognisable, even for more experienced coaches, and appeared to complement each other rather than point in different directions. All former participants in the module gave permission for their critical moments to be published. In this chapter, I attempt to identify recurring patterns within the sample and investigate how coaches can handle these critical moments.

## 2. Summary in the form of a "doubtful" story

I try to listen as carefully as possible to these coaches and to their interpretations of their own critical moments, and then I summarise all 80 of these moments as follows:

'Who am I to think I can do this work?' is the first question asked by every coach, presuming that you can coach someone else, and at the same time finding that presumption very presumptuous. This makes it so difficult to recommend yourself, or to explain your own contribution to a potential new coachee. Even after that, this doubt is tense and exciting: 'when does it start, how does it start, what is going to happen, and will I be capable of saying something back?' And then, <u>when</u> something happens, when the coaching relationship is entered into, when something is said or something is contributed in that relationship, new doubts immediately set in: 'Do I understand, how do I respond, and is it good enough?' Then, the question 'What should I offer?' at the same time as the question 'Do I have to offer something?'.[2] Sometimes, you even start to have doubts about your own doubts, for example, in the form of the question 'Should I contribute my doubts, or not?'.[3] Doubts can also extend to the activity of coaching itself, as in 'is this or that still coaching?', a different expression of 'am I doing it right?'

Difficult confrontations with your own doubts are the moments when your coachee asks you what to do, or when you yourself take the initiative to advise the coachee. But there are also more subtle confrontations with those doubts, when the coachee takes them away, for example, by putting you on a pedestal, flattering you or 'learning an awful lot from you'. That turns out to feel so good that you want that good feeling more often and start to say things that stand you a greater chance of attracting such compliments.

But there are also times when the doubts are relieved, and coaches actively seek out those critical moments: when the "penny drops" or the "breakthrough takes place", that is, when your coachee starts to feel, think or act differently.

The coach who is aware of this frequently realises the extent to which coaching is in fact a single, long succession of critical moments, often in the form of doubts:

> do I have something to offer as a coach, am I good enough, am I doing it right, what is going to happen, and if it happens will the coachee and I be able to handle it, where are the boundaries and can we make sure we are not overstepping them?

These questions follow each other in many different variants. There is the oppressive feeling that something may happen at any time, something that will have important consequences, but we do not know what, which consequences, when or to what extent we will be involved ourselves.

When all of the doubts about coaching as a conversational form fade into the background a little, more specific doubts arise about the situation. A doubt may come up whether the coach will be able to handle this specific coachee. "Difficult" coachees appear to be those who have the wrong expectations, shirk responsibility, or are quiet and introverted.

And even if the doubts about the coaching situation turn out to be manageable, there are still external influences to contend with. Internal coaches in particular often feel pressure from the coachee or others within the organisation to achieve results or to take action in a particular direction; results and actions which are often either outside the scope of the contract or cannot be guaranteed. Team coaching is a special case, in which the various options and dilemmas may be represented by the various people around the table, and thus be more explicit.

All in all, a story full of doubts, doubts about yourself, your professional interventions and the boundaries of your profession.[4] To summarise even more concisely, coaches are mainly feeling two things at many moments: 'what is going on?' and 'do I have an answer to it?', or: 'what do I see?' and 'how do I respond?'

One coherent story emerges clearly from this summary, a story I will call the "critical story of the inexperienced coach and her coachee". However different all of these coaches may be, it appears on further examination that they experience very similar tensions in their work. It is also noticeable that experience and training as a coach does not lead to different tensions in their coaching work: when I ask more experienced coaches about their critical moments, very similar aspects come to light.[5] This brings to mind Rogers' famous pronouncement 'The most personal is the most universal' (Rogers, 1961): in other words, the critical moments in coaching point strongly to a general human experience with a certain form of conversation, namely a "helping conversation". This is an experience familiar even to children, without them being aware that they are coaching or being coached.

### 3. How to handle these critical moments and doubts?

#### 3.1 Analysis

The following contains a transcription of all 80 critical moments in the form of 67 doubts, worded as concise questions. The original critical moments often lead to more than one of the doubts. I take the process of interpretation a step further here, by proposing brief distilled essences that I see recurring in different critical moments. As in real coaching conversations, I reformulate the critical moments "contributed" above and provide them with summarising headings. To each of the resulting groups of similar doubts, I also give a short personal response.

The concise questions below, however, are not strictly doubts in themselves. The doubt arises only if they cannot be answered straightforwardly – if the coach cannot or does not dare to ask the question openly, or if the answer is unclear or ambivalent. Doubts and tensions therefore go hand in hand.

## 1. DOUBTS ABOUT EVERY COACHING CONVERSATION, AND EVERY MOMENT IN A COACHING CONVERSATION

1   What is going to happen now?[6] (i, v, vii, xxxvii, xlvi, lvii, lxii)
2   How is the coachee coming across? (viii, xii)
3   How can I get an idea of the coachee's way of thinking? (xi, xii, xx, xxv)
4   What will I be able to say about this? (vii, xliii, xlv, xlvi, lxii)
5   Can I ask this? (iv, xiii, xvii)
6   What is going on in my coachee? (lxiv)
7   How is the coachee going to interpret this? (v, vii, x, xxi, lx, lxiv)
8   Do I understand enough of this? (xviii, xx, xli, lxiv)
9   Can I keep my coachee's issues central? (xvi, xvii, xlii, lviii, lxii)
10  How do I find tools to use: after all, coaching is more than "just talking"? (ii)
11  Is this the actual/real problem? (xi, xxv, xxxiv, lxii)
12  Is this coachee willing? (v, vii, ix, xxviii, xxxii, lxii)
13  How can I get my coachee to take more responsibility for his/her own issues? (ix, xx, xxviii, xxxii, liii, xxxix, lxii, lxvii, lxxviii)
14  Does my coachee want to change? (xxviii, lxvii, lxviii)
15  What will come out of this conversation? (ix, xxxi, xlvi, lvii)

If these doubts do not run through the coach's head in every conversation, how can she be a good coach? These doubts indicate that the coach is interested in the coachee, in the coachee's issue, in the coaching and in the results of the coaching, so they must be vital to good coaching. Annoyingly, of course, these doubts and the lack of a definitive answer also make the coach uncertain, and permanently unfulfilled. This first set of doubts already shows clearly how important something like "containment" (Bion, 1963) is for the coach: remaining calm, open and authentic even in a situation of terse, even existential questions and doubts.

## 2. DOUBTS ABOUT THE COACHING RELATIONSHIP AND TRANSFERENCE[7]

16  Finding my role and that of the coachee... (i, ii, xix, xxxiv, lxxvi)
17  Am I entering the other person's territory if I bring up the question of behaviour? (xxvi, xxvii, xxxiii, lx)
18  How do I recommend myself? (iii, iv, v, vi, liii)
19  Will I be accepted? (iv, vi, xi, xiv, xv, xxiv, xli, liii, lxviii)
20  What does the coachee think about me and my interventions? (vii, viii, xiii, xli, lxvi)
21  Does the coachee have confidence in me, and how do I develop that confidence? (vi, xi, xiii, xiv, xv, xxiv, lx)
22  Does the coachee have confidence in the coaching? (vi, xxxvi, liii)

*(Continued)*

23  What to do if the coachee becomes emotional about the coaching? (xxxvi)
24  How do I handle undermining of the coaching by the coachee? (ix, xxviii, xxxvi, xlv, lxvii, lxxi)
25  How do I handle denial (specifically of summaries) by the coachee? (xii, xxviii, lxvii)
26  Am I being seduced by my coachee? (xi, xliv, lxxii)
27  What to do if my coachee puts me on a pedestal? (xliv)
28  What to do if my coachee tempts me to "join in the grumbling"? (lii)
29  What to do if I myself become emotional about the coaching? (xxxviii, xxxviv, xli)
30  What if I doubt my coachee's abilities? (li, lxviii)
31  What to do if my coachee irritates me? (xl, liii, lxii)
32  How do I handle introverted coachees? (lxiv, lxv, lxvi)
33  How do I handle awkward or egocentric coachees? (lxviii)
34  How do I bring up the relationship itself? (ix, xxiii, xxvi, liii)
35  When to call it a day? (xii, xl, lxii, lxxvii, lxxix)

It is difficult to underestimate the importance of the relationship between coach and coachee. First of all, the coachee needs a minimum of confidence in and acceptance of the coach in order to work with him or her (18–22). This leads to confidence in the results and hope of improvement, a "placebo effect" which has been demonstrated to account for a substantial proportion of the effectiveness of therapy – even entirely independently of the actual therapeutic work. Second, in 23–28, we see the enormous importance of *transference* and, in 29–33, the equal importance of *countertransference* to the results of coaching. Friction in the relationship between coach and coachee provides insight into the coachee's other relationships. Quite rightly, the contributors point out that the people who are not open to coaching interventions are often precisely the ones who need coaching (see v in Appendix A), and that these critical moments between coach and coachee are precisely the ones that are seen as 'turning points' in retrospect (see, e.g., xxxvi in Appendix A). An important and daring task of the coach is to raise the subject of the coaching relationship itself and the possibility of transference (34).

## 3. DOUBTS ABOUT GUIDING THE COACHING CONVERSATIONS

36  What to do if there is no issue? (xxix, xxx)
37  What to do if the issue is entirely open? (xxix)
38  How to raise the fact that there is "something" wrong, an uncomfortable reaction from the coachee? (xxv, xxvi, lxiii)
39  What to do when I come across deeper layers and stronger emotions? (xxxiii, xxxiv, xxxv, xxxvi, xxxvii, xxxviii, lxxix)

40  How to "press on" if the coachee is not open to reflection? (ix, xvi, xxviii, xlvi, lxiii, lxviii)
41  How to handle a "breakthrough", and the subsequent feeling of satisfaction? (xxxiii, xxxvi, liv, lv, lvi)
42  What to do with my *esprit de l'escalier?*[8] (xxv)
43  Is listening and summarising enough? (xvii, lviii)
44  Can I offer my own interpretation (without being asked)? (x, xvi, xvii, xxvii, lx, lxi, lxxii, lxxiii, lxxv)
45  How can I give my more critical interpretation? (xvi, xxi, xxii, xxvii, xlix)
46  How to voice my opinion? (xlvii, xlviii)
47  Can I offer advice (without being asked)? (x, xxii, xxxiii, xlvii, xlviii, l, li, lx, lxi, lxxiii)
48  What to do if my coachee asks my advice? (xxi, xliii, xliv, xlv, xlix, li)
49  Can I ask for feedback about my approach? (xvii)
50  Do I have to structure the conversation or guide it and, if so, how? (ix, xvii, xxxi, xxxviii, lvii, lviii, lix, lxv)
51  Team coaching: how to involve and coordinate different interests? (xviii, lvi)
52  How do I find a balance between objective and personal themes? (lix, lxvi)
53  How do I find a balance between my objectivity and joint responsibility? (ix, xxxiii, lxii)
54  How do I find a balance in terms of timing, that is, when and how to say something? (lxiii, lxv, lxviii)

Dealing with emotions and the suspicion that 'something' is going on for the coachee is high on the list of a coach's critical moments. You never know for sure: is there 'nothing' there or is there 'something' there? And how do you bring 'it' up in a way that is not too controlling and does not put the relationship under unnecessary pressure from your side? In coaching, the coachee should be central, so coaches do not wish to over-direct the conversation. However, they notice that a summary has a certain "directive" (coach-centric) effect, as does the question of whether there is 'something' going on here, or an interpretation, or feedback, or giving advice.

In many of the doubts above, we can see that coaches feel very responsible for direction, for the balance between different topics during the conversation and for when something is said. Although this is understandable, in my view it is primarily the coachee who should be responsible for those things: coaches should reconcile themselves to the fact that quite fundamentally they cannot direct or plan their coaching conversations. Direction (or control) is an illusion, sometimes on the part of the coach, sometimes on the part of the coachee, and often both. The illusion of being able to direct coaching is one of our defences against the presence of unpleasant tensions and doubts. Coaches may indeed ask what aim or result the coachee has in mind, but they cannot derive certainty from that question about what will happen next. Indeed, objectives set by coachees often mask underlying, more essential needs.

## 4. DOUBTS ABOUT THE BOUNDARIES OF COACHING CONVERSATIONS

55   Where is the boundary with therapy; when to refer? (xx, xxxiv, xxxv)
56   How to work without an explicit contract? (xix, lxix)
57   How to work without the explicit label "coaching"? (lxix)
58   What if my coachee has "feelings" for me? (lxxi)
59   What if I myself become attached to the coaching? (lxxvii)
60   How to coach if a result is demanded by a third party? (xix)
61   What if I also have other roles with respect to the coachee, such as colleague, adviser or manager within the same organisation? (e.g. lxx–lxxvi)
62   What if I want to "tip off" the coachee's manager? (lxx, lxxvi)
63   What if the coachee's manager "tips me off"? (xix, lxxii, lxxiii, lxxv)
64   What if my coachee starts talking about a common colleague? (lxxiv, lxxvi)
65   What to do with information that I have from elsewhere in the organisation? (lxxiii, lxxv, lxxvi)
66   What if I myself want to use information from the coaching elsewhere in the organisation? (lxxiv, lxxv, lxxvii)
67   What to do if the organisation has a negative impact on the coaching? (lxxviii, lxxix)

Doubts 55–60 show the importance of explicit coaching contracts and codes of conduct to which coaches not only adhere and refer, but of which they themselves are conscious during the coaching itself. With the aid of generally accepted ethical rules, these doubts can be answered with relative ease. Other doubts concern examples of transference, such as strong feelings for the coach on the part of the coachee, and vice versa. These are times when, provided it is used properly, the coaching itself can achieve a lot. Doubts 61–67 have as much to do with ethics and the boundaries of the coach's role, especially as they apply to internal coaches. It appears to be even more critical for internal coaches than for external coaches to agree explicitly that everything said in coaching sessions is completely confidential and will not go any further. The answers to doubts 62–67 are therefore quite clear in my view: do not let it happen!

### 3.2 Synthesis

How can coaches learn from their own critical moments? How can they better handle these anxieties and doubts, and perhaps even make use of the most critical moments in their practice? Here are some suggestions and ideas that follow on from the analysis above.

1   **The critical moment says something about the coach, and about the coaching**
    The tension of the coach at any moment in the coaching process says something about the moments he or she experiences as critical, that is, the most sensitive aspects of his or her own activities as a coach. The key question in identifying one's own tensions and doubts is 'what comes from whom?', that is, what part of these

tensions comes from the coachee and what originates from the coach. Tensions arise partly due to a specific sensitivity and/or susceptibility on the part of the coach, partly due to what the coachee does in the conversations with the coach. A good coach tries to distinguish carefully between the transference brought in by the coachee and the transference that s/he him- or herself contributes to the coaching situation. This enables the coach to use his or her own countertransference as an antenna alerting him or her to what the coachee triggers in the coach (see Heimann, 1950).

2    **Critical moments are breakthrough moments**

Coaches themselves often describe their critical moments in retrospect as breakthrough moments (consider, e.g., moment xxxvi in Appendix A, or liv–lvi). Critical moments are very often a blessing for the coaching process, because they are moments where deeper layers and ways of viewing and assessing things differently are found. Take, for example, the moment when an awkward silence descends because the coach is still pondering what to do, or the moment when the coachee suddenly comes out with something delicate that he or she did not dare to mention before.

3    **The more the critical moments, the better the coaching**

It would be lovely if coaches could seek out their own blessings. Although critical moments are potential breakthrough moments, this does not mean that all the coach needs to do is create as many critical moments as possible in order to generate an equal number of breakthroughs. The only coaches who might well subscribe to this assertion are those who work provocatively (see, e.g., Farrelly & Brandsma, 1974). They use their coaching conversations to "deliver" critical moments to the coachee, although this means that the critical moments can become more those of the coach than those of the coachee. The coach may learn something from them, but in most cases the coachee learns less.

The more critical moments the better, therefore, but only if they come from the coachee. Coaching is about getting the coachee to share and (re)experience her or his own critical moments. For the coach, this means being available, asking questions, listening, exploring and building up a relationship in which critical things can be expressed and critical transitions can be felt. Most of all, it means not avoiding or repressing critical moments when they occur. Our coachees do enough of that themselves. The art is to use those moments in the coaching process itself, by contemplating on them and asking questions about them, together with the coachee.

To this end, coaches need a unique combination of preparedness[9] and daring, warmth and an awareness of boundaries. The best short description of these two almost diametrically opposed characteristics that I have found is in the title of the book by O'Neill (2000): *Coaching with Backbone and Heart* – Strength, daring and containment (*backbone*) to examine the critical moment, and acceptance, readiness and warmth (*heart*) to welcome and support it. This leads us back to the vital "common factors" which have been shown to account for more than 70% of the outcome of therapy (see Wampold, 2001). These therapist- or coach-related basic conditions were first studied by Rogers (1961) and consist primarily of empathy, acceptance, warmth and authenticity.

4    **Continuing to learn from critical moments**

We all have a tendency to want to eliminate our tensions and doubts. This applies to our coachees, but equally to ourselves as coaches. Before we know it, we are skirting around or ignoring our tensions, or pinning them down with a firm interpretation. And the more we coach, the more we ourselves build up long-term defences against our anxieties and existential doubts without realising it (see the following chapter for more on this). This is perhaps the main reason why inexperienced therapists often appear to perform better than experienced ones, partly because they set to work with more enthusiasm, involvement and vulnerability (see Dumont, 1991).

In this study, I was not able to investigate the differences between less and more experienced coaches (this comes later, in Chapter 3). But it does seem that the relatively inexperienced coaches in our sample complemented each other nicely and cleverly cover the full range of critical aspects in coaching.

What are the actual benefits of experience in coaching? We can conceive of the following differences between more and less experienced coaches:

1   It is evident that more experienced coaches become both calmer and more sensitive as a result of training. However, they may also become more jaded and lose their edge at the same time!
2   Experienced coaches may sense critical moments sooner, and develop a "suspicious" antenna that alerts them to such moments. However, critical moments are always most critical for those encountering them for the first time!
3   A process of self-selection probably takes place: the coaches who remain receptive and continue to ask questions about their coachees and themselves will stay in the profession, while others will seek a change of career. However, it may also be the very people who are susceptible to flattery or suffer from a "helper's syndrome" who tend to stay in the profession!

All in all, therefore, the value of experience in the coaching profession is not unambiguous. Only by very careful experiential learning, ongoing supervision and their own coaching can coaches translate experience into more professional action. What is more, in the 80 critical moments listed in Appendix A, a number of subtle forms of transference remain implicit or are lacking, forms that more experienced coaches would probably identify more readily, such as seducing the coach with flattery,[10] working hard for the coach, competition with the coach, "using" the coach for non learning purposes or "flights into health" during the coaching.

Due to the phenomenon of transference, everything a coachee does during coaching conversations is relevant to the coaching objectives and other current relationships of the coachee. Equally, everything the coach feels during sessions is relevant to the coachee. Critical moments for the coach are therefore of the utmost importance for their coachees. What is the situation, then, with the critical moments described in this chapter? Do they also tell us something about the coachees of these coaches? My experience of facilitating and participating in supervision groups of external coaches tells me that they do. Time after time, a critical moment as reported by the coach says something about the contribution made by that coach's coachee. As in the supervision of coaches, the purpose of the coaching for the coachee is often not to repress, deny or avoid that tension – or whatever defence the coachee wants to apply to it. The main question in the coaching of critical situations is 'how do I keep this tension in the room?', or, in other words, 'how do I keep my coachee in doubt?', or 'how can I extend the time to examine this doubt as a doubt and continue to learn from it?'

This is why I believe that the effectiveness of inexperienced coaches will be determined primarily by their ability to doubt, not to know what is coming next, and to greet what comes next with questions. Like Descartes in his famous *Meditations*, the coach experiences a significant turning point when she shifts her own attention from the many doubts and uncertainties that assail her during the coaching and towards the activity of doubting itself, which can be regarded as the starting point and *raison d'être* of her own professional behaviour. Descartes' famous saying *cogito ergo sum* can therefore be rephrased for coaches as "I doubt therefore I coach", so this research would encourage coaches to coach with that ongoing and deliberately maintained doubt as their only certainty.

---

## SUMMARY OF CHAPTER 2: "I DOUBT THEREFORE I COACH"

In the first phase of the research into critical moments in coaching, we asked 72 relatively inexperienced coaches to answer the following question:

> Describe briefly one **critical moment** (an exciting, tense or significant moment) with one of your coachees. Think about what was critical in the coaching journey, or a moment when you did not quite know what to do.

Analysis of the 80 descriptions of critical moments yielded the following results:

- Critical moments appear to be moments when something unusual happens or the coach is put to the test more than is usual.
- Some coaches report that all moments in coaching are in fact critical moments.
- Critical moments appear to be primarily associated with **doubts**.
- These doubts relate to the relationship, how to lead the session and the limits of coaching.

The 67 specific doubts found in the 80 critical moments were grouped as follows:

- Doubts about every coaching conversation, and every moment in coaching.
- Doubts about the coaching relationship and transference.
- Doubts about directing the coaching conversations.
- Doubts about the boundaries of coaching conversations.

The 67 specific doubts identified also appear to hold the following lessons for coaches:

1　The critical moment says something about the coach, and about the coaching relationship.
2　Critical moments are potential *breakthrough moments*.
3　The more the critical moments, the better the coaching.
4　Coaches can only continue to *learn* thanks to their critical moments.
5　Preparing oneself for critical moments implies coaching with "*backbone and heart*".

## Notes

1  The Dutch version of the question was shorter because the one word "*spannend*" sufficed for the four different adjectives in English. We chose to keep those adjectives in in all subsequent English uses of the questions (as reported over the next chapters) to cover the whole range of tipping, pivotal or critical moments as uniformly as possible.
2  As described in critical moment lvii in Appendix A.
3  As described in critical moment xxix in Appendix A.
4  Only 11 of the 80 critical moments do not refer directly to doubts in the coach.
5  Compare with the moments in Appendix B: similar themes but generally with fewer doubts.
6  The numbers of the descriptions in Appendix A to which the question relates are given in brackets.
7  Transference is the phenomenon whereby relationship patterns from outside the coaching relationship influence that relationship itself, where something can be learned from those patterns. The concept was introduced by Freud.
8  This term was introduced by the French philosopher Diderot in *Paradoxe sur le Comédien* and describes the feeling that sometimes seized diplomats and dignitaries during the French Enlightenment as they left one of the Parisian *grands hôtels particuliers* after a tense meeting and then – typically on the stairs on their way out – suddenly realised what they 'should' have answered at the crucial moment. The expression aptly captures the experience of thinking of a clever comeback when it is too late. The phenomenon is usually accompanied by a feeling of regret at not having thought of it when it was most needed or suitable.
9  Also called "containment" (Bion, 1963) and "negative capability" (Bion, 1970).
10  In *Fearless Consulting* (De Haan, 2006), I write at greater length about the temptation of flattery and the extent to which the experienced, successful consultant or coach is exposed to it.

# Chapter 3

# Critical moments in coaching

## What experienced coaches have to say

## A. Anecdote

An international production company had recently been taken over by a private equity firm that was advocating a robust growth scenario. To facilitate this growth, it was investing in leadership by bringing in a new CEO and supporting the incumbent management. In one form of support, board members were offered a series of eight executive coaching sessions. Four different coaches were commissioned to agree contracts with the four directors who wished to take up the opportunity. Part of the coaching was a three-way conversation at the start of the second session, in which the new CEO offered his first impressions of the working relationship over the past six months. The four coaches were regularly supervised by a qualified supervisor from their consultancy firm.

Let's call the first director Albert. This man has already had a long career in the company's technical department. He was a consummate engineer capable of effecting skilful repairs and assembling whole machine parts with his own hands. But after heading the technical department he first moved to Head of Production and now Chief Operations Officer because he saw these as his most ambitious next steps. However, Albert himself is the first to admit that management was never his real ambition; there were simply no other promotions or career steps open to him within the company if he was not also proficient in general management.

As far as Albert is concerned, the first session is mainly about a new machine that has just come into production. He has even brought along a YouTube clip of it that he is keen to show the coach. Only during the second session does the coach discover that Albert has had three complaints lodged against him, mainly by operations and engineering staff on the shop floor. In the end, these complaints will be dismissed as unfounded. Albert had insisted that new rules on dress codes and working hours should be strictly followed, in some cases wiping out years of tradition. He had not tolerated any dissent, antagonising many people in the process. Indeed, each time someone broke the rules he had explained them again in minute detail, both verbally and in writing, to the great irritation of both staff and managers at various locations. In short, he treated many of his staff as 'machines' that needed to be 'fixed'. Right from the very first coaching sessions, a peculiar dynamic emerges in which Albert wants to talk about engineering and production while the coach feels obliged (towards the CEO as well) to continue focussing on leadership and communication. It became a polite but uncomfortable struggle which – with some back and forth and negotiation – did usually result in a common agenda. Inspired by his own supervision, the coach tried to listen deeply and attentively to what Albert was bringing, but then the hour soon filled up with technical talk. It gradually became more difficult to schedule follow-up appointments with Albert, but in the second-last session they were able to address this openly and had a real heart-to-heart about Albert's nascent ambitions concerning professional engineering organisations outside his company, including platforms and conferences hosting the latest technology. He turned to the coach to learn how to get people on board with his plans for the future. 'Only now am I noticing that you can really get something out of coaching', he sighed in the very last session. Better late than never, said the coach.

The second executive, Boris, is currently the commercial director but was told years ago by the previous CEO that he would make a good successor. However, the same thing had been said at the same time to the marketing director, who has recently left the company. Boris is struggling with his motivation. He has had a brilliant career in the company over several decades, in various sales and marketing posts, knows the industry like no-one else and still has the ambition to take that next step. But he's not sure what the new CEO has in mind for him. On the one hand, he is getting positive signals, having been invited to spend more time in Singapore, where the CEO and head office are located. On the other hand, he is not seeing any prospect of promotion. The coaching sessions help him to develop alternatives outside the company but ultimately, after a few job offers that look more senior on paper and are better paid, he does not opt for this route. Instead, he decides to continue devoting himself to the company at the tail end of his career, despite the uncertainty that has arisen with the new owners. The coach feels good about the contract, which has also extended beyond the current post, towards alternative employers, because she made it clear at the outset that the sessions are confidential and the coachee can bring to coaching whatever he wants.

Charles is responsible for distribution and logistics and feels permanently overburdened. Even before the coaching began, he agreed with the CEO that he would 'do something about time management'. The coaching sessions seem like a good opportunity for this, so he agrees with the coach that he will map out his own use of time as a first step. In the second session, it turns out he has not yet done so. At the start of the third session he again has to apologise: he has been far too busy. This difficulty in mapping out his time seems to confirm that he really does have problems with it, and during the coaching sessions he talks about the hundred-plus emails he still has to answer, a long list that never actually disappears, and about his problems with prioritising. When the coach asks about what his top priorities should be, "time management" turns out to be at number 2, and priorities 1 and 3 are currently badly neglected as well. Again he decides to really tackle this, but between sessions three and four and then again between four and five he still does not get around to it, although he says that he has 'made a beginning'. However, in the fifth session he does manage to report a positive development: he delegated something in difficult circumstances. In China, an apparent logistics crisis was emerging around one of his factories but, despite the insistence of his fellow board members, he decided not to travel to the country. Conversely, and in line with his intentions in coaching, he delegated the matter to his Asian colleagues, who are now on site. The coach welcomes this as a potentially favourable development, but remembers Charles saying before that he does not like to travel internationally any more. So the coach wonders to what extent the success of this sole case of delegation was due to Charles' own travelling preferences. In the next session, it becomes clear that Charles had miscalculated: shortly after the fifth session, his CEO had ordered him to travel to China and handle the situation there in person. The crisis had deepened in the interim and Charles now felt compelled to stay in China for much longer. Not a great success, and grounds for a degree of tension between coach and coachee in the sixth session. This time, however, Charles really does intend to start mapping out his time use....

Dominic is the HR director and the coaches' sponsor, and sometimes shows concern about the course of the project. Another of his responsibilities is to prepare and streamline new organisational structures, which will have a major impact on Albert's responsibilities and the future products of the factories he manages. He discusses his plans and the various options during the coaching sessions. Albert clearly knows nothing about this; Dominic first wants to be sure of his plans and to coordinate with the CEO. The coach has the sense that Dominic also wants to make him somehow jointly responsible for the restructuring and the difficult decisions. Indeed, the coach raises this a couple of times, but Dominic does not see it that way. The coach feels burdened and discusses this with Albert's coach in supervision. He finds Dominic very open about his ideas regarding the reorganisation and progress of the project, but much less so about his own development needs and vulnerability. In the end, the coach decides to raise the question of whether the sessions feel safe for Dominic, but simply receives a polite response: Dominic assures him that the coaching is having huge benefits, and helps him to get a lot off his chest. Indeed, he asks for extra sessions, but even this does not dispel the coach's doubts. In the end, the coach plays devil's advocate and asks how Albert might feel with so much uncertainty in the organisation, and with so little discussion of it between him and the CEO or Dominic. This leads to a breakthrough with Dominic, who calls Albert later on the same day.

In supervision, all four coaches report how much they struggled in their work. Sometimes the issues brought in are unclear and they do not know if their coachees really trust them enough. In other cases, the themes are clear, relevant and personal, but the challenge was more to help change some deeply ingrained personal patterns such as with Albert and Charles. There were some obvious successes. For example, they heard from various quarters that cooperation between two of the management team members who had been avoiding each other (to the great detriment of the team) was improving.

Sometimes the coaches wanted more influence. They were keen to talk to the owners of the company, or facilitate a team meeting with the board. But with their supervisor's help, they realised that this would take them beyond the scope of their assignments and possibly detract from their genuine even if messy effectiveness as executive coaches.

## B. Essences

Following my recent study of critical moments of relatively inexperienced coaches (previous chapter and De Haan, 2008c), it seemed a worthwhile exercise to embark upon a similar study among more experienced coaches.

The question asked in the first study (see Chapter 2) was:

> Describe briefly one <u>critical moment</u> (an exciting, tense or significant moment) with one of your coachees. Think about what was critical in the coaching journey, or a moment when you did not quite know what to do.

The very same question was posed in a personalised email to 110 experienced coaches (61 women, 49 men) from my own network, that of the Ashridge Business School and that of my colleague Yvonne Burger. The criterion stipulated in the email was that coaches should have at least eight years' coaching practice behind them after completing their formal training or accreditation. Many of them were not formally accredited, however, because such accreditation was not common practice a decade or more ago. Five respondents replied that they did not meet the criteria and 47 coaches responded (43%), communicating a total of 78 moments. The coaches who responded are among the best and most experienced coaches I know.

After that study and the first analysis, we explored the question again with a different group of 28 very experienced coaches, from the networks of my Ashridge business school executive-coaching colleagues, using in-depth telephone interviews. This yielded another 49 descriptions of critical moments, giving a total of 127 critical-moment descriptions of experienced coaches available for analysis. Moreover, in the second group we also recorded the entire history of the "critical moment", that is, the run-up to the moment and the meaning and outcome for the coaching relationship, which was often dramatic. In the interviews, we also focussed on the topic of supervision. We asked the coaches whether and, if so, why they had raised and discussed the events with their supervisor, and what kind of help did they receive from supervision. The detailed analysis of these temporal aspects (previous history and post-history) follows in Part C of this chapter, and a brief description of each moment can be found in Appendix B. A summary of the analysis of these two new data sets follows below.

My analysis of these 127 critical moments of experienced coaches appears to indicate that positive changes occur through coaching mainly when:

1   There is sufficient trust to allow intuition to do its work.
2   The coaches' intuition can come up with fresh observations.
3   The coaches develop their ability to put things into perspective.
4   The coaches (have the courage to) reflect their observations back in such a way that the coachee can hear them.
5   The coaches can develop a relationship with the coachee that is well-defined yet allows both parties room to move.
6   Which is a relationship that results in more trust to allow intuition to do its work (*da capo*).

If this works, the coach generates a self-fulfilling, iterative process of increasingly sensitive and in-depth coaching.

Most of us – whether we are coaches or not – have a personal relationship with "moments of change" or "turning points": moments when our lives and/or careers changed course and we learned how to function on a new level. Other coaches such as Kets de Vries (2013) have also written about such pivotal "tipping point" moments as belonging to the coaching's "good hour". Carlberg (1997) defines "turning point moments" from the point of view of the therapist or coach as those moments when the coach notes something qualitatively new in relation to the coachee's behaviour or to the relationship between coach and coachee. Carlberg reports how he has identified two common threads in all of the turning points that he has studied:

1   Experienced therapists appear to relate turning points to unpredictable and un-
    usual incidents in an otherwise fairly predictable therapeutic relationship. After
    these incidents, they need to step outside the system to review the situation.
2   Experienced therapists always experience a deeper "emotional meeting" at these
    moments, an "intersubjective phenomenon between two subjects, each influenc-
    ing the other, which prepares the way for change to take place".

Carlberg here follows Daniel Stern's "process of change study group" (see, e.g., Stern,
2004; Stern et al. 1998), which calls such moments "now-moments", "weird moments" and "moments of meeting". Although I could not investigate Carlberg's suggestion directly, I did go back to the data to look at reported breakthroughs. In the
first set of 78 critical moments, I can identify 26 major and minor breakthroughs, 20
of which (77%) display explicit evidence of both unpredictability and a deeper emotional meeting, either positive or negative. This appears to support Carlberg's conclusions, especially because "unpredictability" and "emotional meetings" always go
hand in hand also in my data. However, the other six breakthrough moments (vi, xx,
xl, xliii, xlv and lxi; see Appendix B.1) contain neither demonstrable unpredictability
nor a demonstrable emotional deepening. In addition, I actually found one example
of a critical moment that did not contain a breakthrough but did contain both unpredictability and a deeper emotional meeting (lxxviii).

Let us compare the two groups studied once again: 49 coaches in their first year
(Chapter 2) and 75 coaches with more than eight years' experience (this chapter).
Differences that emerge straight away from a reading of all 209 "critical moments"
collected (to date) are as follows:

• Less experienced coaches appear to have *more doubts* during coaching, including
  doubts about their own suitability for the role of coach.
• More experienced coaches *still struggle* with their critical moments, but do so with
  more self-confidence, sometimes giving the impression that some major drama is
  required before the experienced coach in question perceives a true critical moment.
• More experienced coaches appear to have a different sort of self-awareness that is
  more linked to the desire to assert that they are doing a good job. While the critical moments of the less experienced coaches were more often "egodocuments",
  some of those of experienced coaches appear to be more a case of "demonstrating
  accountability". This may, of course, be partly due to the context of the study,
  which was different for the inexperienced and experienced coaches.
• At the end of the previous chapter, I predicted that experienced coaches would write
  more about the seduction of the coach by flattery, working hard for the coach, competition with the coach or "using" the coach for non-learning purposes or "flights
  into health"[1] during the coaching – and this material does indeed show that experienced coaches more often mention such forms of more subtle transference.

Two of the moments reported here by experienced coaches come explicitly from the
start of their coaching careers (Appendix B.1, xii, lxii) and a third participant wrote
that, in his view, critical moments occur primarily in a coach's first few years.

There remains much to discover about change through coaching in the moment
itself, though the engaging lists of critical moments in Appendices A and B give an

indication of the type of moments that coaches experience as critical. It would seem that the quality of coaches is determined primarily by their ability to tolerate anxiety and to tackle the ongoing struggle with new tensions and new uncertainties.

Critical moments born from struggles, potentially leading to rupture in the coach-coachee relationship, are at the same time potential opportunities for dawning insight and positive changes, first within the coaching relationship and then also for the coachee herself. The coach's "containment" of the coachee's anxieties at these moments appears to be a critical factor in their outcome. Critical moments are by definition difficult, emotional and risky, so coaches and coachees can seek different forms of support when dealing with their moments. Less experienced coaches may be reassured to know that highly experienced colleagues still feel anxieties in similar situations, and still struggle with bringing situations to a successful conclusion and with their own role in the process.

The increased emotionality that occurs in the coaching relationship around the critical moment itself seems to be an important factor in successfully facilitating the coachee's learning process. Learning with the help of coaching is just as much an emotional process as a cognitive one (see Maroda, 1998). If the coaching relationship can "contain" these emotions, then shared reflection on the event is possible. This increases the chance that the coachee will consider new possibilities, both in this relationship and more generally in other relationships and in the workplace. This confirms what Safran et al. wrote in 1990: 'the successful resolution of a rupture in the relationship can be a powerful means of overcoming the client's dysfunctional patterns'. It is important that coaches themselves understand their own patterns and scripts (Berne, 1972; Lapworth, Sills, & Fish, 2001), so they are able to receive the coachee's emotions and give them a place.

Supervision gives coaches the space to process moments they find difficult or critical. Supervision too, therefore, succeeds or fails depending on the provision of that space, or "containment" (Bion, 1963). Our finding that many critical moments were still raised in supervision even following a positive outcome indicates that coaches – and probably their coachees as well – still consider it important to receive reassurance, to feel competent and to have their working methods confirmed, even after the anxiety has subsided. And it also seems to indicate that handling these kinds of critical moments is not part of a coach's everyday skills and competences, if only because in these circumstances it is necessary to see the process in a radically different way, and/or to trust the process at a deeper level and to remain present, even when faced with new and uncomfortable experiences. In order to find that trust and presence, a different conversation space and a different interlocutor, that is, outside the coaching relationship itself, is sometimes a vital requirement.

The analysis in the next part of this chapter shows that the experienced coaches we interviewed by telephone process their critical moments mainly by seeking confirmation, comfort and reassurance. And who would say they are wrong to do so? The critical moment has occurred, the moment itself cannot be adjusted after the fact, and it is reasonable that the top priority should be to regain or develop self-confidence and resilience. A large percentage of coaches do not take the event to supervision, while others focus on seeking reflection and new understanding following their critical moment. Like Asclepius in his guise of the "wounded healer" (Jung, 1946), all of these coaches attempt to transform their own wounds into a higher degree of mastery in the profession.

## C. Research among experienced coaches: "I struggle and emerge"

### I. Introduction: research into critical moments of experienced coaches

The study group in this chapter consisted initially of 47 predominantly external coaches who were surveyed by email. More than 30 of these are independent coaches, the next largest cohort consists of seven coaches accredited and working at Ashridge, and two are internal coaches. Of the 47 coaches, 25 are based in the Netherlands, 18 in the United Kingdom, 2 in Germany, 1 in the United States and 1 in South Africa; 28 women and 19 men responded. In total, these 47 coaches contributed 78 critical-moment descriptions. A later study (Day et al., 2008; and see Section C.2 of this chapter) put the same question to a group of 28 highly experienced coaches (average experience as a coach: 11.3 years; nationalities: 18 British, 5 Dutch, 2 Irish, 1 Israeli, 1 North American and 1 Australian). This time, the coaches were recruited from the new co-authors' networks and each was interviewed extensively by telephone. This enabled us to add 49 critical moments to the list of "critical moments of experienced coaches" (i.e. the collection grew to 127 descriptions in total). Thanks to the interviews, we were able to trace the background and outcome of those new moments (see Appendix B.2 for telephone transcripts of the critical moments themselves). The interview contained four follow-up questions on each critical moment, with the researcher asking the participant about the context, events, outcomes and their (or their coachee's) actions. We then asked whether the incident in question had been taken to supervision and, if not, why not; if it had, what happened next and what were the outcomes and learning benefits?

The aim of the study was to obtain a greater understanding of the processes that lead to change as a result of coaching. Change through coaching is usually investigated by means of quantitative outcome studies (for a summary of most of the outcome studies before 2013, see De Haan & Duckworth, 2013), which make it possible to determine the degree of effectiveness, and sometimes – in very balanced and well thought-out meta-studies; see Wampold, 2001 – the conditions under which greater effectiveness can be achieved. What is not possible with outcome studies, however, is to gain any understanding of the complex processes of coaching that often extend over several sessions and are influenced by countless factors both internal and external to the coaching itself. It is almost impossible, using these measurements of effectiveness, ever to gain an insight into the exact factors that lead to *specific* coaching results, in other words, into the (multiple) causality of coaching. This is why I opted in this case for a method that, rather than collating large numbers of very general and discrete comments on coaching (usually consisting of ratings on a Likert scale), studies the personal side of coaching and focusses on critical moments in coaching: turning points and dilemmas as perceived by the coach himself. In so doing, I followed the exhortation of Rice and Greenberg (1984), who wrote in their book *Patterns of Change* that

> What is needed is a research method that can tap the rich clinical experience of skilled therapists in a way that will also push them to explicate what they know, yielding a rigorous description of the important regularities they have observed.

The type of study on which this chapter is based is *narrative* and *qualitative* in nature (see Smith, 2003), so what I was primarily looking for here is *meaning*, in an *inductive* manner. The researcher is not an objective observer in such research, but participates as a subjective "colleague" in the material (in this case, the critical moments), by imposing a sequence, identifying patterns and inferring interpretations[2]. By asking respondents to describe a moment, we are determining the "unit" of coaching to be studied: the moment, the event and the ultrashort time period. However, the descriptions given by the participants in the study clearly show that those moments are always linked to a whole conversation, to a coaching relationship and sometimes even to many years of an executive coaching career. The contributions differ in many respects, though: some cite the most critical moment of their life, dating back ten years or more, while others simply mention the "critical moment that happened yesterday, and another one from today".

All of the coaches gave consent for the anonymous use of their critical moment, and took steps themselves to ensure that their incidents were untraceable. The only changes I made were to edit every moment into a single paragraph, to remove spelling and stylistic errors and to translate the Dutch contributions into English as literally as possible (see Appendix B.1). In some cases, I also deleted some of the background information which was not directly relevant to the moment but related to the background of the coach or to my study, for example. I did not contribute a "critical moment" myself because I did not wish to influence the study material with my own preferences, biases and ideas.

The research question was again worded as follows:

> Describe briefly one <u>critical moment</u> (an exciting, tense or significant moment) with one of your coachees. Think about what was critical in the coaching journey, or a moment when you did not quite know what to do.

I acknowledge that these are self-reported critical moments from the coaches' point of view, which inevitably leads to distortions. We only know the stories from one side, the same side that made the selection. We do not know what the coachees in these same moments would have said. Further distortions may be due to the effects of "everyday memory", which unconsciously tends to distort the reporting of critical events towards a much more positive self-image (Goodman et al. 2006)

The coaches taking part in the first study also offered the researcher some unsolicited advice, such as:

- 'Are you sure you get the "tough cases" as well, this way?'
- 'Taking stock of the results of critical moments for the person being coached can also yield interesting information. As a coach, you are keen to record the positive effect of a critical moment, but what is ultimately important is whether the person being coached experiences it'. (This comment ultimately led to the research described in Chapter 4.)

Before moving on to the overview and analysis of the moments, I would like to start with some more of the valuable comments made by the participants in their email responses:

- 'Even though I've been doing this work for years and notice I'm becoming more and more skilful at handling these moments... I still find it exciting'.

- 'I certainly do know moments like that, and I have to say I like them'.
- 'A critical moment can occur at any stage'.
- 'Apparently I find difficult situations hard to think about or remember! I've never had a situation where I broke out in a sweat or was completely stumped. No-one ever says anything aggressive, no-one ever walks out, there are never any awkward silences or a total energy drain'.
- 'My impression is that there must have been more critical moments, but I think they often occur in your first few years as a coach; as time goes by you find yourself at a loss for words less and less often'.
- 'I don't usually experience much excitement in the coaching although, as a teacher of other coaches, I admit to saying: if it's not exciting, there's nothing happening'.
- 'I realise of course that it's not about breakthroughs on the part of the coach, but nevertheless...'.

## 2. Summary of all 127 critical moments

As in Chapter 1, I go one step further after listening to these coaches and collecting their critical moments, by giving a broad summary of all 127 critical moments from the two studies with experienced coaches. This summary is as follows:

Experienced coaches appear to have much fewer doubts than coaches who are just starting out (De Haan, 2008c). They approach their field of work, the coaching conversation and the coaching relationship, with more confidence than the relatively new coach, usually with an attitude of "I struggle and emerge". They are aware that they will have to monitor a lot of things closely if they are to achieve a genuine coaching conversation, and that they will have to keep connecting and deepening during every coaching conversation in order to safeguard the coaching from moment to moment. They also realise that there will be surprises, unsought discoveries[3], unintended learning effects and unforeseen setbacks. They know that they may meet strong emotions, in both their coachee and themselves, and that it is worth their while – however difficult it may be – to grasp hold of those surprises and emotions and to exploit the opportunity presented by the surprises to deepen the contact.

More generally, these coaches experience coaching as something that cannot be taken for granted, that has to be earned and protected, and that, due to a wide range of factors beyond the coach's control, may sometimes have to be abandoned or on other occasions may bear exceptional fruits. Coaching is therefore a constant struggle, but one that can be faced with confidence, because, in one way or another, it does usually result in benefits for the coachee, and hence also for the coach. The struggle begins right at the start of the coaching relationship, and the accompanying psychological contract, when all of the potential environmental factors, uncertainties and emotions already play a role. It continues later, during the coaching conversations, when the coach feels she owes it to her profession to embark upon a "risky" intervention, for example, when:

- Directing or otherwise influencing the process and the method of working;
- Making explicit and reacting to what is happening here and now;
- Extending the conversation to other, similar experiences of the coachee;
- Making connections with the same behaviours displayed elsewhere by the coachee (transference);
- Identifying or making use of countertransference.

### 3. How to handle these critical moments?

#### 3.1 Analysis

The following contains a transcription of all 127 critical moments in 110 concisely worded "anxieties". Again, I take the interpretation a step further, by proposing distilled essences that I see recurring in various critical moments. As in real coaching conversations, I reformulate the critical moments "contributed" above and give them summarising headings. To each of the resulting groups of similar anxieties, I also give a brief response. Unlike the critical moments of less experienced coaches, not all of the anxieties and anxiety signals that coaches experience here can be reworded in the form of doubts or dilemmas: they are often *facts*, facts of which the coach is absolutely certain, but which pose an obstacle or cause positive anxieties.

In this list, I have, as far as possible, resisted the temptation to discuss all anxieties in terms of the coachee (with attributions as defences, projections, resistance, "difficult" behaviour, progress, relapse, etc.). It would have been easy to give in to that temptation. Equally, it would be entirely feasible to view the anxieties from the coach's perspective only. However, since they always arise in a *relationship* between coach and coachee, with other people and organisations more in the background, I consider the best description to be that where the relationship remains as central as possible.

### I ANXIETY ABOUT THE BOUNDARIES OF COACHING (CONTRACTING, TRIANGULATION[4], ETC.)

1  Key conditions are not right for coaching (ii)
2  Conversation unhealthy for both parties (lv)
3  Trust comes under pressure (l, lxxii, lxxviii)
4  The coach's options are limited by confidentiality agreements (viii, ix, x, lxxvii)
5  Preconditions (iii)
6  What will fellow coaches think about me and my methods? (vi, xxxvi)
7  Awkwardness because coachees meet in the waiting room (i)
8  Different expectations or needs within the triangular contract (v, vi, vii, viii, ix, x, xli)

   Additional anxieties from the telephone interviews:

9  A request to share notes. (Twice)
10  What information can I share with whom in a triangular contract? (Twice)
11  Triangular contracts: new boss "sees no need for coaching".
12  Re-contracting from coaching to psychotherapy, and then regrets from coachee.
13  Anxiety around taking a personal history of the coachee.
14  A coachee's anxiety about limits of coaching.

It is clear that, for experienced coaches, coaching – and hence the emergence of critical moments – begins before the conversations themselves, even before the first meeting. Many anxieties were highlighted on the fringes of coaching: before the start, between sessions, *vis-à-vis* other interested parties, and after the coaching under the scrutiny of fellow coaches or supervisors. Coaches learn how important it is to manage such key conditions and boundaries properly, and have them under control first, before embarking on the coaching *per se*. Many anxieties about the boundaries of coaching occur at the start, when those boundaries are being laid down jointly, during both formal and informal contracting. However, it is noticeable that these boundaries also cause anxiety later on, at the start and end of every meeting, for example, and in relation to other parties not actually present during the coaching conversations.

## 2    ANXIETY AROUND SATISFYING OUTCOMES

15 Relief, enthusiasm or relaxation as the result of cooperation (xii, xvi, xix, xxi, xxix, liii, lvi, lviii, lxvii, lxxviii)

16 Breakthroughs and turning points (xv, xvii, xviii, xxii, xxxiii, xxxiv, xxxv, xxxix, xlii, li)

17 Confident expectation that things will turn out well (xiv, xlix)

18 Considerable vulnerability achieved in the conversation (xix, lv)

19 Different elements come together and are expressed in the way the coachee handles the session itself (li)

20 Pleasantly surprised: the coachee corrects me (xii)

21 Pleasantly surprised: the coachee wants to continue (lvi)

Additional anxieties from the telephone interviews:

22 Coach pleasantly surprised at the great progress the coachee has made.

23 Strengths of coachee become more apparent.

24 A rise in self-worth and self-belief.

Many of the anxieties reported relate to satisfaction and success, a welcome initiative by the coachee, a breakthrough, or a deeper level of cooperation. These are therefore very positive anxieties, although for many experienced coaches they are also anxieties in a more worrying sense, because they know the pitfalls of success – loss of concentration, becoming distracted, coaches being "taken in" by the coachee's positive feedback, loss of realism and grandiosity in attributing the coachee's successes to yourself, actively and unconsciously undoing the coachee's success,[5] to name but a few. Some coaches are therefore cautious about identifying a successful change (see, e.g., xlii), although others do attribute a lot to themselves (see, e.g., xxix, xxxiii).

The phrase "turning point" was mentioned three times in the 78 written descriptions, as were the words "breakthrough" and "shift". Critical moments are often associated with periods of profound change in coaching. Coachees often seem to come back to such moments and they run through the coaching like a sort of connecting theme (see, e.g., xxxiii, xxxix).

## 3  ANXIETY ABOUT THE COACH'S OWN ROLE AND CONTRIBUTION

25  Anxiety related to the coach's own uncertainty about what to do (ix, xi, xxxviii, xliii, xlvii, lii, lxxvii)

26  In conjunction with the coachee, not knowing what to do… (viii, xxxiii, lii)

27  Uncertainty about what will enter the coachee's consciousness (xxxii)

28  Uncertainty about what I am getting into (xix)

29  Uncertainty: am I being inviting enough? (lxxv)

30  Uncertainty: what now? Is it going quickly enough? Is it exciting enough? (xliii, lix, lxi)

31  Uncertainty: what will best serve the coachee? (vii, xlix, lxxiv)

32  Uncertainty: can I keep up with the coachee and understand what his/her issue is about? (lvii, lxi)

33  Uncertainty: can I help the other person, am I failing him/her, am I doing enough? (xviii, xxiii, xliii, liii, lviii)

34  Uncertainty: does the coachee need me? (xlix, lviii)

35  Uncertainty: is this in fact (professional) coaching, am I the right coach? (vi, x, xxv, xlvii, liv)

36  Anxiety about my own motives in coaching (lx)

37  Worry about failing to fill the allotted time with coaching (liii)

38  Anxiety about the coach's view of his/her role: knowing better than or "rescuing" the coachee (lii, lx)

39  Sense of responsibility in being taken into someone's confidence, especially when significant consequences are expected (lxii, lxvii)

40  Sense of responsibility in a tragedy (lii, lxxiv)

Additional anxieties from the telephone conversations:

41  Is the coachee really making the choice himself, or am I pushing the choice?

Even experienced coaches are sometimes very uncertain. They may be uncertain about what is happening in this conversation (anxieties 25–30), what this coachee needs (anxieties 31–34) or what is and is not part of their own role and contribution as a coach (anxieties 35–38). It is touching to note that even experienced colleagues have doubts, about what to do or whether they are doing it well, and that, just as much as less experienced coaches, they sometimes have major doubts about themselves and their own contributions as coaches. Perhaps this uncertainty typifies the experienced coach who has managed to avoid becoming jaded despite repeating situations and events. Research has shown that there is a risk of coaches, or at least psychotherapists, becoming less effective as they gain in experience (Dumont, 1991).

A feeling of being responsible can increase the uncertainty even further – for example, when the coachee takes you into his confidence or shares something illicit with you, when she is affected by a major and traumatic event, or when she takes important, irreversible decisions as a result of the coaching (anxieties 39 and 40).

## 4 ANXIETY ABOUT THE COACH'S OWN INTUITION

> 42  At the outset: difficult to assess a new coachee (xi, xii)
> 43  At the outset: can I make a connection? Have we established trust? (iv)
> 44  Can I trust my feeling, inspiration or intuition? (xiii, xx, xxvi, xxxiii, xl, xlix)
> 45  There is more going on here, and do I dare to take a guess at it? (xix, xlvi)
> 46  Searching for something new that will shed new light (xvi)
> 47  Can I have confidence that "internal" changes are sometimes the most important result of coaching? (xxi, lviii)

The coach's own intuition is mentioned so frequently by the participants in this study that it merits separate examination. What we are talking about here are hunches or thoughts (compare Freud's *freie Einfälle* or free associations) relating to the material contributed by the coachee, but also to suggestions or methods that may help the coachee, that is, interventions which may benefit the coachee. In fact, all of the critical moments demonstrate that coaches work very intuitively, because they rarely if ever give a rationale for the great diversity of ways in which they coach, and if they refer to a foundation in specific approaches or methodology (such as solution-focussed coaching in xxxix and xlviii, and person-centred counselling in lvi), this appears to be more a reference to the coach's toolkit than to an approach specifically tailored to this coachee or this conversation. In short, coaching will remain a largely intuitive area of work until it can be demonstrated conclusively what works in what circumstances.

## 5 ANXIETY ABOUT WHAT COACHES CONTRIBUTE, OR DO NOT CONTRIBUTE, THEMSELVES

> 48  Gathering courage to help the coachee to gather courage (xxxii, xl)
> 49  Can I refrain from judging despite having opinions? (xx)
> 50  Anxiety about facilitating decision-making and not taking part in it (lxiii)
> 51  Having the nerve to explore further, by listening or by asking a personal question (xviii, xx, xxi, xl, lxxi)
> 52  Am I being too controlling, am I not disempowering the coachee? (xii, xiii, xxxviii, lxviii)
> 53  Is this a step too far? (xxxii)
> 54  Does it help if I start to talk about myself? (lxxiv, xxx)
> 55  The anxiety of stagnation, impasse, emptiness, silence, and breathless anticipation (vii, xiv, xxxii, xxxiv, xxxviii, xlix, lii)
> 56  Anxiety (including uncertainty and anticipation) about making a suggestion (ii, xxxii, xxxiii, xxxiv, xxxv, xxxvi, xxxviii, xxxix)
> 57  Anxiety about saying what I think and feel about the coachee (or their story) (xxiv, xxvi, xxix, liv)
> 58  Anxiety about reflecting back what the coachee has said (xx, xxii)
> 59  Anxiety about challenging the coachee by stating their merits (xxii)

60  Anxiety about bringing up patterns displayed by the coachee, here and now with me (xxiii, xxv, xli, xlii, xliii)
61  Anxiety about asking about a parallel between this conversation and other situations the coachee has experienced (xxv, xliii)
62  Anxiety about laying down the coach's own conditions in a non-negotiable way (iii)
63  Anxiety about placing my coachee and the coaching relationship itself under pressure (iii, xxviii, xl, xlv)
64  Anxiety about referring (or taking the decision to refer) a coachee (iii, xxv, xlvi, xlvii, xlviii, liv, lxxiv)

Additional anxieties from the telephone interviews:

65  Being very directive – e.g. when my coachee is at a very low point, when teaching emotional distance and resilience, when a push is "what she really needed". (Three times)
66  Reflecting back what the coachee does, here with me.

Many specific coaching interventions are described as causing anxiety. In the same order as the anxieties identified above, these are: withholding opinions or control, exploring, talking about yourself, doing nothing (tolerating the silence), making a suggestion or proposing a way of working, practising directness and openness (including supportive feedback, patterns here and now with the coach, parallels with other situations experienced by the coachee), laying down key conditions, placing the coachee and the coaching relationship under pressure, and referring – more or less the entire spectrum of coaching skills.

## 6 ANXIETY DUE TO SPECIFIC BEHAVIOUR OF THE COACHEE

67  What to do if the coachee has already achieved everything? (lviii)
68  Difficult to establish and maintain contact (iii, xxvi, xxviii, xlviii)
69  Flogging a dead horse (vii, xli)
70  Torrent of words and rationalisations from the coachee (xxv, xxxiv, xxxix, xl, xli, xlviii)
71  Standing by speechless while the coachee drops a bombshell in team coaching (xliv, lxxvi)
72  The feeling of being manipulated (lxxvii)
73  Team coaching: coachees don't want to take the path that I think is the right one (lxxvi)
74  It is suddenly about me, the tables are turned (lxx, lxxi)
75  Unsettled by sexual advances from the coachee (lxx)
76  Feeling guilty because the coachee criticises me or makes a special effort for the meeting (xliii, lv)
77  My advice is not taken up (xxxi)
78  The coachee asks for something I am unable to offer (lxxvii, lxxviii)

79  Anxiety due to a coachee who starts to control proceedings (xii, xxxvii)
80  Intense emotions and surprises (xxi, xlix, lii)
81  Intense emotion, distress or a cry for help and comfort (xlix, liv, lvi)
82  The coachee is angry or critical (xviii, xl, xliii, l, lv, lxxi)
83  Being corrected by the coachee (xii)

Additional anxieties from the telephone interviews:

84  The coachee is physically threatening. (Twice)
85  The coaching becomes very personal and this upsets the coachee. (Twice)
86  The coachee tells me what to do.
87  The coachee flatters me.
88  The coachee pulls me into criticising him (to become a "wicked stepmother").
89  I am concerned for my coachee's overall health.
90  The coachee is ambivalent, sends out mixed messages, which "de-skills" me.

Here, we are entering the territory of transference: all behaviour displayed by the coachee during the coaching for which it is worthwhile at least exploring the hypothesis that it comes from elsewhere or also occurs elsewhere, that is, outside this situation with this coach. The participants in this study report a wide variety of transference phenomena, ranging from the entirely innocent (such as 77) to the hugely unsettling (e.g. 75). I myself would in any case typify anxieties 67–76 as resistance, that is, as largely unconscious defences against the coaching itself, which can be seen as located within the coachee but also (more appropriately I think) as being co-created within the coach–coachee relationship.

## 7 ANXIETY STEMMING MAINLY FROM THE COACH

91   My ability to put things into perspective appears to be deficient (lxix)
92   My opinion, my ethics are an obstacle (lxxii)
93   I am bewitched by my own suggestion (xxxi)
94   Doubts about the qualities of my coachee (xxvii, lxxvii)
95   Mistrust of the coachee (l)
96   Mistrust of the coachee's manager (v)
97   I am bewitched by the pressure on the coachee (xvii)
98   My own anxiety is an obstacle (xxxvii)
99   My own emotions are influencing the coaching situation, for example, because they chime with what the coachee is saying (lxxiii, lxxiv)
100  My own subconscious is sending out the wrong signal (lxxiv)
101  I need positive feedback (lxi)
102  The situation is not exciting enough for me (lix)
103  I observe too little response or signs of a learning effect (lxi)
104  My discomfort is an obstacle (lix)
105  My distractedness is an obstacle (lxiv, lxv)

> 106   My inability to comply with the contract is an obstacle (lxvi)
> 107   My possible competition with my coachee is an obstacle (lvii)
>
> Additional anxieties from the telephone interviews:
>
> 108   How to say this helpfully, without triggering a defensive response?
> 109   I cry, and that sets the coachee off.
> 110   Endings are an issue for me, which led me in this case to prolong the coaching.

Virtually all anxieties rooted in countertransference are unique and individual, specific to this coach and to this situation. They are not easily generalised, even though the phenomenon whereby the coach's own agenda or emotions play a role in the coaching is a relatively universal one. It is fascinating to note that, precisely when factors inherent to the coach are truly an obstacle, when there is a good chance that relevant information will emerge in the countertransference (see Heimann, 1950), we have often lost the ability to practise the necessary openness about our own observations. This is reminiscent of Bion's prescription to work 'without memory or desire' (Bion, 1970). Reading through the critical moments, many of them show how difficult that is in practice. In the light of Bion's pronouncement, one might say that the coach's own memories (own opinions and doubts, and own emotions resulting from what has happened to the coach) play a role in some way in anxieties 91–100, and her own desires play a role in anxieties 101–107. In fact, as one coach writes, each of these cases concerns the failure of the coach's own ability to put things into perspective, the loss of the 'evenly hovering attention' (Freud, 1912) which is so essential to effective coaching. However, it is important again to see these phenomena which occur during coaching, not so much as entirely stemming from the coach but as being co-created within the coachee–coach relationship.

### 3.2  Synthesis

What insight can we derive from this study of critical moments? What are the mechanisms that lead to such moments, and what are their consequences? What can these moments teach us about the processes of change through coaching? And how can coaches better handle tensions of this kind and so make better use of critical moments in their practice? We have certainly not heard the last word on this, but, in the meanwhile, we *can* present a number of suggestions and ideas on the basis of the above analysis. Each of the four paragraphs below opens with a quote from one of the experienced coaches in this study. Since these are recurring challenges that experienced coaches cannot avoid but need to handle as well as possible, time after time, I refer to them here as "struggles".

#### 3.2.1 THE STRUGGLE TO STAY "FRESH AND RECEPTIVE"

> I also have a belief that things will work through to a positive conclusion which helps me if I'm feeling a bit stuck or unsure.
>
> (xlix)

Developing and using their own intuition is certainly an important theme for experienced coaches. Can we perceive, feel and sense something we are not yet aware of, perhaps even something that the coachee is not yet aware of, something that summarises the coachee's issues at a deeper level?

The participants in this study often associate intuition with trust, the trust that allows them to bide their time until something presents itself or until something sheds new light on the issue. They describe how they can increase their trust by being quiet, creating a safe situation and approaching the coachee with an open mind. They contrast that situation, imbued with trust, where intuition can thrive, with moments of stagnation and uncertainty. There is a clear association between trust and flexibility, having options and self-confidence, and between lack of trust and rigidity, stagnation and uncertainty.

I believe that for experienced coaches, trust primarily means staying fresh and receptive, with the same keen anticipation and unbiased outlook they had when they started their coaching career. It means not following fixed patterns and certainly not holding preconceptions believed to have been "acquired" in earlier coaching assignments. This applies to the coaches' attitude to every coachee and every conversation, but equally to every moment of coaching: if they can remain attentive, fresh and receptive, trust will automatically follow.

### 3.2.2 THE STRUGGLE TO RETAIN AND INCREASE THE COACH'S ABILITY TO PUT THINGS INTO PERSPECTIVE

> Surpassing my own frame of thinking and ability to put things into perspective.
>
> (lxix)

Anxieties can permeate the coaching conversations by many different routes: they may stem from the material contributed by the coachee, the coachee's presentation, the moment itself, or from "memories and desires" of the coach. All of these tensions form both a basis or opening for new insight, and an obstacle to or diversion from the gaining of that insight. Tensions can point to the current emotional state and the elusive insight, but they may also inhibit intuition and the ability to think clearly. One problem with this study is that it only provides evidence of the tensions of which coaches were aware, not of those that went unrecorded by the coach. It is likely that many more tensions arise during coaching, tensions that coaches are simply not aware of – or are only partly aware of, due to vague irritations, fatigue and distractions. The earlier study (De Haan, 2008c) also showed how important it is to be sensitive to these half-perceived tensions, in order then to use them in a way that will benefit the coaching.

In my view, *external* tensions (stemming from the coachee's material and presentation) obstruct the coach only if they give rise to strong *internal* tensions, that is, if they influence the coach's ability to put things into perspective, her detachment and her patience. It is therefore vitally important for the coach to learn how to handle her own internal tensions – to allow those internal tensions to exist, to note their presence but at the same time to reserve some attention for new perceptions, hunches, making connections and other coaching interventions. This enables us to broaden our frame of thinking and our ability to put things into perspective, which is vital because coachees are more different from ourselves as coaches than we think. Our powers of logic have a strong tendency to lead us to regard people as similar, and to assume that others are similar to ourselves, that they feel and react just as we do. However, we are often wrong about that, not to mention the (many) situations in which we coach someone from a different culture or a completely different background and profession than ourselves, where the differences in outlook are more explicit or prominent.

### 3.2.3 THE STRUGGLE TO CONTRIBUTE "CONTAINMENT" TO THE RELATIONSHIP

> You set the tone, you lay down your key conditions in a non-negotiable way: you can get off to a flying start or you can pack up and clear off.
>
> (iii)

Many participants in this study write about managing the relationship that they offer their coachees, about managing the boundaries of the relationship through contracting and the continuing "psychological contract": the unanimity and trust that coach and coachee share, in other words the "alliance" that coach and coachee attempt to forge with each other. They write about the tensions that arise when this working alliance is tested, such as when the basic conditions are disputed, their mutual trust comes under stress or the coaching begins to resemble a game of chess with arguments and rationalisations.

I believe that the term "containment" is a good summary of what is needed for a confident working alliance. Bion (1963) employed this term to signify remaining calm, receptive and authentic even in a situation of terse, even existential anxieties and doubts, which is in keeping with what participants in this study seem to be striving to achieve. Participants describe:

- on the one hand, the need to welcome, to be sympathetic and to give unconditional support, even in the case of problematic issues and strong emotions;
- on the other hand, the need to define a stable context, to have firm boundaries and to persevere, even if the coachee would prefer not to hear certain things.

> This is precisely the dual meaning of "containment": setting boundaries, on the one hand, but, on the other hand, within those boundaries, creating space for development and change.

### 3.2.4 THE STRUGGLE TO CONTRIBUTE THE COACH'S OWN OBSERVATIONS

> Touching a chord that makes the coachee open up rather than clam up.
>
> (xxvi)

The need for fresh observations and intuitions has already been mentioned, but perceiving and identifying does not seem to be the hardest part: actually *saying* it, that is, expressing observations, appears to be much more difficult for experienced coaches. Indeed, it is often the simplest and most striking things, such as the predominant emotion in a story, a lack of eye contact or a downturn to the mouth, or the quality of the rapport between coach and coachee, which are the riskiest things to mention.

Clearly, the coaches who write about this find that as many as possible of their own observations need to be communicated, but in such a way that the coachee can listen to and consider them. As many of the critical moments illustrate, with some coachees this is a tall order.

I believe this is where one of the boundaries lies between real coaching and an "ordinary" good conversation: it is so much easier not to mention some things we have observed, and instead just to keep to friendly and welcoming words. A professional coach does not shy away from actually pushing towards critical moments in the coaching process, and tries to bring anxieties to light as far as possible if they remain implicit. Moreover, I believe that this is an outstanding example of an area where experience helps, because once we have successfully attempted to communicate challenging observations to coachees, we strengthen our nerve to keep doing it in future.

### 4. The temporal aspects of the critical moments

Thanks to the in-depth interviews, we are able for the first time to examine further questions about critical moments, such as what happened before and after the moment described and what were the effects more broadly on the coaching and the coach? The temporal pattern of each critical moment was investigated by breaking each interview report down into codified phases or stages in the developing relationship between coach and coachee. The purpose of this analysis was to investigate the temporal process of the unfolding relationship, for each moment reported. We looked at specific patterns in the stories that were told, and characterised those patterns in terms of phases in the coaching relationship. The only aspect of the stories that we could not put into relational terms was the "interior monologue" of the coach that comes through in the descriptions, which we identified as "unshared" or "private" reflection.

In the process of analysing aspects such as context, events, actions and outcomes associated with the critical moment, we became aware that the dynamics of the unfolding *relationship* between coach and coachee seem to be significant for the *outcome* or consequence of the critical moment.

On the basis of the events, actions and outcomes reported, therefore, we devised relational codes for the different phases of the coaching relationship that we identified in the material. Nine codes covered all of the different transitions. We should point out that it would be difficult and in many cases impossible to identify retrospectively the individual contributions made by the different parties in the relationship, including third parties (e.g. within the coachee's organisation). It was impossible to determine 'who did what' based on the descriptions alone: who was responsible for a breakthrough, distancing or final breakdown of the coaching relationship. Coaching turns out time and again to be a joint process, and it is therefore easier to focus on the relationship *per se* in the description. The relationship is a more easily defined "unit" than coach and/or coachee.

The nine codes that describe each different phase of the relationship are:

PI: *presenting issue* (often a problem, emotion, event or action). All critical moments start with this phase; there is always a trigger or shift at the start. This code is therefore only used at the beginning of each moment.

CA: *counteraction*, sometimes also called "defence" or "defensive behaviour". This code represents an action taken as an immediate, unprocessed response to a previous action or emotion. The effect on the relationship is a reactive hold on the previous state, so essentially an ongoing state of the presenting issue – the actions, issues or raw emotions from before.

IM: *interior monologue*, often expressed in the form of an internal (and sometimes "ethical") dilemma. In their descriptions, coaches naturally convey this only about themselves. Indeed, we only have these data in the form of thinking-after-the-fact, so we do not know what state the coaching relationship was in. The only thing we can say is that IM often seems to go together with "distancing" (see DI below) or some form of "unshared reflection", including in the coachee, as reported by the coach.

DI: explicit *distancing* in the relationship, sometimes expressed as the coachee not turning up, or the contract being discontinued, or the request for referral to another coach.

RE: *explicit* and shared *reflection*, where coach and coachee explore the actions, issues and emotions, and/or the state of their own relationship.

DE: *deepening* of the relationship between coachee and coach, sometimes expressed as 'new issues were shared', sometimes as recontracting, often as more calmness and dissipation of conflict.

CH: *change* for the coachee, the kind of change that brings satisfaction and fulfils the coaching contract, sometimes expressed as new insight, sometimes as a new way of working together, sometimes as a breakthrough, a promotion, a decision taken or a new plan.

BR: *breakdown* of the relationship, which is also the end of coaching.

UF: *unknown future*. We used this code not to signify any question marks about the future of the coaching relationship (as there are always multiple question marks), but only to express a certain type of outcome at the end of the relationship, which is unspecified, ongoing and (as yet) unresolved. This code therefore occurred only at the end of the process.

Using this method, the 49 critical moments generated 49 strings of codes, for example, "PI – CA – BR" or "PI – CA – RE – DE" or even "PI – RE – CH – PI – RE – UF", the shortest string containing three codes and the longest six. These strings illustrate a range of recognisable temporal patterns within coaching relationships and make those relationships amenable to comparison, even though they are, of course, very different.

Each description had an opening phase, with a presenting issue (PI), often followed by counteraction (CA) or sometimes distancing (DI); then an intermediate phase which might contain many different states, sometimes shared reflection (RE) or more counteraction (CA), and sometimes more distancing (DI); and then an end phase which was usually one of the following three types:

1   a positive outcome: deepening of the relationship between coachee and coach (DE) and/or a satisfactory change for the coachee (CH);
2   a negative outcome: breakdown of the relationship (BR) and/or distancing in the relationship (DI);
3   an unknown outcome (UF), because the critical moment is still fresh and still moving towards some form of resolution.

Explicit distancing in the relationship (DI) only occurred as an outcome in two cases, as it usually led to a breakdown (BR) or an ongoing situation (UF).

When we distinguished the descriptions that had some form of shared reflection (RE) from those that did not, we noticed that in this collection of critical moments, shared reflection led to a fundamentally different outcome of the critical moment (see Table 3.1). In other words, the completed sequences (i.e. those that did not end in an open situation or UF) were divided sharply into two categories. The first category contained a pattern of interaction that involved no reflection and thus observed the following pattern: presenting issue (PI) followed by more actions, issues and emotions (CA) and lastly either a distancing or a breakdown in the relationship. The second category contained a point of reflection (RE) towards the end of the description, initiated by either the coach or coachee. Here the pattern was different: presenting issue (PI), followed by a range of other phases leading up to shared reflection (RE), then a deepening of the relationship (DE) and/or a positive change for the coachee (CH).

There is only one critical moment where shared reflection (RE) leads to breakdown (BR). Even in this case the breakdown is a consensual process of referral to another coach, with whom positive results were later achieved. On the other hand, there are as many as 11 moments in which ongoing PI/DI/CA without reflection (RE) leads to distancing (in one case DI and in ten cases BR) and in which the issues and problems, emotions, actions and counteractions and new emotions, and finally distancing, continue to dominate. Table 3.1 also shows that none of the 28 moments that lead to a positive change (CH) and deepening (DE) of the relationship can do so without shared reflection (RE) preceding that positive outcome.

Our collection of detailed descriptions suggests that in many of the critical moments, there was a point of *rupture* (PI, CA) in the working alliance (Greenson, 1965) between coach and coachee. This took the form of a professional and/or emotional disturbance in or suspension of their relationship. At these points, our participants reported that they felt anxious and full of doubts. If they responded to the coachee's emotional state by pushing back or avoiding the "here-and-now" emotional reality, this resulted in distancing and further disruption of the relationship. In these moments, the coach's response to the coachee's emotional reaction paralleled or reversely paralleled the coachee's response. For instance, irritation is met with (counter-)irritation or reversely, with feeling intimidated, rather than with interest or curiosity.

Table 3.1 The final stages of all temporal patterns in the 49 critical moments, indicating the outcome of the temporal process

| Outcome: final phases of the temporal process | Number of critical moments with this outcome |
| --- | --- |
| PI/DI/CA → DI | 1 |
| PI/DI/CA → BR | 10 |
| PI/DI/CA → DE/CH | None |
| PI/DI/CA → UF | 6 |
| PI/DI/CA → RE → DI | None |
| PI/DI/CA → RE → BR | 1 |
| PI/DI/CA → RE → DE/BR | 28 |
| PI/DI/CA → RE → UF | 5 |

In a number of incidents, for example, the coach reported that she responded to the coachee's irritation by becoming irritated herself or by blaming the coachee. This pattern of responses in the coaching relationship only seemed to amplify the levels of emotion in the relationship. In the descriptions, we observed how this increase in the level of (unprocessed) emotion resulted in a loss of trust and ultimately, in some cases, in the end of the coaching session or even the relationship. Where the relationship broke down, both coach and coachee seem to be left with feelings of frustration or even hostility. The level of emotion and anxiety becomes so overwhelming that neither coach nor coachee are able to generate sufficient *containment* (Bion, 1963) to handle the anxieties within their relationship.

If, however, the coach was able to reflect on the situation and their own emotional state and respond in a manner that did "contain" the coachee's emotion, then the eventual outcome tended to be a deepening of the relationship and tangible results for both parties, in the form of change for the coachee (and sometimes the coach). Regardless of the source of the initial rupture, our analysis of these critical moments suggests that the key to whether the relationship broke down or was strengthened seems to lie with the coach and coachee's ability to reflect together and thereby to manage their relational space. By doing this, they create the possibility of generative learning, a moment of insight or growth for the coachee. Moreover, the working alliance is strengthened and deepened, a change which is often accompanied by a noticeable shift or an improvement in the coachee's state of mind (Greenson, 1965).

Specific interventions of coaches who were able to overcome the rupture in the coaching relationship were very diverse, and included:

- confronting or challenging the coachee with interest and acceptance,
- providing feedback to the coachee in the "here and now" about what they are noticing or observing,
- sharing their own feelings with the coachee and inviting them to reflect on possible links between those feelings and the coaching relationship or the coachee's feelings,
- helping the coachee to clarify their thinking and feelings, and
- proposing a future conversation to discuss the rupture and the relationship.

## 5. The contribution of supervision

### 5.1 How did supervision help participants to respond to critical moments?

After asking our participating coaches about their experience in and around the critical moment, we asked them whether they had taken their moments to supervision (or whatever form of continuing professional development they undertook) and what their experiences had been. Of the 49 moments described, 47 were recounted by coaches who had supervisors (or peer supervisors) and 34 of those moments (72%) were taken to supervision. The majority of the interviewees undertook supervision at least once a month, either in a group or individually.

These coaches' use of professional development such as supervision and peer review was investigated by categorising:

1   The different forms of professional development, such as training, supervision, peer review and self-study.

2   The reason or reasons given for discussing critical moments during development activities.
3   The coaches' experience of working through the moment in development activities.
4   What happened as a result of that professional development.

### 5.1.1 PARTICIPANTS' MOTIVATION FOR USING SUPERVISION

When asked why they chose to take their moments to supervision, the most common responses from participants were:

1   to seek reassurance, guidance and a way forward (11 moments);
2   to examine their own response to the critical moment (9 moments);
3   to understand themselves better (6 moments).

The participants seemed therefore to be using supervision mainly to work through their anxieties and doubts in some way, and to better understand their own emotional responses. For critical moments that had emerged suddenly, supervision took on a role of helping the individual to make sense of their experience and their reaction, and to gain reassurance that they had handled the moment competently. For those moments that had evolved more gradually, supervision provided an opportunity for coaches to plan a strategy for working with the coachee. One participant, for instance, gave the following account of their motivation for using supervision: 'I was at a loss about what to do. We explored my need to be more assertive about his engagement in the coaching process. His attitude and approach was not personal towards me but was part of a pattern or phenomenon for the coachee'.

Thirteen critical moments which could have been taken to supervision were not. However, our participants did cite many additional forms of support, such as informal consultation with colleagues, talking to partners, action learning and self-reflection using a diary. Coaches often used these forms of support to help them make sense of a critical moment, especially when practical and timing constraints, or the formal relationship with the supervisor, prevented them from taking their experiences to supervision.

When asked why they had not taken the moment to supervision, the most frequent response from participants was that they were 'okay with the outcome' (eight moments). This reinforces our finding that the main trigger for a coach to take a moment to supervision is their own anxiety and doubt about their work with a coachee. However, three participants did acknowledge that they had avoided taking a moment to supervision because they were 'not good at asking for help' or 'were concerned about being criticised by their supervisor' (compare Lawton, 2000). That barrier is much lower if coaches feel good about their own attitude or response during a critical moment. Here are some typical examples of moments that were taken to supervision – critical, but not *too* critical:

*   'Because of the positive nature of the meeting I was left asking myself "what am I missing?"'
*   'I wanted to "go round the loop" and check if what I had done was right. Raised it as an area in my mind which causes me more anxiety than it apparently caused my coachee'.
*   'It felt extremely risky. Somewhere I felt I had done well, but it still felt risky. I think I looked for affirmation'.

To summarise, the motivations of these experienced coaches for using supervision to support their response to a critical moment are often to help them to deal with their own doubts and anxieties that arise from the moment, especially when the outcome, for them, was positive. Many of the participants also tell us that they were looking for reassurance from the process of supervision. Supervision may therefore provide important "containment" for the coach in helping them, in turn, to contain a coachee's anxiety and heightened emotion.

In view of these findings, we subsequently had to ask ourselves whether participants in the telephone interviews had, in fact, shared their most critical moments with us...?

### 5.1.2 PARTICIPANTS' EXPERIENCES WITH SUPERVISION

We then asked about these coaches' experiences with supervision, and how supervision had helped them to handle their critical moments. Reassurance appears to come first among the responses to this question, followed by management of the coachee relationship. See Table 3.2 for the most common responses to this question.

The approaches during supervision most commonly mentioned are as follows:

1   The coach talks about his own experience and receives feedback, support and advice.
2   The coach attempts to make sense of his own experience.
3   The coach puts into words what he took away or learned from the supervision session.

The coaches also reported that they were given the space to reflect and to become aware of new aspects of the situation. They believe that they usually got the reassurance and support they were looking for from supervision. For example:

- 'Supervision helped highlight the role of religion and spirituality. This had a big impact. It really changed our line of inquiry'.
- 'Supervision gave advice about how to attend to my coachee and leave my own opinion out of it'.
- 'I presented, others listened, asked questions, went to the roots of things, both internal (therapeutically) and external (organisationally). They gave me confirmation. They "carried" me through (just like I "carried" my coachee)'.

*Table 3.2* What happened during supervision according to the coaches interviewed

| Summary of supervision by the coach | Number of coaches with this experience |
| --- | --- |
| 1. Reassurance received | 11 |
| 2. Management of the coachee relationship explored | 9 |
| 3. Instructions or advice received | 5 |
| 4. Scope for clarification found | 4 |
| 5. New interpretations found | 4 |
| 6. Self-understanding increased | 3 |
| 7. Understanding of the coachee's situation increased | 1 |
| 8. No noticeable outcome | 1 |

It is clear therefore that coaches use supervision for reassurance, confidence building and benchmarking their practice against that of another coach. Supervision also raises their awareness and adds perspective, whether this is self-awareness, context awareness or process awareness.

### 5.1.3 WHAT DID PARTICIPANTS LEARN FROM SUPERVISION?

Table 3.3 presents an overview of the learning outcomes described by the participants in this study as a result of their discussion of critical moments during supervision or other continuing professional development activities.

If we compare these findings with the original reason for taking issues to supervision, we notice that learning about coaching relationships occurs more broadly than anticipated by the coach. Perhaps in some cases the critical moment is seen more as a *relational* moment as a result of supervision. Here are some more examples:

- 'There is a big gulp when you're going to say something and going to massively reframe something. Unless you have the courage, they will not have it'.
- 'Take time to build a relationship. Stay with the process of the relationship and the work gets done'.

Participants also described that reviewing critical moments in supervision helped them to learn something about themselves:

- 'To be still more cautious. Don't take it personally. That is very difficult. My personal confidence was shocked'.
- 'That I must be careful not to think everything is my fault'.
- 'About holding, containing when someone is in survival mode as opposed to competency mode. You can ask too much when they are in survival mode. Try and trust my intuition on this. I realise I do work more intuitively than I thought.'

Our interview accounts point to a process of "internalisation" for these coaches, as if they were taking on the responsibility for any anxieties or conflicts during the work. They often describe their issues as personal, whereas we as external observers would tend to describe them as relational issues with joint responsibility of coach and

*Table 3.3* What did the coaches believe they had learned during supervision?

| Learning outcome for coach due to supervision | Number of coaches with this outcome |
| --- | --- |
| 1. More about coaching relationships | 15 |
| 2. More about myself | 8 |
| 3. The value of reassurance | 6 |
| 4. To trust myself | 6 |
| 5. Ethical considerations | 4 |
| 6. Personal values | 3 |
| 7. Boundaries of the role of coach | 2 |
| 8. Clarity of argument | 2 |
| 9. Motivation | 1 |

coachee. This might explain why the coaches so often cite "reassurance" as an outcome of supervision, that is, reassurance that they are not completely on their own.

Supervision appears to be important for two reasons. First, the process maintains the psychological health of the coach in the context of difficult emotional "material". Second, it helps the coach to identify what "material" belongs to them and what belongs to the coachee, thereby reflecting on the extent of their own contribution to the coaching relationship.

The question remains of course whether formal supervision is more or less effective than other forms of professional or personal support. Our participants tell us in any case that we should not underestimate the importance of informal support, given its immediate availability and the large degree of confidence and trust involved.

## 5.2 Conclusions on the possible assistance that supervision can offer

The critical moments chosen and described by the participants in our study confirm that a key challenge for coaches is when they experience a rupture in or threat to the coaching relationship, which appears to induce substantial anxiety and doubt on the part of both coach and coachee. As described in De Haan (2008c – i.e. the previous chapter), such moments are often moments when the coachee is about to make a breakthrough, see something in a different light, interpret something differently or otherwise enter new territory. In our view, it is important that the coach does not back away in such moments, but remains active in the relationship despite the increasing anxiety, including his own anxiety. In fact, this is essentially what differentiates a coaching conversation from any other "good conversation". A professional coach stays with moments of anxiety and doubt and uses them to facilitate breakthroughs, despite the real or perceived risk to the relationship. As we have shown above, ongoing shared reflection (Reason, 1994) is a prerequisite for this.

Our analysis of the 49 critical moments from live interviews seems to confirm earlier research into the development of the working alliance (e.g. Horvath & Marx, 1990; Safran, Crocker, McMain, & Murray, 1990; Safran, Muran, & Wallner Samstag, 1993). That earlier research provided strong evidence for the existence of a rupture-repair cycle in successful counselling and therapy, although we have to add that meta-analysis has shown that coachees tend to find the working alliance more stable than do therapists and observers (Martin, Garske, & Davis, 2000). It is therefore important to study the process around critical moments from the perspective of the coachee as well, and we have now embarked on research in that area (for the results, see the following chapter).

At supervision, the coach will express her anxieties and doubts in terms of questions such as 'What is going on?', 'What is going on for my coachee?' and 'How can I best tackle this situation?' There are no right or wrong answers to these questions, and no set formulae or solutions. Supervision is more focussed on affording the coach the space to explore her own questions. If supervision is not available, coaches seek alternative support mechanisms such as trusted colleagues, peer consultation sets and partners.

This research clearly shows that critical moments of coaches are challenging both to coaches and their coachees, and that even experienced coaches may feel uncertain about the impact they are having on the coachee and the relationship. This insecurity is partly overcome through getting the reassurance of friends and colleagues, but may be most effectively addressed through the process of supervision. The level of emotion involved, and the diversity of the critical moments reported, which often show a clear connection with transference and countertransference dynamics, is a strong argument for the use of supervision as a better delineated and more professional form of reflection.

Supervision would appear to be most useful to the coach if it occurs within the time frame of a critical moment or rupture in the coaching relationship. If the experience is still fresh, the coach gains both reflection and increasing insight, but also a way of responding, of generating *containment* for herself and her coachee, and of preventing her own defensive behaviour. If more time elapses and the "incident" has developed into a "breakthrough" or the end of the relationship, there appears to be less of a need to take the experience to supervision, although the coach may, of course, still have much to learn from it.

Supervision can help coaches explore their management of the coaching relationship, and to understand themselves within the context of that relationship, their own needs and wants within that relationship, and their own motivations. This can increase their self-confidence because they are comforted by finding:

- that they react just as others would in the same situation; or
- that they can convert their intuitions and emotions into helpful interventions; or simply
- that they can trust their own anxieties and emotions as guides to their intuition.

In addition, supervision can help identify those situations which are not suitable for further coaching interventions and where the coach should refer the coachee on. And supervision can help coaches to choose their own path when ethical questions and dilemmas arise. Supervision is therefore a mechanism for providing "containment" for the coach which can enable the coach, in turn, to provide "containment" for the coachee.

There remains much to discover about change through coaching in the moment itself, though the engaging lists of critical moments in Appendices A and B give an indication of the type of moments that coaches experience as critical. It would seem that the quality of coaches is determined primarily by their ability to tolerate anxiety and to tackle the ongoing struggle with new anxieties and new uncertainties.

Like the Zeeland resistance fighters in their battle against the elements and the Spaniards, the coach experiences a significant turning point moment when she shifts her own attention from the many struggles that occupy her during the coaching, to the struggle itself, which can be viewed as the starting point and *raison d'être* of her own professional activity. On behalf of these experienced coaches, therefore, I adopt the well-known motto of the province of Zeeland: "I struggle and emerge" (*luctor et emergo*), and encourage coaches to coach with careful attention to the struggle itself.

The analysis in the second part of this chapter showed that the experienced coaches we interviewed by telephone process their critical moments mainly by seeking confirmation, comfort and reassurance. And who would say they are wrong to do so? The critical moment has occurred, the moment itself cannot be adjusted after the fact, and it is reasonable that the highest priority should be to regain self-confidence and resilience. In addition, a large percentage of coaches do not take the event to supervision, while others focus on seeking reflection and new understanding following their critical moment. Like Asclepius in his guise of the "wounded healer" (Jung, 1946), all of these coaches attempt to transform their own wounds into a higher degree of mastery in the profession.

---

### SUMMARY OF CHAPTER 3: "I STRUGGLE AND EMERGE"

In the second phase of the research into critical moments in coaching, we asked 47 + 28 (= 75) coaches with at least eight years' experience to answer the following question:

> Describe briefly one **critical moment** (an exciting, tense or significant moment) with one of your coachees. Think about what was critical in the coaching journey, or a moment when you did not quite know what to do.

Analysis of the 78 + 49 (= 127) descriptions of critical moments yielded 110 specific **anxieties,** grouped as follows:

- Anxiety about the boundaries of coaching
- Anxiety due to satisfaction
- Anxiety about the coach's own role
- Anxiety about the coach's own intuition
- Anxiety about what coaches contribute, or do not contribute, themselves
- Anxiety due to specific behaviour of the coachee
- Anxiety stemming mainly from the coach.

The 110 specific anxieties identified appear to indicate that positive changes occur as a result of coaching mainly when:

1   There is sufficient *trust* to allow intuition to do its work.
2   The intuition of the coaches can lead to *unbiased* observations.
3   Coaches also develop the maximum possible *ability to put things into perspective.*
4   Coaches (have the courage to) put forward their observations in such a way that the coachee can hear them.
5   Coaches can develop a *well-defined* relationship with the coachee yet one that offers *room to move.*
6   Which results in more trust to allow intuition to do its work (*da capo*).

Differences emerging from a comparison of the critical moments of inexperienced and experienced coaches:

- Less experienced coaches appear to have more doubts during coaching, including doubts about their own suitability for the role of coach.

- More experienced coaches still struggle with their critical moments, but do so with more self-confidence.
- More experienced coaches appear to have a different sort of self-awareness that is more linked to the desire to assert that they are doing a good job.
- Experienced coaches are more likely to highlight more subtle forms of (counter-) transference.

It was possible to describe all of the extended accounts of the 47 critical moments from in-depth interviews in just nine **relational phases**, which kept recurring in different orders: action, counteraction, interior monologue of the coach, distancing, shared reflection, deepening, change, breakdown and unknown future.

It also emerged that **all** moments with a favourable outcome, a deepening and/or a change, contained a phase of shared reflection prior to that outcome. Moreover, almost all of the moments that ended in a breakdown **lacked** such a stage of shared reflection.

Participants' **motivations** for taking these critical moments to supervision:

1   to seek reassurance, guidance and a way forward (eleven moments);
2   to examine their own response to the critical moment (nine moments);
3   to understand themselves better (six moments).

## Notes

1  Some of these forms of "resistance" have been described by Freud.
2  The choice of *moments* as research material stems also from my own personal experience of coaching, that is, I find it is often moments that have worked for me, that make a difference and are referred to many times subsequently.
3  Unsought discoveries that are reminiscent of the old story *The Three Princes of Serendip* (Merton & Barber, 2003). In the eponymous fairy tale, three princes from the exotic island of Serendip (Sri Lanka) keep accidentally discovering things they are not looking for, leading Horace Walpole to coin the term "serendipity".
4  Triangulation is sometimes the result of triangular contracts and relationships: tension within a binary relationship (e.g. between coachee and coach, or between the coachee and his manager) is diverted towards the third party within the triangular contract. The tension thus escapes being resolved within the relationship where it originated (for more on triangulation, see O'Neill, 2000).
5  Some of these forms of "defensiveness" have also been described by Freud.

# Chapter 4

# Critical moments in coaching

## What coachees have to say

## A. Anecdote

Why does a coachee come to coaching? There are as many reasons as there are different coachees. Because the offer is there within her company, because she sees that someone else who works with a coach is doing well, because her boss or HR is pushing for it, or even out of boredom or the need for promotion? There are many reasons for coaching, and usually multiple reasons at the same time, which are also at odds with each other. Plus there are mixed feelings about the coaching itself and about how much (or little!) it will yield. All good reasons for ambivalence, and for the need for coaching to prove itself in some way and to become worthwhile. In my experience, coaching becomes worthwhile only gradually, when understanding begins to dawn, when a new insight is gained that the coachee can work with. Something I can still be thinking about after the session, or a new activity that I plan and then actually do. So an idea or suggestion that is not too unhinged, too fanciful or too shocking that the coachee would dismiss it out of hand, but challenging, stimulating and also recognisable enough to consider. Here are some examples from my own practice, which I have deliberately anonymised or compiled from a variety of profiles.

Connor is an ambitious CFO who has been assigned an external coach because his reputation within the company is waning. However, the coach needs to be able to "tell him the truth and not handle him too much with kid gloves; otherwise I'd be worried that his coaching will turn into having a nice chat and this is not acceptable", as was stated in the HR director's email requesting a matching process. When we reach the point where interviews can start to determine the goals of the coaching, it turns out he has already lost his job. But the company is generous enough to continue paying for the coaching as a means of support towards his next work environment. Connor is visibly shaken but is clearly open to the tales of a broken reputation collected by the coach. He listens and stays relaxed and even has a range of ideas for the future, for example, to devote time and attention to various projects and hobbies he never got around to. This remains the case throughout the coaching assignment. During the eight sessions, Connor never shows any concerns about his future, despite the fact that he will be unemployed at first and will also have to change country together with his family. This self-confidence was not misplaced: he lands a similar role in another company fairly quickly and on his own initiative. Connor does, however, have various questions about 'how this came about' and how to interpret the feedback: feedback about his lack of availability, inability to distinguish between main and secondary issues, failure to keep to agreements, overfamiliarity with direct reports and not getting much done despite having ideas galore. How should Connor interpret all of these opinions from the coach's first round of interviews and what should he really tackle? Gradually, using psychometric tests, we arrive at an interpretation that may be of use to him. But it's not his own first interpretation, so some persuasion is needed from the coach. At first, Connor mainly believes that office politics did for him, that better networked people had priority on the board, that he focussed too much on the details of the work, while even his fellow board members could not really follow his superior vision, but that things are now all the worse for them because they still do not see what is really going on (he makes quite an effort to keep meeting some former colleagues). Based on his own impressions and the psychometric tests, the coach ends up on a completely different track, namely that of "passive aggression": deep down, Connor is unwilling to assume some of his responsibilities or finish tasks because he is too frightened of (the prospect of) being held to account. Too anxious to make a real commitment. He also has extremely broad interests and an ability to associate that go far beyond his everyday (mainly numbers driven) work. They both spend many sessions talking about the situation, whether the psychometric data are relevant, or whether Connor's own impressions are more important – or even if both can be true. It is only when examples of forgetfulness arise in the coaching relationship itself and Connor actually misses a session, and when the coach shares the same experience as the ex-colleagues (failure to keep agreements despite promises and good intentions), that they come to a shared hypothesis and the proverbial penny finally drops for Connor.

Caroline is a top economic researcher who has been working in financial services for some time now, just below board level. She is extremely successful as a researcher and also as a project leader on major international projects, often involving finance ministers from different countries. She has requested external coaching due to a difficult relationship with her boss, whom she regards as a micromanaging technocrat. She also wants to reflect on what it means to be a high-flying woman in a male environment; she has the impression that people expect her to be softer, kinder and nicer, as a woman among men. She receives several emails a week from her boss and also has to account for herself once a week in a one-to-one work meeting. She feels far too capable and autonomous for that. Moreover, as far as she is concerned, her boss does not add anything, in either the meetings or the emails. After a telephone interview where I feel rather tested and interrogated, it is the day of our first encounter and Caroline shows me the results of a 360-degree feedback exercise. She is a bit scornful about it and acts like it's 'just one of those things'. In between interviews with direct reports and colleagues, I read the feedback, and I am rather shocked. These are descriptions of someone who cannot be trusted, only ever thinks of herself and pays you no attention unless she needs something from you. On top of this, according to her colleagues, she raises her voice and slams doors. One of the live interviews on the day turns very emotional when her employee says he does not trust her at all and so cannot trust me as her "coach" here in the room either. I had trouble recognising what people were saying because I had found her much more open, friendly and reflective, even though she had been somewhat acerbic during our first contact. It becomes a day full of anxiety for many of us including me, because I have to report to her at the end of the day, and I am starting to worry about her reputation in the office. I go through all the feedback with her and urge her initially to try to relax at work, take some distance from her conflicts and perhaps engage in more sport or meditation. Caroline only realises she might have a problem when she sees the shocked and slightly alarmed reaction of her coach, and she promises to take things a bit easier and seek contact again with a few people at work. This is followed by five really good coaching sessions in which she learns to appreciate her boss's requests as a kind of "tax" that she has to pay in order to do her "prestigious" international work within this company. As a high performer she may have to be in a high-rate tax regime, she now understands. She also gradually becomes more tolerant of her boss and his emails, and actually accounts to him on a weekly basis, which helps him to relax, in turn. I remember in our last session we talked about *Antigone* (Sophocles, 5th century BC), a drama that she read and reread endlessly as a teenager and which she is now able to link to her rebellious and almost aggressive behaviour at work. She can now relate her anger more closely to her ideals and ultimately opts for a different sphere of work, more within humanitarian economy.

Pavel's coaching goals were not immediately clear, and even his job seemed rather vague. He was Director of Transformation and sat in a large, bare room in a nondescript office environment, with two assistants in a large lobby out front. There seemed to be hardly any connection between his office and the remainder of the rather lively international company's office space. Although he explained his responsibility within the company several times, as his coach I couldn't really form a picture of it. Apparently his position was a temporary one, created for around two years due to a company restructuring and demerger; it was intended to prepare for a fresh management team for a new, streamlined business that would likely be put up for sale. The feeling of distance between us persisted for a long time. I knew he had requested my services because I had coached someone else on the same Board the year before. So I knew he had confidence in coaching, but I did not observe any motivation, or any demotivation either, just a kind of flatness, remoteness, as if this was a task lower down on his to-do list. Both during the sessions and in the days afterwards, I struggled with the coaching contract: there were almost no learning goals to summarise, just a vague idea about looking for a new, more senior position in two years' time. The sessions did gradually become more open and I got the impression that Pavel was slowly starting to feel more at home, and safe enough to say more about what was really preoccupying him. In the end, this turned out to be a feeling of being "superfluous" and not contributing anything to the Board except the idea of a future and a strategy, without him really being able to work on it. And I could empathise with that feeling, because that was how I'd felt with him during our first few sessions. His personality profile indicated a certain recklessness and wilfulness, which I could not really infer from our sessions, because Pavel was always extremely polite and charming. As is usually the case, there was apparently a whole drama going on below the surface which we very slowly started to touch on….

What these coachees have in common is that something very positive happens when their own perception or interpretation becomes slightly disrupted and they are persuaded of a different way of looking at things. As a coach I often wonder how you get that different view, how you shine light under that door into the dark internal room, how you find an opening in those proud peacock feathers, and a new perspective in that self view or world view that to me as an outsider, sometimes (to be honest) seems surprisingly confident or even immutable….

Sometimes you really need to exercise patience as a coach, to slowly uncover the highly personal 'tragedy' of the coachee that underpins the coaching issue. Psychometric tools can help in this respect, both to gain a different intuition for yourself and to show the coachee something new in an acceptable way. But it is true that a coach needs to take care not to become a kind of guide to the information that sounds very factual but ultimately says very little (Metselaar & De Haan, 2015).

One can safely assume that coachees wish and need to learn something new although they do not know what it is, and that they can only learn it if it emerges from their own reflections or is presented in such a way that it can easily be fitted into their own self-understanding.

It is often surprising how we are all the same at the deepest level. We are all familiar with the basic emotions, such as the Big Four ("mad, sad, glad, scared"), and countless shades of emotion such as the many varieties of love, longing, shame and aversion. We all recognise themes around change, psychodynamics and struggles with ambivalence. At that deepest level we are, as Carl Rogers has said, all the same ('the most personal is the most universal', Rogers, 1961). But at the level just above that, it's about how we interpret this universal human condition and our ambitions and emotions, as well as the emotions we feel or choose for our day-to-day experiencing (the "climate" of our personality versus the "season" of our mood), and the conflicts we enter into, the issues we take to coaching; in this, I notice that we are extremely different. It is as if we are all composed of the same primary colours: everyone has all of the colours, but each of us uses them to create our own highly personal pastiche.

Coaching of leaders is often about these highly personal, unique patterns that leaders do not share with anyone in their own environment and that make them feel pretty isolated. If coaching can bring some recognition and meaning to this, then half the work has already been done, or perhaps much more than half.

## B. Essences

In this third phase of the research into critical moments during coaching, we examine them for the first time from the perspective of the coachee. A vast amount of research has been done into the coach's experience of coaching conversations. But how does the coachee experience those conversations? This is the account of an initial exploratory study of a highly relevant but virtually uncharted issue in executive coaching: what is it that coachees experience as critical, significant and pivotal, in coaching conversations?

The growing interest in executive coaching, exemplified by a wealth of publications, has provided us with a plethora of models for the various aspects of coaching, such as:

- Basic rules for approaching conversations (see, e.g., Kilburg, 2000; or Downey, 1999);
- Basic rules for structuring conversations (see, e.g., Whitmore, 1992; De Haan & Burger, 2005);
- Basic ways of intervening within conversations (see, e.g., Heron, 1975; or Clutterbuck, 1985).

These and many other formalised approaches and categories give us an insight into how professional coaches (may) think about their work. However, even though we now seem to know a great deal about what coaches do and how coaches conceptualise, what do these models actually tell us about the coachee's experience of coaching conversations? How does the coachee experience the process of being coached? How does the coachee view coaching?

Other than the coachee surveys as mentioned in Chapter 1 (Blackman, 2006; Bush, 2005; Gyllensten & Palmer, 2007; MacKenzie, 2007; Terblanche, Albertyn, & Coller-Peter, 2017; Timson, 2015), we rarely find the coachee's opinion in the coaching literature. Nevertheless, we *are* beginning to know more about the effectiveness of coaching for coachees, or the results that are achieved (for overviews of outcome-research articles, see De Haan & Duckworth, 2013; Feldman & Lankau, 2005; Jones, Woods, & Guillaume, 2015; Kampa-Kokesch & Anderson, 2001; Waldman, 2003). Coaching seems to be particularly effective, and perhaps this is why so many professional managers and consultants are attracted to this form of organisational development. But even if we know about coaching outcomes, what does this tell us about how those outcomes are (or can be) achieved? What does it tell us about specific interventions during a coaching conversation? To be able to say something about this, we need to study the interaction between a specific coachee and a specific coach, that is, within real-life coaching conversations and coaching contracts, from the perspective of the coachee.

This chapter therefore sets out to find some preliminary answers to the following three open questions about the executive-coaching profession:

1   How do coachees experience executive-coaching interventions?
2   What outcomes are generated for coachees in the real time of coaching?
3   What model(s) do coachees (implicitly) operate on?

Little or no research has been done in this area as yet. This study is therefore only a first exploration and our conclusions will necessarily be tentative and somewhat hypothetical. We believe, however, that this is important territory that lends itself to broader research programmes. After all, coaching is undertaken for the benefit of the coachee. It is therefore crucial to understand the coachee's perspective on coaching as thoroughly as possible. From our own experience, we know that the coach's perspective on coaching is completely different from that of the coachee; in other words, we experience coaching very differently depending on whether we ourselves are the learner or the facilitator of learning. We believe that all or most outcomes achieved by coaching ultimately result from "sub-outcomes" at conversation level (Rice & Greenberg, 1984), and coaching therefore succeeds or fails based on the results achieved from moment to moment. To begin to understand how the various outcomes of the whole journey are achieved, we therefore need to gain some understanding of these sub-outcomes – the effectiveness from moment to moment. Moreover, we believe that it is probably easier to describe sub-outcomes than overall outcomes, because, in the former case, there are likely to be fewer variables involved.

To the best of our knowledge of the literature on executive coaching, this study moves into new and uncharted territory, but it is not without important precursors. Our work has been inspired by thorough investigations that have taken place in the fields of psychotherapy and narrative psychology, which we briefly summarise here.

Many clients of coaching told us they experience moments that they would describe as "critical", although many do not. When coachees do report a critical moment, their description is often about a new personal realisation or insight they have gained, whether this is issue-related or self-related. It is striking how these realisations or insights are often accompanied by emotions such as elation or relief, or the sensation of a confidence boost. In this regard, they are similar to the "epiphanies" that Denzin (1989) surmised.

By giving coaching clients the opportunity to describe their experiences in detail, we also learned more about the occasions where coaching did *not* work: occasions which may be obscured by the many apparently successful assignments, and by the generally encouraging outcomes with regard to effectiveness of coaching. Just like the coaches in the previous chapter, some participants in our study report negative coaching experiences, both linked to critical moments and in the absence of critical moments (four negative experiences in the descriptions, and two explicitly negative experiences in the "no" responses).

It is not so surprising to us that coaches and coachees gave very different answers to the same question about a "critical moment" in coaching. One has only to consider the essentially complementary nature of the coach-coachee pair, a pair that can be compared to, on the one hand, a "container" or "vehicle" (the primary etymological meaning of the word coach, going back to the Hungarian place name Kocs) and, on the other, the "contained" or "passenger" (De Haan & Burger, 2005). Executive coach and coaching client perform very different roles during the coaching. Coachees concentrate on themselves and their issues or queries, and coaches are focussed on offering help with those issues and queries.

More research is needed into coaching, among both coaches and coachees, and it would be good if we could combine coachees and their coaches in a single common paradigm. We are still at an early stage, but our research already allows us to draw some provisional conclusions with regard to the critical moments of coaching clients:

- Critical moments, tipping points, breakthroughs or epiphanies may not necessarily be so relevant or important to coachees. They do not always feel that there were such critical moments in the coaching work. Sometimes creating a sense of support and reflection is adequate.
- Through critical moments, coachees primarily (hope to) find personal realisations, such as new perspectives on their issues or new understanding of themselves and others (see Table 4.1).
- Coaching leads to both incremental change and transformative change, which is achieved through ongoing personal realisation (see Section C of this chapter). Perhaps there is more truth than we sometimes realise in the idea that coachees 'value advice and solutions, when free to reject them', to quote Llewelyn (1988).
- The coachees in this study often relate their positive outcomes to an increase in insight and realisation (see again Section C). This is not a trivial conclusion, as many approaches in executive coaching are geared towards other outcomes (such as problem-solving, strengthening of existing solutions, remedial help or active support). It seems that the insight-focussed (analytical) approach to coaching (see De Haan & Burger, 2005; or Brunning, 2006) is most favoured

by these clients of coaching. However, given the wide range of coachees' experiences (Table 4.1), it is important to define the concept of "insight" broadly enough and to extend it to new facts, new instruments, new strategies, decisions and the comprehension of others, as well as the insight into yourself, your own motivation, defences and hidden assumptions, which is usually most associated with insight-focussed work.

However, our main recommendation is to conduct more research and gather more descriptions of critical moments of coaching clients. These should help us to answer questions such as the following:

1   Are the low response rate and high proportion of "no" responses merely incidental features of this research, or is this a real phenomenon that merits further investigation? On the one hand, the high proportion of "no" responses may be due to the fact that participants were contacted by a direct mail approach (by email) and were not really involved in the research programme, and that they had no relationship with the researchers (such as all of the participants in the research reported on in Chapters 2 and 3). On the other hand, a possible explanation might be that coaching is a much more incremental process for coachees – where there are no moments that stand out for them – than for coaches. Psychotherapeutic research has also shown that clients experience the relationship as flatter and more stable than do their therapists (Martin, Garske, & Davis, 2000).

2   Do coachees and coaches look at the coaching conversation in fundamentally different ways? This first study seems to indicate that they do. However, we are aware that the data sets used for the various studies (see Appendices A, B and C of this book) were obtained from different target groups, under different circumstances, and in different ways. What is needed is a study such as that by Llewelyn (1988) in which the perspectives of coachee and coach are examined on the basis of the same coaching conversation (we undertake this kind of study in the next chapter).

3   Why do coachees refer so little to the coach and the relationship when everything is going well, while other research (summarised in Wampold, 2001) shows that these "common factors" are highly relevant?

After the present study, we started a new research programme in 2008 to directly compare the descriptions of critical moments by coach and coachee (see Chapter 5 and De Haan et al., 2010b).

It seems that the coaching clients in this study find the question about critical moments less self-evident than do the coaches we asked before; and that, if they do report critical moments, they refer mainly to a new realisation or a new insight. For coaching clients, things only really happen when they look at something differently, when they start thinking about something in a new way, or when they are able to make an unanticipated decision. Just like for the Greek philosopher Archimedes, the watchword for these managers is "eureka": "I have found it!", exclaimed in the warm bath of their coaching conversations when they create unanticipated new insights, answers and solutions to long-standing issues.

## C. Research among coachees: "I suddenly realised"

### I. Introduction: earlier research into "moments of change" in other disciplines

It is interesting to note that the study of "moments" or "events" of effectiveness (sub-outcomes) started relatively late in all professions that focus on change through helping conversations. The first important research into events within professional helping conversations took place in the field of group psychotherapy. Irvin Yalom (1970) started the systematic study of the nature of helpful events for clients, asking clients to classify these events with the help of a preconceived classification. Later, Bloch et al. (1979) abandoned the preconceived classification so that they could inquire more deeply into the clients' experience of "most important events" in psychotherapy. Llewelyn (1988) undertook a major research project in individual psychotherapy, interviewing 40 patient-therapist pairs and collecting 1,076 critical events (both helpful and unhelpful) from 399 sessions. She found highly significant differences between the selection and description of the events by therapists and by patients. These differences turned out to be greater when the outcome of the psychotherapy was relatively less helpful for the patient. Llewelyn used Elliott's (1985) taxonomy to classify the events, and found that

- Patients valued "reassurance/relief" and "problem solutions" more highly;
- Therapists valued "gaining of cognitive/affective insight" highest;
- Both patients and therapists valued "personal contact" highly.

Llewelyn (1988) writes in her conclusion that patients seem to be more concerned with solutions to their problems, and that they value advice and solutions more, provided they feel free to reject them. Therapists, on the other hand, seem more concerned with the aetiology of the problems and potential transformation through the patient's insight.

Related research into significant (both helpful and non-helpful) events in individual psychotherapy can be found in Elliott (1985), Elliott et al. (1985), Mahrer and Nadler (1986), Llewelyn et al. (1988) and Timulak and Keogh (2017). Mahrer and Nadler (1986) give an overview of "good moments in psychotherapy" found by various researchers. The other articles looked at the nature of therapist/counsellor interventions which clients rated as being more and less helpful. All of these researchers were able to make a comparison between helpfulness of specific events and outcome, so they provide links between "sub-outcomes" and "overall outcomes". Our research too seems to confirm this discrepancy between therapist and patient perspectives on a shared experience (in our case, the coaching conversation). One recurring finding in the literature mentioned above was that coding of clients' accounts can be rated reliably by therapists/researchers, something we also found in this research.

Another discipline where critical moments in individual change processes have been studied is that of biographical research, for example, studies of significant events in the lifetime of a famous person (see, e.g., Mandelbaum, 1973), or sociological field research into critical moments of groups of individuals that are known to be in transition, such as adolescents (see, e.g., Thomson et al., 2002). Interestingly, critical moments can be defined more objectively in retrospect: in terms of the importance the moment demonstratively has on the ensuing biography. In other words, a moment often becomes "critical" because we notice in retrospect that it "proved to be" significant as it worked itself out. Critical moments have been elucidated theoretically in a variety of ways, for example, as "turning points" (Mandelbaum, 1973), "epiphanies" (Denzin, 1989), "fateful moments" (Giddens, 1991) or "social career breaks" (Humphrey, 1993) in narrative sociology, and as "turning points" (Carlberg, 1997) or "moments of meeting" (Stern, 2004) in psychotherapy.

### Our own earlier research into "moments of change" in coaching

Our own earlier research focussed on the coach's experience of critical moments (see Chapters 2 and 3). By "critical moment" we mean a sudden shift or interruption to a coaching journey: one that feels significant and urgent, exciting or disturbing. It seems that coaches frequently find these critical moments to be turning points in their work with coachees; either they are generative or they lead to a deterioration in the coaching relationship (Day et al., 2008).

Our first investigations with executive coaches (De Haan, 2008c, 2008d) showed that critical moments are usually:

- Unexpected and unforeseen by the coach;
- Associated by the coach with heightened emotions for both coachee and coach;
- Experienced as tension-provoking in the relationship between coach and coachee;
- Associated by the coach with feeling doubt or anxiety about how to proceed or respond in the moment.

Coaches often reported that frequently their coachees were experiencing insight and learning during or after these moments, although in a minority of cases, they led to the breakdown of the relationship and even the termination of the coaching. When comparing moments that resulted in good outcomes and breakthroughs to moments that resulted in the breakdown of the coaching relationship (see previous chapter), we observed that the key difference seemed to be presence or absence of shared reflection at the point of tension. When coach and coachee were both able to reflect on what was happening in the moment, or on what had just happened, learning and insight was often the result. When, however, either the coach or the coachee allowed their anxiety to result in, for example, conflict or withdrawal, a breakdown in the relationship often resulted.

From a theoretical perspective, the research demonstrates the importance of the dynamics of the co-created relationship between coach and coachee and the importance of "reflexivity" in coaching. By "reflexivity" we mean the ability to experience and reflect on one's own inner world, and to view it as if we were an outsider, *during* points of heightened emotion.

With this new research study on critical moments in coaching, we aimed to investigate whether coaching clients are aware of critical moments during the coaching and, if they are, what are their experiences of these moments. The two main questions in this study are therefore:

- What critical moments do clients of coaching experience? and
- What descriptors do they use in their reports of those moments?

We are aware that there are important differences between psychotherapy and executive coaching (Spinelli, 2008). However, we hypothesised that the perspectives of coachees and coaches could be significantly different, similar to what is known about critical events in psychotherapy (see Llewelyn, 1988; or the review study by Weiss, Rabinowitz, & Spiro, 1996). To begin our enquiry, we set out to explore the specific language of the coachee who engages in coaching conversations. In other words, we were interested in how coachees would describe their experiences of coaching, and what we could infer from their word choice about their attitudes, thinking or sense-making. Coachees might employ a language that matches that of both inexperienced and experienced coaches, or perhaps not (see, e.g., De Haan, 2008a; Heron, 1975; Kilburg, 2000). If the coachees' frame of reference proves to be radically different from what coaches say about critical moments, we should be able to infer that from their use of language when describing events. In that case, a different model of the coaching experience might be called for to describe their experiences – separate from the existing models created for and used by coaches.

## 2. Method

We embarked on two different inquiries in order to get first-hand accounts of coachees' experience of critical moments in coaching relationships. The first stage was a short survey asking participants whether they had experienced a critical moment as a coachee and, if they had, to provide a short description of it. The second stage consisted of interviews with selected individuals who had described a critical moment and some who had indicated they had not experienced a critical moment at all.

We opted for a "fresh" set of coachees that did not form part of any of our previous research on critical moments, and that we ourselves have not had anything to do with as a coach. For this reason, we offered our short survey first to all members of the Ashridge alumni network. The Ashridge alumni are all ex-participants of educational programmes of the Ashridge Business School (14% from one of our MBAs and 86% from one of our other open enrolment leadership programmes). We do not teach on the Ashridge MBA or leadership programmes, so we ourselves had no previous contact with those we invited to participate in the survey. There were 3,015 alumni on the Ashridge Alumni Register, mostly leaders and managers working in the fullest range of industries, with the largest subsets from Financial Services (16%), Consulting, Professional and Business Services (13%) and Pharmaceuticals, Chemical and Biotech (9%); 25% were female and 75% were male. We asked these alumni the following research question, once as an advert in the Alumni monthly bulletin, and once in the form of a more personalised email:

'Our earlier research into coaches' perspectives focused on the frequent experience during the coaching process of what we are calling "critical moments". These moments often turned out to be important times in the coaching journey, so we are very interested to know if coachees also have these experiences. Our definition of a "critical moment" is "an exciting, tense or significant moment" and it could be either an actual moment or a period of time. Our questions to you are:

1   Have you ever experienced something that felt like a "critical moment" (an exciting, tense or significant moment) during your coaching? [Yes/No]
2   If so, please describe briefly one (or more) critical moment. What was it about this moment that made it critical for you?

NB: In our research report we will take away all identifying elements from the descriptions, so we can promise complete anonymity. Please let us know if you'd like to receive our report before publication. We will be more than happy to share our findings'.

This short written enquiry was emailed to all 3,015 members of the Ashridge alumni network. When response rates turned out to be a little low for analysis, we topped up the data set by sending the same email to 166 graduates of the Ashridge "Coaching for Organisation Consultants" programme (another group with whom we had not ourselves done any individual coaching) and to 20 current coaching clients of Ashridge Consulting (with permission from their coaches). The response rates were 51 from Ashridge alumni (1.7%), 10 from coaching programme participants (6%) and 6 from current coaching clients (30%). So the full data set consisted of 67 completed responses. This set comprised 20 (30%) "no" moments (participants reporting they had not had any critical moments during their coaching) and 59 critical-moment descriptions from the remaining 47 participants.

Based on this data set of 59 critical moments (see Appendix C for some examples), our enquiry proceeded as follows:

1   Using grounded theory (Corbin & Strauss, 1990), we came up with 40 short codes describing critical aspects in the critical-moment descriptions.
2   All members of the research team (the four authors) coded the data set using as many of these codes as deemed relevant for each critical moment. Following Elliott (1985), we thought a sort method would have oversimplified the actual complexity by imposing mutually exclusive classification. The four codings were correlated for inter-rater consistency, and first conclusions were drawn from the frequencies of codes.
3   We held in-depth telephone interviews with five participants who had described a critical moment and with three participants who had indicated they had not experienced a critical moment at all.
4   From the initial critical-moment descriptions and the interview transcripts, we analysed the use of metaphor by extracting a grand total of 252 metaphors from this extended data set.
5   The full set of metaphors was categorised by two of the authors (AD and CB); this provided a rough classification and the metaphors were then divided into 15 categories on the basis of extended conversations and a Q-sort method (Smith, 2003).
6   On the basis of the patterns that emerged in the content analysis and in the metaphor analysis, we devised a simple model of the language that these coachees most often employ to describe their critical moments.
7   Finally, we tested this model by having two of the authors (EH and CB) categorise all metaphors afresh, on the basis of the eight dimensions opened up by the model. For this purpose, the 15 categories were dropped and the cards bearing the metaphors were shuffled. EH and CB then agreed to divide the metaphors

over a two-dimensional field with a total of eight categories, again using a Q-sort method (Smith, 2003). Only two of the metaphors seemed too vague to be clearly assigned to any of the eight categories.

## 3. Results

### Overview of the 59 real-life critical moments

Appendix C contains half of our collected data set of critical moments. It is a random selection of 28 of the 59 critical-moment descriptions, with only minor changes made by us, in terms of style and spelling. We have left out the longest descriptions, which in some cases went up to 500 words, or a page of typed text. Other than the critical-moment descriptions, we also show six of the (longer) "no" responses.

### Content analysis of the critical moments

We coded each critical moment to identify themes and significant participant comments. The whole team of four authors took part in the creation of the codes as well as (each individually) in the coding itself in order to be able to check for inter-rater consistency. We arrived at 40 codes that described the whole data set (see Table 4.1). The four observers (the authors) together used combinations of these 40 codes a total of 788 times to code the 59 moments, which amounts to an average of 3.3 codes per critical-moment description. All codes were used at least once. Table 4.1 shows the frequency of use of the codes, for all four observers.

To determine inter-rater reliability, we computed Cohen's Kappa (Cohen, 1960) and also Fleiss's Kappa (Fleiss, 1971) which give a multi-rater statistic. The scores are in Table 4.2. As is well known (Dollard & Auld, 1959), Cohen's and Fleiss's Kappas are very sensitive to the number of codes and cannot be expected to be very large with such a high amount of codes. However, the average Kappa from Table 4.2 is 0.44 and therefore the average improvement over chance was 45-fold. We may safely conclude that our codes have been most reliably used by the four observers to categorise the critical moments. High reliability between raters of "helpful events" was also reported in psychotherapy research (Elliott et al., 1985; Llewelyn, 1988).

Reading through the critical moments, and looking at the result of our coding, our first conclusions were as follows. Across the 59 reported critical moments, respondents were most likely to assert that the critical moment contained an instance of increasing awareness, whether relating to themselves, their pattern of behaviour or the consequences of their behaviour in their organisations. Many participants referred to a "realisation" or "revelation" (the word "realise" occurred 24 times in our collected data, "insight" eight times, and "revelation" once; these expressions covered 16 of the 40 codes, accounting for no less than 43% of our coding – see Table 4.1). Elliott (1985) reports something very similar in his collection of "helpful events" from psychotherapy: by far the largest of his clusters is the one he calls "new perspective", which is defined very similarly to our "personal realisation". One of our participants says 'Yes, I have had that "critical moment" as described above, although I referred to it as the moment "I saw the path clear"' (see example 25 in Appendix C). We noticed two major areas of personal realisation:

*Table 4.1* The table shows all 40 codes, divided into four categories: Personal realisations, Experiencing personal changes, Other experiences through the coaching and Actions by the coach. The right-hand column shows the percentage of uses of the code by all four observers together (all uses by the four observers = 100%)

| Codes | Typical experiences related by coachees | Frequency (%) |
|---|---|---|
| | 1. Personal realisations | |
| | (1.A About issues) New knowledge/understanding/insight | |
| 1 | Content/facts | 4.6 |
| 2 | New action/behaviour that can be used | 4.8 |
| 3 | New strategy/approach to adopt | 4.4 |
| 4 | Working with others/their behaviour/work roles | 4.6 |
| 5 | About others and their personalities | 0.8 |
| | (1.B About self) Self-knowledge | |
| 6 | Revelations/blind spots | 10.4 |
| 7 | How others view me | 1.3 |
| 8 | Own defensiveness/excuses | 0.9 |
| 9 | Consequences of own behaviour | 2.5 |
| 10 | Hidden motivators | 0.9 |
| 11 | Influence of old patterns/past experience | 3.9 |
| | (1.C About this coaching) | |
| 12 | The coach/coaching not being supportive | 0.5 |
| 13 | The coach/coaching leaving me to my own devices | 0.9 |
| 14 | The coach/coaching not being good enough | 1.1 |
| 15 | The coach/coaching breaking confidentiality | 0.5 |
| 16 | The coach/coaching being unsure | 0.4 |
| | 2. Experiencing personal changes | |
| 17 | Acceptance | 1.5 |
| 18 | Change of style/behaviour | 9.4 |
| | Decisions | |
| 19 | Reaffirming current decision/position | 1.0 |
| 20 | Making a new decision | 3.6 |
| 21 | Revoking a decision | 0.5 |
| | 3. Other experiences through the coaching | |
| 22 | Relief | 1.6 |
| 23 | Growing confidence/self-belief | 5.3 |
| 24 | Overcoming fear | 1.0 |
| 25 | Just speaking/talking during the coaching | 1.3 |
| 26 | Just partaking in the experience of it | 0.6 |
| 27 | 'Elation' | 1.6 |
| 28 | Sensation of time slowing down | 0.6 |
| 29 | Working through challenges or 'training in' new behaviour | 1.5 |
| 30 | Painful awareness/realisation | 5.8 |
| | 4. Actions by coach, who offers: | |
| 31 | Tools/experiences | 5.3 |
| 32 | Pertinent or insightful questions | 3.8 |
| 33 | Quality of listening | 0.1 |
| 34 | Personal feedback | 1.3 |
| 35 | Advice | 2.5 |
| 36 | Suspension of advice/judgement | 1.1 |
| 37 | Metaphor | 1.3 |
| 38 | Direct confrontation/challenge | 3.4 |
| 39 | Tangible support | 1.4 |
| 40 | Space/freedom | 1.6 |

Table 4.2 Kappas[1] for inter-rater reliability in the coding of critical moments

|                | Rater CB | Rater CS | Rater EH |      |
|----------------|----------|----------|----------|------|
| Rater CS       | 0.46     |          |          |      |
| Rater EH       | 0.48     | 0.49     |          |      |
| Rater AD       | 0.32     | 0.40     | 0.47     |      |
| Multi-rater agreement (Fleiss's Kappa): |          |          |          | 0.24 |

1  Personal realisations about issues (18% of assigned codes – see Table 4.1). This includes new knowledge, understanding or insight into a situation, understanding of others or ideas about strategies. See, for example, critical moments 5 and 12 in Appendix C.

2  Personal realisations into and about self (20% of assigned codes – see Table 4.1). This includes recognising unhelpful patterns of relating, personal "hang-ups" or impact on others. See, for example, critical moments 6 and 18 in Appendix C.

These realisations or insights were often accompanied by strong emotions, including "painful awareness", "elation", "liberation", "relief" and "boost in confidence". Similar to our earlier findings with coaches (Day et al., 2008), the realisations often emerged suddenly or abruptly in the process.

We were surprised that very few of the respondents who described "positive" critical moments referred to anything the coach had done around this time. This is in marked contrast to the earlier research with coaches (see, e.g., De Haan, 2008c, 2008d), where the participants nearly always described their own actions and their coachees' responses before, during and after the critical moment. At the same time, it was interesting that in the case of "negative" critical moments, all participants did mention the coach, specifically the (in their view) unhelpful or insensitive actions by the coach that damaged the trust in the relationship and led to the negative outcome. Therefore, in the negative critical moment, the coach was mentioned much more often (see, e.g., descriptions 4 and 14 in Appendix C).

## The use of metaphor

We became intrigued by the way participants used metaphors to describe their experience of critical moments. Frequently, they used images or ideas from one area of life or "conceptual domain" to help them to describe their emerging experience during or after coaching (Lakoff, 1993). In total, we found 252 metaphors across both the 59 critical-moment descriptions and the transcripts from the eight in-depth interviews.

We categorised all the metaphors used by participants into 14 different clusters each representing a common conceptual domain. Fourteen clusters were enough to capture all metaphors except for one singular one which had been used ten times by a single participant (the word "gremlin"). Here are the 14 clusters of metaphors, in order of decreasing occurrence (the full data set of metaphors can be obtained from the authors):

1  Journey (e.g. "Sort of avenues that were open to me"): 36 occurrences.
2  Physical Space (e.g. "Point in time"): 35 occurrences.
3  Revelation (e.g. "Light bulb moments"): 26 occurrences.
4  Visual (e.g. "The pathetic façade I thought I was projecting to the world was completely see-through"): 25 occurrences.
5  Agency (e.g. "In charge of your own destiny"): 20 occurrences.
6  Release (e.g. "The sense of liberation I felt"): 18 occurrences.
7  Resources (e.g. "'Toolkit' to explore options"): 15 occurrences.
8  Frame (e.g. "A different framework"): 14 occurrences.
9  Challenged (e.g. "Stretch me"): 13 occurrences.
10  Connecting (e.g. "Decouple events"): 13 occurrences.
11  Tackle (e.g. "Take the trucks across the bridge"): 10 occurrences.
12  Fight (e.g. "Your platoon is just a single unit in a larger group"): nine occurrences.
13  Hearing (e.g. "Listen to myself"): four occurrences.
14  Money (e.g. "Value offering"): four occurrences.

So our collection of descriptions of critical moments in coaching contained a wealth of metaphors that our earlier coding could not convey. At the same time, we were struck by the overlap between the results of these two very different ways of analysing the data. "Realisations" dominate the coding categories, while the very similar "revelations" (including "visual" and "hearing" insights) are prominent in the collection of metaphors. It seems worthwhile to explore the possibility of a coaching model that covers a substantial part of both the codes and the metaphors.

## 4. Discussion

Although the 59 detailed descriptions of critical moments form a broad database of research data, we need to keep three things in mind:

1  As far as we know, this is the first study of its type in the field of executive coaching, so no comparison data are available.
2  The response rate was low, especially among the alumni, where senior managers who did not know us and possibly had not been coached were asked to respond to a direct mail request.
3  20 of the 67 coachees who did respond (30%) reported that they had not experienced any critical moments. We cannot tell whether the low response rate is due to little experience of coaching or not remembering critical moments. Or perhaps it is due to us asking a separate closed question about whether they have experienced critical moments, which we had not done before.

The combination of comments (2) and (3) above seems to indicate that coachees *tended not to experience critical moments*, although 70% of our respondents reported at least one critical moment. When we examine the 59 critical-moment descriptions more closely, we do so in the knowledge that only further research will enable us to determine how relevant critical moments really are for clients of coaching. The discussion below is therefore mainly intended to inspire further research. We conclude with a summary of recommendations for other coaches and researchers in this field.

### Summary of findings

In summary, the data contributed by 67 clients of executive coaching suggest to us the following:

- Coachees report very different phenomena from their coaches in response to literally the same question about critical moments in coaching. For one thing, coachees seemed to be less interested (than the coaches in our earlier research) in discussing the patterns of interaction during coaching. A second important difference is that coaches spoke to us at length about their doubts and anxieties (Day et al., 2008; De Haan, 2008c, 2008d), while coachees mostly speak about the personal realisations and understanding of themselves and others that they gain during coaching. In other words, coaches focus more on emotions and anxieties, while coachees focus more on outcomes and insight.
- Coachees report a lot fewer critical moments than coaches: 30% of the participants in this research had not experienced any critical moments. One participant summed this up by 'Only once did I experience a critical moment, which considering I have had many hours of coaching, seems that this may be a bit over estimated'. Lower prevalence of critical moments can be partly explained by the fact that professional coaches often have more than one coachee and generally spend more hours in coaching than their coachees.
- Coachees' critical-moment descriptions are more diverse than those of coaches, for example, many of the descriptions relate to the outcome or "harvest" of the moment and not to the moment itself. Coachees seem less interested in making sense of what was happening in the relationship and more focussed on what was happening for them and for their issues. This relates to the next point as well.
- Coachees mention much less often the coaching process and their counterparts in the relationship, while realisation, insight and awareness come much more to the fore. In other words, coachees are not recognising explicitly that their coach played a direct role in this process. Perhaps the coachee finds it very difficult to identify specific interventions or behaviours of the coach leading up to or during a critical moment. Also, coachees will be focussing so much on their own issues that the process or the coach's contributions may not figure as strongly as their own reflections, realisations and breakthroughs. In this, we confirm another conclusion of Llewelyn (1988): 'it is clear that coachees were more concerned with the results of the procedure than with the process by which it occurred'. Indeed, one definition of "good coaching" is that it should facilitate the coachee to find his or her own solutions and that the coaching process should therefore run relatively smoothly and invisibly for the coachee. It seems as if that is a tenable conclusion based on our data.

### A tentative coaching model of the coachee

The tentative findings outlined above are based on a limited volume of data. However, they seem to argue for a completely new way of understanding how coaching is experienced by the coachee, in contrast to the experiences of coaches, which were investigated previously (De Haan, 2008c, 2008d).

A number of models that are used in the coaching profession introduce distinctions that may guide the coach in approach and intervention. Frequent examples of such polarities are as follows:

- The distinction between *directiveness* and *non-directiveness*, alternatively presented as a distinction between "push" and "pull", or between "exploring" and "advocating", or "question" and "advice";
- The distinction between *challenge* and *support*, alternatively presented as a distinction between "confrontation" and "invitation", or between "overcoming weaknesses" and "building on strengths";
- The distinction between *content* and *process*, that is, between the topic matter of the conversation and the conversation itself; alternatively, between expert contributions and open exploration;
- Distinctions between *past* and *future*, between *closeness* and *distance*, and between *accepting* or *changing*;
- Several other distinctions and polarities that have been put forward are reviewed in Appendix A in De Haan and Burger (2005).

Some of these distinctions or polarities may speak to the coachee as well, but our contention is that most of these are less relevant for the coachee than for the coach. On some of these dimensions, a coachee may not feel as if he or she has equal freedom of choice as a coach (e.g. push/pull or content/process); on others, the coachee simply has or wants both (e.g. past/future or challenge/support). From our (albeit limited) data, it seems that the main distinction or polarity for the coachee is between issue/problem and issue/problem resolution. The coachee's agenda is usually none other than to find new answers to old queries. Data on critical moments for coaches invite many of the above distinctions (see De Haan, 2008d), but these initial data on critical moments for coachees call for quite new and different distinctions. It is time to explore those coachee distinctions, both empirically and theoretically.

From the nature of the codes, and especially those that occurred relatively frequently in the coding of coachee descriptions of critical moments (see Table 4.1), we infer that the main differences identified by these coachees related to realisation/insight, change, instruments and decision-making or action. Around half of the insights relate to the coachee's problems, the other half to the coachee himself. Similarly, the change experienced sometimes seems to be internal, sometimes external. The image created in us by reading the descriptions and codes was that of a voyage of discovery, with some discoveries being internal, others external, some emerging gradually or incrementally, others more suddenly and leading the coachee into deeper investigations or less-explored territory. Based on this interpretation of our data and the most frequently assigned codes, we arrive at the following two essential polarities that we recognise in all the coachee data. Both relate to personal change and both have already been described in different contexts:

## (I) CHANGE THAT IS ALTERATION VERSUS CHANGE THAT IS GENERATION/DESTRUCTION

We were reminded of Aristotle's (4th century BC) distinction between two fundamentally different forms of change. He argued that change can consist of:

a A change in attributes, such as movement from A to B or acquisitions (whether quantitative or qualitative), sometimes called "progress" or "journey". This form of change is basically an alteration and is often referred to as "accidental change" or "incremental change". Examples are critical moments 2 and 25 (Appendix C).

b A change in nature or substance, sometimes called "transformation". This form of change is basically generative or destructive and is often referred to as "substantial change" or "transformational change". Examples are critical moments 16 and 23 (Appendix C).

### (2) INTERNAL PROCESSING VERSUS EXTERNAL PROCESSING

We were also reminded of Jung's (1920) distinction between introversion and extraversion, taken up by Kolb (1984) in his model of experiential learning. This distinction relates to two types of personal learning as a precondition for change:

a Internal processing (introversion, intention) means looking inward to generate a different perspective, by concentration and reflection. Examples are critical moments 9 and 19 (Appendix C).

b External processing (extraversion, extension) means moving outward to generate a different perspective, by experimenting and acting. Examples are critical moments 6 and 25 (Appendix C).

The two-by-two matrix spanned by these two polarities has been drawn up in Figure 4.1. For us, the diagonals in the model are also clear polarities:

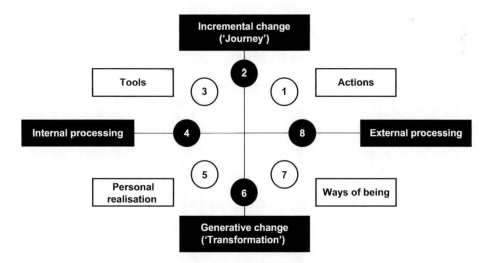

Figure 4.1 Word choice used by coaching clients to describe their experience of critical moments in coaching. The two poles (incremental versus generative change and internal versus external processing) and the four dimensions that they create (action, tools, realisation/insight, ways of being) are based on the 59 critical-moment descriptions and the codes most frequently used to designate those descriptions. © Ashridge Executive Education 2017.

1   (left-top to right-bottom) Tools and ways of being can be seen as complementary ways of defining oneself: an ontological coaching dimension (Sieler, 2003) distinguishing between "appearing" and "being" (*phenomenon* versus *noumenon*).

2   (left-bottom to right-top) Insight and action can be seen as theory and practice in behaviour: a hermeneutic coaching dimension distinguishing between theory-in-use and espoused theory (Argyris, 1991).

### Using the tentative model as a taxonomy of coachee metaphor

Once we had developed a model that covered much of the content of the critical-moment descriptions collected from coaching clients, we wanted to investigate whether it could also be applied to their use of metaphor. We took the same 252 metaphor cards we had collected and looked at how well they fit into the "tentative model". We were pleased to find that only two metaphors could not be easily placed in the two-by-two matrix in Figure 4.1 (these were two cards bearing the words "Summer Umbrella" and "Critical Factors"). Table 4.3 shows the way that many metaphors

*Table 4.3* Occurrence of metaphors in the eight dimensions of our 'Model of the ways a coachee may experience executive coaching' (as summarised in Figure 4.1)

| No. | Dimension | Total number of metaphors assigned | Patterns in/Examples from metaphor data |
|---|---|---|---|
| 1 | Acquisition of new action (Agency) | 72 | Fighting, Revisiting/Evaluating, Constrained, Controlling, Choosing/Altering, Facing up to/Owning, (Dis)Connecting/ (De)Constructing |
| 2 | Incremental change (Journey) | 34 | Start → Route → End, Quest(ing), Nautical passage (gentle), Travelling companion, Sudden easing of the way |
| 3 | Acquisition of solutions and tools | 25 | Framing/structuring, Making sense, Conceptual domain/context, Foundations/base, Reality/Truth/Authenticity, Measurables, Tools, Experience |
| 4 | Internal processing (focussing inwards) | 4 | Pattern, Structure, Organisation |
| 5 | Personal realisation (Enhancing insight) | 61 | Revelation, Realising, Perspectives/Context, Visualising/Focussing, Thinking patterns/styles, Building conceptual resources |
| 6 | Generative Change (Transformation) | 4 | Sudden "coming together", Expansive thinking |
| 7 | Way of being in the world (Becoming a different person) | 47 | Reviewing one's foundations and personal context, Adapting to what comes along, Striving and enduring against challenges, Making sense and clarifying meaning in interaction |
| 8 | External processing (focussing outwards) | 3 | Creating, shaping, offering (packaging and bundling product) |

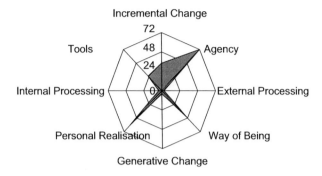

**Number of metaphors**

*Figure 4.2* Diagram showing the amount of metaphors that can convincingly be attributed to one of the eight ways in our model in which coachees experience executive coaching (using the data from Table 4.3).

can be linked with the eight dimensions in Figure 4.1. In Figure 4.2, these results are plotted to show the spread of metaphors that emerged in the research. It is also noteworthy that the participants' metaphors seem to focus mainly on the diagonals: the fields of "Tools", "Actions", "Personal realisation" and "Ways of being" have the highest occurrence of metaphors, and only one of the four axes (the "Incremental change" dimension) captures a similar amount of metaphors.

The way in which we investigated the rich content that the coaching clients shared with us, as described above, reminds us to some extent of … coaching. First, we tried to understand what the coachees wanted to tell us in terms of content, by summarising it in our own words and using concise "codes" for different descriptions given by coachees. Then we developed a heuristic model based on our understanding of what the coaching clients had told us. Finally, we used this model to help us understand how they said it (the words and metaphors they used). We thus tried to understand the volunteered "critical moments" from two radically different angles: content and use of metaphor. As is so often the case in executive coaching, we found a strong connection between what was said and the way it was said, between message and language, between content and metaphor. And as also noted in Chapter 1, there is once again a striking resemblance between the fields of "coaching" and "qualitative research", where both consist of an open and honest, courageous and creative exploration of the material brought forward by the coachee.

It seems that the coaching clients in this study find the question about critical moments less self-evident than do their coaches; and that, if they do report critical moments, they refer mainly to a new realisation or a new insight. For coaching clients, things only really happen when they look at something differently, when they start thinking about something in a new way or when they are able to make an unanticipated decision. Just as for the Greek philosopher Archimedes, the watchword for these managers is "eureka": "I have found it!", exclaimed in the warm bath of their coaching conversations, while they create new insights, answers and solutions to long-standing issues.

### SUMMARY OF CHAPTER 4: "I SUDDENLY REALISED"

In the third phase of the research into critical moments in coaching, we received from 67 former clients of coaching their answers to the following question:

> Have you ever experienced something that felt like a **critical moment** (an exciting, tense or significant moment) during your coaching? If so, please describe briefly one (or more) critical moment. What was it about this moment that made it critical for you?

Twenty of these coachees did not recognise the question and did not provide descriptions of critical moments, while the other 47 respondents volunteered a total of 59 critical moments (see Appendix C), which were then analysed.

The most common ingredient of coachees' critical-moment descriptions was "realisation", "insight" or "revelation": these words and similar ones covered no less than 43% of all codes we assigned.

In around half of the cases, this **"insight"** mentioned by the coachee was related to her- or himself (i.e. she had realised something new about herself); in the other half of cases, it was related to the issues she or he had brought to coaching. Moreover, this dawning insight was often accompanied by strong emotions, including "painful awareness", "elation", "liberation", "relief" and "boost in confidence".

The 20 coachees (30% of the sample of respondents) said they obtained more constant, ongoing help through coaching and were generally positive about the coaching they had received.

Finally, three critical moments were noticeably negative about the coaching conversations in this respect. In all three, there was a reference to the (inadequate) person or contribution of the coach. In the other moments, the coach was hardly ever mentioned.

Analysis of the moment descriptions and of the metaphors used by coachees yielded a **coaching model of the coachee**, that is, a first model of coaching dictated by the way in which coachees themselves experience coaching. The two axes of this model span the following dimensions: (1) *change of aspects (mere mental change)* versus *essential change (transformative change)* and (2) *internal* versus *external processing* aspects of experiential learning.

## Note

1 Landis and Koch (1977) suggest that any Fleiss's Kappa over 0.24 should be regarded as "fair agreement", even with a much smaller number of codes than we have in our study.

# Chapter 5

# Critical moments in coaching

## Looking for a *Rashomon* effect

## A. Anecdote

*Rashomon* is a 1950 feature film by Japanese director Akira Kurosawa and one of the first Japanese films to enjoy immediate success in the West. Its theme is the impossibility of reconstructing the past from different testimonies. The film is still considered a masterpiece by many, for example, it is the favourite film of renowned Hollywood director Paul Verhoeven. *Rashomon* describes a particular event, the attack and rape of a woman and the murder of her Samurai husband, as seen by different witnesses who contradict each other. They cannot all be right, and yet every version of the violent incident seems credible. The film's existential plot has made *Rashomon* synonymous with the relativity of "the truth". All of the witnesses' stories seem perfectly logical and defensible, but there always turns out to be an underlying motive (lust, revenge, honour, greed, fear) for them to tell the story in this particular way and not another. The question remains: is there actually such a thing as 'objective' truth?

It is enlightening to view coaching conversations and relationships through the *Rashomon* lens:

> This is how I experience our conversation. But how does the other person experience it? On the surface of the relationship, we both see the same things and hear the same words. But how do we understand those words, how do we interpret them for ourselves? Etcetera.

In this way we can associate to our own experience of the coaching, and hidden aspects of the relationship (such as the underlying motives in the *Rashomon* story) also come into play. I often notice a relationship that at first glance seems straightforward and is spoken about as if it were straightforward, including, for example, defined contractual agreements, a clear purpose and agreed goals, with one person in the role of coach and service provider and the other in the role of client, owner and protagonist. Still, this very relationship can look very different from the inside. And also different to each party involved. A huge amount of work goes on below the surface. This is where we bring in our own anxieties and indirectly all the relationships we have "practised" with in the past.

Below the surface is the domain of transference and countertransference, where we as coachee and coach approach each other much more symmetrically, as two independent human beings each with our own needs and vulnerabilities. Here, very different stories are told. Here, basically, we continue to play out many earlier, significant relationships, especially if they are somehow unfinished or unsatisfactory. To navigate properly within any coaching relationship, we need to be open to this almost unknowable domain and remain genuinely curious about underlying motivations and anxieties. Otherwise, in the "above-ground", explicit relationship, we will not achieve results that actually work.

Let me dig around in my memory and find that undercurrent. Those taboos and buried tensions, the soft and dark underbelly of my coaching conversations, which I acutely felt at the time but rarely dared to address explicitly. Let me try to recall something of that more somatic experience, the rushes of adrenaline, sweat and anxiety in my body, the simmering aggression, the attacks on the bearer of bad news, the mutual idealisations, the need for status and the stalking, the battle over who becomes the hunter and who the prey, heterosexual men deliberately choosing attractive female coaches or coachees, women feeling intimidated within the coaching relationship, etc. Let me try to write a little *Rashomon* story based on my own coaching conversations.

It is well established by now that we bring all sorts of unresolved patterns from previous relationships with us into our coaching sessions, hidden below the surface. Racker (1968) remains an authoritative text on transference and countertransference. He observes that there are basically only two underlying impulses in a relationship, which are also the hardest to overcome (in this case, to reflect on together rather than acting them out) during coaching conversations. These are the impulses of sex/love and power/violence. At the core, they may be parts of the same drive, because within coaching they are both clear attempts of subjection. In other words, under the surface we can perceive "personal growth" on a very primitive and territorial level.

### So... Sex

The worst thing that ever happened to me in coaching was in a first session, when I was so overwhelmed by someone's physical attractiveness that my fountain pen began to leak incessantly and in minutes my hands were covered in black ink. A very Freudian slip that happened "of its own accord". For the rest of the session, I tried to keep talking as normal, but I felt ashamed and was more concerned with my hands than with coaching. In the end, the coachee did not choose to continue in any case.

I am familiar too with the phenomenon of stalking and of wanting to get ever closer to the coach of one's choice. In fact, I went out of my way to continue seeing my first therapist after successful treatment, for example, by joining a course he was teaching. And for years I have not been able to go on holiday without having to turn down special messages and requests to do a bit extra for someone, that is, with coachees signalling their secret wish that I would still be available on my holiday. And I often hear coaches in supervision talk about how they are "pursued" by coachees who keep signing up again for more sessions, but actually are mainly seeking closeness and intimacy; their benefit from those additional sessions in terms of coaching objectives usually turns out to be very limited.

As a supervisor, I see many examples of sexual distraction from the task of coaching – colleagues who turn their coachees into life partners, coachees who choose a coach based on physical appeal and coachees who start to flirt (or unexpectedly misinterpret warmth and attention as a "pass"), often precisely at those times when the coaching conversations are difficult and tough decisions need to be taken. See also Gray and Goregaokar (2010) as a study of sexual phenomena during coach-client matching.

And then there is mutual idealisation within the coaching relationship which I believe is sexual in nature, for example, the senior executive who has found a senior coach. The coach is proud of his coachee, and the executive is proud of his coach. Both have substantial reputations and each has now "landed" the other. I remember a coachee where this was very much the case. So much so that it took me perhaps eight to ten coaching sessions to say what I had seen in terms of a vulnerability in his leadership, namely that he had a strong need in all his relationships to keep everything "nice": warm, pleasant and agreeable, which made him sit on the fence when it came to conflict and challenge. Something I probably would have offered much earlier in the absence of those mutual expressions of estimation. As is invariably the case (a "parallel process", see Searles, 1955), the same thing happened in our relationship: I found our sessions pleasant and warm, but did not realise that critical moments only occurred in the coachee's stories, never between us. I had noticed this tendency on his part to soothe with warmth and courtesy but had never mentioned it, so much was I basking in the (reflected) glow of this coachee. Until, that is, he and I both came in for heavy criticism. My coachee had lost the support of his supervisory board and had been fiercely criticised for his conflict avoidance and for failing to implement certain painful changes in the organisation. This board meeting also raised the circumstance of the coaching, which had then been going on for almost a year. My coachee told me how I as his coach had been accused of only making things worse. He was very disappointed by this, not only in himself but also in the coaching. The meeting immediately led to a series of telephone conversations between us in which his threat to stop and find another coach hung constantly in the air. In the end, we both put on our hair shirts and only then did we really get to work. Suddenly a much more challenging side emerged within myself, one which I knew from other coaching relationships, but had not thought necessary here because I conveniently believed my coachee was already so calm, distinguished and accomplished.

### And power

Once I was contracted to gather impressions of the plant manager in a production company in preparation for our coaching sessions. There had been a lot of criticism in the interviews, especially that the manager did not intervene enough in cases of indiscipline or harassment and other goings-on between workers in the factory. I reported back as sensitively as I could and mentioned the essence of the feedback – with plusses and minuses. Imagine my surprise when the plant manager first turned bright red in the face, then stood up, left the room and headed straight for the executive wing of the company and the operations chief to complain about me. 'I've been working here for twenty years and have never heard anything like this', was his biggest gripe. He had not received any direct feedback on his performance for over 20 years. And after 20 years, he did not want to change that either, because he asked the director to dismiss his coach. In the end that did not happen: the plant manager and I worked together for many months at the request of the COO, although we never developed a truly warm relationship. It was more based on power and resentment. Eventually, he did realise that he had let a lot of things slide and lacked authority on the shop floor. He agreed to step aside in favour of a successor who could act more firmly when things got out of hand between the operators.

Often, organisational power permeates the coaching room, with very different goals from those from within the coaching. I remember Matthew who headed the crucial "home country" of an investment bank, but had been sidelined by the new CEO. Ahead of our meetings, I received various items of information about Matthew from the CEO and the HR director. Matthew turned out to be an enthusiastic coachee and worked quickly and energetically on his learning goals, some of which had been dictated by the CEO. However, as time went on, it became clear to me that the focus was not on the coaching, but on the complex negotiations to disentangle from the bank. Matthew owned a large percentage of the bank's shares and would benefit enormously from staying on for another year. Hence, at least in part, his enthusiasm for coaching and hence the continuing involvement of the HR director, who expressed dissatisfaction with the effects of the coaching. After working together for six months, Matthew and I felt we had achieved all the learning goals and Matthew proposed a three-way discussion with the CEO. The latter did not take up this invitation but was very keen to evaluate things for himself. He specified that I should send him my evaluation in writing. On his part Matthew was now working with a lawyer and also wanted a review meeting with me and a written report of that. So, at the end of the assignment, two different stories emerged about the coaching relationship: stories that might one day be contrasted in court, just like in the magnificent *Rashomon* movie.

But even on a much smaller scale, I often observe "power" and "competition" in coaching relationships. Being constantly contradicted by your partner in conversation, or infusing the conversation with tall tales to impress or win the other person over. Sometimes it is "airtime" as well, where my sense is that the coachee fills up the hour with a stream of words and associations, offering very little time for the coach to make a comment, possibly out of fear about what this comment might be. These can be major obstacles to coaching, unless you are able to raise the interaction itself and make it part of the learning process. Often it is the case that the kind of exercise of power you experience from your client as a coach will also be experienced in a similar form by others in the coachee's organisation.

### And a special mention for money

Money is where sex and power come together, so money tends to signify much more than just spending ability, a healthy budget or even a sense of comfort. Only by understanding the hidden associations of money, and the extent of control and pleasure that money often represents to the unconscious, can we understand how someone could worry about another wage rise when they are already home and dry. How often have I seen that the "desire" for a promotion or better salary is the main reason to enter coaching, and then becomes the primary reason to stay away from the coaching goals, in other words the desire itself becomes the main obstacle to really being coached. Blind fascination for what others might offer you can be very distracting from your own coaching agenda, even if that was where everything began for the collaboration.

For coaches, it is all the more important to understand the attraction of sex, money and power, and also to comprehend the deeper meaning of these sorts of "emoluments", that is, the ability of these drives to fill apparent gaps or acquire alternative means of control. They can give you a "handle" on other people or on your work objectives which is ultimately corrupting as it goes beyond more open and rational ways of achieving the same. If coaches cannot understand the motivations behind this blind (because largely unconscious) desire, we will achieve little in our conversations, and, if we cannot name these aspects somehow or try to interpret them in terms of transference and a deep deficiency in previous relationships, we will never get the conversation that we should have and the only one that may have a chance to generate real growth in the client's circumstances. This demands a great deal of an executive coach, something that in my experience can only be acquired through intensive training and supervision, namely the art of understanding the whirlpool of desires and raw emotions while not allowing yourself to be carried away by it.

For a place to start, we often ask coaches on our training courses to think about a coachee they are currently working with. And then to imagine being marooned with this coachee on a deserted island. Visualisations like these, shifting the mind from brief, contained conversations to having to deal with each other full-time, often have a powerful effect. Try it with your own current coachee. Sniggers and laughter are never far away when we present this thought experiment to a group of coaches. Everyone recognises the undercurrent when they transport themselves and their client to such an island, but only a few remain aware of it during their coaching conversations and are able to handle it in an ethical and reflective way.

## B. Essences

After collecting coachee accounts of critical moments in coaching, our research gained a new impetus. These accounts clearly showed a different picture than that presented by the coaches. Coachees focussed much more on the learning process and learning outcomes (see Chapter 4), while coaches were more concerned with emotions in the coaching relationship and their own doubts and struggles (see Chapters 2 and 3). The question arose whether coaches and coachees would show the same differences when considering the *same* coaching relationship or the *same* coaching conversation. In other words, do they take quite different things away from a shared coaching experience, as the previous studies showed? To measure this, we began studying critical moments immediately after the coaching conversations. This chapter reports on the results of that research. The first study consisted of interviews with coach and coachee, independently of each other, immediately after their shared coaching conversations. We did this with 21 coach-coachee pairs, resulting in 86 new descriptions of critical moments (examples are in Appendix D.1). Next, we studied critical moments recorded by coach and coachee immediately after each of their ten coaching sessions. This study also yielded 32 critical moments, from both participants (all these critical-moment descriptions are in Appendix D.2). These moments form a case study and also enable us to follow the development of critical moments over the course of a coaching relationship. An overview of our findings is given below, with a more detailed analysis in part C of this chapter.

This study of critical moments as reported immediately after "live" coaching conversations yields encouraging results in a number of respects. First, it was encouraging that analysis of the critical-moment descriptions given by coaches and coachees leads to unambiguous conclusions that are statistically reliable. It is good to see that qualitative research into large numbers of descriptions can generate firm conclusions. Second, it was encouraging to see that coachees and coaches normally *agree* on the moments that matter in their coaching conversations. Despite all of the constructivist and narrative tendencies in the modern specialist literature, it is nice to see that, while coachee and coach may each have their own story, these independent stories show a large degree of overlap – justifying the hope that there is an underlying, more objective story about each coaching conversation and its effectiveness. Third, it is good to know that exceptional critical moments, often coinciding with disruptions in the coaching relationship or existential doubts on the part of the coach, probably require different skills and a different approach than the more "everyday" critical moments in this latest research. In contrast to Gaston Bachelard's statement, often quoted as a defence of constructivism, "Nothing proceeds from itself. Nothing is given. All is constructed" (Bachelard, 1938), these coaches and coachees seem to uncover a shared truth when making sense of their shared conversations.

Content analysis of the longitudinal case study, seen from the perspective of both coachee and coach, shows that previous patterns observed in hundreds of critical-moment descriptions of coachees and coaches from hundreds of coaching relationships can even be demonstrated within a single coaching relationship. This shows that general process research into critical moments in coaching can also be relevant to specific coaching relationships.

This case study of critical moments in ten successive coaching conversations begins to give us an understanding of how anxieties can develop during coaching relationships. The case study has a clear beginning, middle and end, anxieties emerge and are resolved in the coaching relationship, and there are demonstrable patterns in the frequency of critical moment types from session to session. It seems that the success of coaching is strongly determined by the ability of both coach and coachee to offer answers to recurring relational problems, such as "how do we create enough openness and trust to get to work", "how can we continue to listen and learn even if something painful or unexpected is said" and "how do we hold on to the created reflective space so we can do our best work, even if we believe the initial question has already been answered". Coach and coachee must constantly redesign their partnership, renegotiate their interaction, and continuously navigate the cliffs and currents of the coaching process with due attention. Like the little prince and the wild fox in Antoine de Saint-Exupéry's famous story, the two protagonists in executive coaching need to build a unique relationship full of friendship and respect, but at the same time with enough frankness and distance to learn from each other. In other words, coach and coachee need to "tame" each other and continue to do so for the benefit of their coaching relationship:

> It was then that the fox appeared.
> 'Good morning,' said the fox.
> 'Good morning,' the little prince answered politely, though when he turned around he saw nothing.
> 'I'm right here,' the voice said, 'under the apple tree.'
> 'Who are you?' the little prince asked, and added, 'You're very pretty...'
> 'I'm a fox,' the fox said.
> 'Come and play with me,' the little prince proposed, 'I'm feeling so sad.'

'I can't play with you,' the fox said, 'I'm not tamed.'

'Ah! Please excuse me,' said the little prince. But upon reflection he added:
'What does <u>tamed</u> mean?'

'You're not from around here,' the fox said, 'What are you looking for?'

'I'm looking for people,' said the little prince. 'What does <u>tamed</u> mean?'

'People,' said the fox, 'have guns and they hunt. It's quite troublesome. And
they also raise chickens. That is the only interesting thing about them. Are you
looking for chickens?'

'No,' said the little prince. I'm looking for friends. What does <u>tamed</u> mean?'

'It's something that's been too often neglected,' said the fox. 'It means, to create
ties.'

'To create ties?'

'That's right,' the fox said. 'For me, you're only a little boy just like a hundred
thousand other little boys. And I have no need of you. And you have no need of
me, either. For you I'm only a fox like a hundred thousand other foxes. But if
you tame me, we'll need each other. You'll be the only boy in the world for me.
I'll be the only fox in the world for you...'

(Antoine de Saint-Exupéry, *The Little Prince*, 1943,
start of Chapter 21, translation Richard Howard)

## C.  Research by session: two versions of the same conversation

### I.  Introduction: research into critical moments immediately after coaching conversations

Executive coaching – the professional development of executives through one-to-one
conversations with a qualified coach – is a discipline within the broader field of organisation development (OD) which is comparatively amenable to research. Executive
coaching conversations are usually explicitly contracted and bounded in both time
and space (fixed duration, similar intervals, quiet and dependable space, away from
the coachee's organisation, etc.). Most coaching manuals suggest keeping the space
for conversation as much as possible neutral, uncluttered and comfortable, without
interference or distraction (Hawkins & Smith, 2006; Starr, 2003). Coach and coachee may spend some 10–20 hours in this same environment, in addition to sporadic
email and telephone exchanges. The executive coach does not normally have a lot of
contact with others in the coachee's organisation, unless there are additional coaching
clients in that organisation or the coaching is part of a larger-scale organisational
change programme. This relative simplicity, and the underlying unities of space, time,
action and actors, create a relatively bounded *laboratory* in which consulting interventions can be studied. This is what makes executive coaching particularly exciting
to investigate.

In order to understand the impact and contribution of executive coaching and
other organisational consulting interventions, it is not enough to just understand
general effectiveness or outcome. One also has to inquire into and create an understanding of the underlying coaching processes themselves, from the perspectives of
both coachees and coaches. The executive coaching profession is still young and

although there are several studies on coaching outcome (e.g. Evers, Brouwers, & Tomic, 2006; Ragins, Cotton, & Miller, 2000; Smither et al., 2003), all rigorous quantitative research papers with large enough samples, control groups and independent variables can probably be counted on the fingers of two hands. For recent overview studies that together cover some 20 serious coaching outcome research papers, see Kampa-Kokesch and Anderson (2001), Feldman and Lankau (2005), Greif (2007), De Haan and Duckworth (2013) and Jones, Woods, and Guillaume (2015). However much pioneering work has been done in recent years, there is really no comparison with the related but much more established field of psychotherapy which boasts many hundreds of solid research papers (for an overview of outcome research in psychotherapy, see Wampold, 2001).

This traditional outcome research reduces the whole of the coaching intervention to only one number, or perhaps a set of numbers, for example, averages of psychometric tests. However, outcome research has to be silent on what happens *within* a coaching relationship: the many gestures, speech acts and attempts at sense-making that make up the whole of the intervention. At best, outcome research can help us to predict in a statistical manner what the average expectation is for the outcome of a series of coaching conversations on a one-dimensional scale; at worst, it may not even tell us that. What interested us in this study was therefore how outcomes are achieved *within* the coaching intervention, that is, within and between individual coaching conversations. This is the realm of "sub-outcomes" (Rice & Greenberg, 1984): outcomes achieved in individual moments or sessions of coaching.

As mentioned earlier, researching the coaching *process* is not as straightforward as researching the coaching *outcome*. While reducing the whole of a coaching relationship to one or a few quantifiable "outcomes" (e.g. a rating by the coach, the coachee, the coachee's boss, an independent observer) allows a clear-cut and specific definition of that variable, when it comes to coaching process one has to deal with manifold "sub-outcomes" (Rice & Greenberg, 1984). Moreover, studying an ongoing process will influence that process, which makes it harder to conduct field research.

A field study into the process of executive coaching therefore inevitably entails a number of problems. It is nevertheless of vital importance for coaching practitioners to understand better what happens inside their conversations, what both partners in the conversations pay attention to and what they think is achieved through engaging in coaching. This chapter sets out preliminary answers to the following main research questions:

1  What is the nature of "key moments" that coachees and coaches report immediately after their session together?
2  In what ways and to what degree are the reports by coaches and their coachees different?
3  How do the results obtained with this new sample of "critical moments" collected immediately after the end of a conversation compare with findings from earlier studies?

Although to the best of our knowledge of the executive coaching literature, comparison studies into coaches' and coachees' experiences of coaching have not been undertaken before unless with general surveys about the whole coaching experience (see, e.g., Bickerich, Michel, and O'Shea, 2018; Machin, 2010; O'Broin & Palmer, 2010), they are not without important precursors in psychotherapy. Admittedly, psychotherapy has distinctive professional qualifications, different ways of working and a different knowledge base (Spinelli, 2008). In both executive coaching and psychotherapy, however, a one-to-one conversation is held with someone who provides result-oriented professional assistance. Given this similarity, it makes sense to explore the results of similar research from the other field. Yalom and Elkin (1974) famously wrote up their two-year therapy journey, so that for some 75 sessions we have a first-person account from both therapist and client written up independently and shortly after each session. Feifel and Eells (1964) gave one of the very first accounts of therapy sub-outcomes as reported by both patients and therapists. In their overview, they report 'a thought-provoking contrast in the patients' accent on insight changes compared with those on symptom relief and behaviours by therapists' (Feifel & Eells, 1964, p. 317). In a more extensive study where patient and therapist reports after single sessions were compared (Orlinsky & Howard, 1975), 'patients and therapists agreed in rating insight and problem-resolution as the dominant goal of the patients, with relief as a prominent although secondary, goal' (p. 66). Stiles (1980) did a direct-comparison study of sessions, by comparing clients' and therapists' ratings of sessions that they had together. By correlating ratings, he was able to show that clients' positive feelings after sessions were strongly associated with perceived 'smoothness/ease' of the sessions, while therapists' positive feelings were associated with 'depth/value' of the sessions. Broadly, clients and therapists tended to agree in their characterisations of sessions. Caskey, Barker and Elliott (1984) have compared patients' and therapists' perceptions of preselected individual therapist responses and they found reasonable agreement between patients and therapists on therapists' impact and intentions, as well.

Particularly relevant from the perspective of this inquiry is the direct-comparison study of key moments of therapy by Llewelyn (1988). She interviewed 40 patient-therapist pairs and collected 1,076 'critical events' (both helpful and unhelpful) from 399 sessions (an average of 2.7 per session). She found highly significant differences between the selection and description of the events by therapists and by patients. These differences turned out to be greater when the outcome of the psychotherapy was relatively less helpful. Llewelyn used Elliott's (1985) taxonomy to classify the events, and found that

- Patients valued "reassurance/relief" and "problem solutions" more highly;
- Therapists valued "gaining of cognitive / affective insight" highest;
- Both patients and therapists valued "personal contact" highly.

Llewelyn (1988) concludes that patients seem to be more concerned with solutions to their problems, and that they place higher value on advice and solutions, provided they feel free to reject them. Therapists, on the other hand, seem more concerned with the aetiology of the problems and potential transformation through the patient's insight.

Earlier research of critical moments of coaching conversations followed a narrative and retrospective approach. De Haan (2008c, 2008d), De Haan, Bertie, Day and Sills (2010a) and Day, De Haan, Sills, Bertie and Blass (2008) asked three groups of coaches and one group of clients of executive coaches to describe briefly one *critical moment* (an exciting, tense or significant moment) from their coaching journeys.

The studies to date have found quite divergent material with coaches and coachees clearly submitting different descriptions and also placing a different emphasis within the descriptions (see De Haan et al., 2010a, or Chapter 4). The results of previous investigations prompted the present direct-comparison study as a way to explore and clarify some of the differences and also to test the conclusions from earlier chapters, with the help of a new data set. Direct comparison in real time is, of course, not possible without seriously interfering with the executive coaching sessions themselves. In order to minimise interference, coach and coachee were interviewed only once and directly after a session. Other than logistical issues, potential relational difficulties were anticipated as the research would impinge on very sensitive, private and confidential relationships. To quote Elton Wilson and Syme's (2006) pertinent book *Objectives and Outcomes* (page 82):

> Asking clients for their opinion is a process fraught with controversy, with many therapists asserting the possibility of harm to the therapeutic alliance or, conversely, affecting the transference. In addition, clients may wish to please or praise their therapists or even to covertly attack their therapist. Unfortunately, a practitioner's own observations may be laden with assumption and a defensive need to prove their own worth or the effectiveness of their own theoretical and methodological approach.

The same can very well be true for asking coaches and their coachees about their findings, while they are still engaged in a long-term coaching intervention. One would expect the reports of key moments from their recent conversation to be influenced by what they think of the overall quality of the work and the relationship, by what they expect us as researchers to be looking for, or even by their relationships with us and our institution. We do believe however, that by asking them specifically for 'critical' or 'key' moments within the sessions, this halo effect will be diminished by comparison to asking them about the sessions in more general terms.

Following De Haan et al. (2010a – see Chapter 4), the main hypothesis for this study was that the perspectives of coachees and coaches will be significantly different, as is also the case for critical-event studies in psychotherapy (see, e.g., Caskey et al., 1984; Llewelyn, 1988). We were expecting not only substantial differences in the moments that were selected for recall, but also in terms of the emphasis within the moment descriptions. To our surprise we actually found that coachees' and coaches' data in this study were very similar, that in more than 50% of cases the same moment, event or topic was described, and that there were also substantial similarities in emphases between the coaches and their coachees.

## 2. Method

Since 2002, we have opted for the study of so-called 'critical-moment descriptions' as a way of understanding the impact of executive coaching engagements, following similar methods as pioneered by Flannagan (1954), Elliott, James, Reimschuessel, Cislo and Sack (1985) and Llewelyn (1988). Critical moments are remembered as exciting, tense and/or significant moments after coaching conversations. They can be assumed to be a reflection of change through executive coaching as it happens in conversation. Descriptions allow pattern analysis, both qualitatively and quantitatively, and they afford comparison procedures between different data sets. As a comparison with the previous research on critical moments in executive coaching conversations, a setting was devised that allows as much as possible to directly compare coachees' and coaches' perceptions of key moments in their sessions, in such a way that the distortions of memory (Goodman et al., 2006) would be minimised by gathering the critical-moment descriptions as quickly after the session as possible. We contacted directly and personally about 20 executive coaches of our acquaintance and agreed with 14 to work with us on this research programme. Each of these coaches agreed to be interviewed and selected a coachee who would also be interviewed straight after the coaching session they had together, for a maximum of 30 minutes. Two of the 14 coaches contributed two client sessions, and one contributed seven client sessions (all different coachees). The coach who contributed seven sessions with seven coachees did not preselect and just offered us data from all her coachees within one particular organisation. All interviews were recorded, and in one case the recording equipment did not work so that these data had to be discarded. All in all, the sample size was 21 coaching conversations, yielding 42 recorded interviews.

Of the 14 coaches participating in this inquiry, two were Ashridge staff, five were Ashridge associated coaches who do a lot of executive coaching work for Ashridge, three belonged to a wider network and four were in the second year of their MSc in Executive Coaching at Ashridge. Nine of the coaches had been accredited by Ashridge, and all had over two years of experience as an executive coach, with an average experience level of more than ten years. The coaches selected coachee, coaching conversation and interview day – the researchers worked as much as possible around their requirements and preferences. Three of the participating coaches were male and 11 were female. Of the 21 participating coachees, 6 were female and 15 were male. Most coachees and coaches were British/Irish; there was one Israeli and one Australian coach and one South African coachee. The average number of sessions that coach and coachee had already had with each other was 5.4 – with a minimum of two and a maximum of 15. On average coach and coachee had worked with each other for almost ten months.

As the authors have developed their thinking about critical moments in executive coaching over the years, they decided not to participate in the study as coaches, or as coachees, or even as interviewers. Two MSc students in Organisational Behaviour at Birkbeck University, Heather Reekie and Monica Stroink, were willing to run all the interviews, as they collected material for their own Master's dissertations. All interviews were conducted in private rooms, mostly close to the location where the coaching had taken place. Some were over the telephone. The interviews with coachee and coach were done as much as possible by both students to avoid potential biases. Logistically, this was not possible in three cases – mostly due to the fact that coachee and coach were promised an interview straight after the coaching session, so there would be least memory loss. In some cases, one of the students was not available immediately after the interview, so four coachee interviews (approximately 10% of the total sample) were conducted by one of the authors.

Unexpected logistical challenges followed from the fact that, for every pair of interviews, two different researchers had to travel to the right location or phone in at the right time. This sometimes meant hiring a second consulting room. Even with the logistics under control, the interviewees were subjected to detailed questioning having just come out of presumably intensive and exhausting coaching encounters. Nevertheless, 42 interviews with coachees and coaches took place shortly after their sessions, which generated 86 descriptions of critical moments (see Appendix D.1 for a selection of these descriptions).

All interviews had the same structure and they were all transcribed (except one). The interviewees were asked the following core questions about the critical moments in the session they had just had before the interview:

1    Looking back on the session, what seems to be the important or key or critical moment(s) of your time together? What happened? Please can you provide a brief description of the moment(s).
2    What tells you that this was a critical moment?
3    What was your role in that moment?
4    What was your partner's role in that moment?
5    How do you think this moment will impact on the future? (i.e. the future of these conversations or what you take from the coaching)

In this way, the interviewers were able to obtain 86 critical moments from 21 sessions, that is, an average of just over two per interview and 4.1 per coaching session. Exactly half, that is, 43 of these moments were obtained from coachees and another 43 were obtained from coaches. This chapter reports on the descriptions of key moments as they are found in the transcripts, that is, mainly answers to questions 1 and 2 above, and occasionally more data were taken from answers to the other questions, when this yielded additional clarity.

From this data set, the inquiry proceeded as follows:

1    Using grounded theory (Corbin & Strauss, 1990), we came up with 30 short codes describing critical aspects in the critical-moment descriptions.
2    Five in the research team (the four authors and one MSc student) coded the data set using as many of these codes as they wanted per critical moment. The five codings were correlated for inter-rater consistency, and first conclusions were drawn from the frequencies of codes.
3    The same method of grounded theory was again followed to come up with a much smaller code set, containing only 12 more disparate and mutually exclusive codes, which could be used not only for this data set, but also for all four previous data sets (Day et al., 2008; De Haan, 2008c, 2008d; De Haan et al., 2010a).
4    All five sets of critical moments, totalling 352 critical moments, were coded on the new codes using a sort method (exclusive coding of only one code per critical moment), by two of the authors (CB and EH) and by one outsider, a colleague not previously introduced to this research (AC).

## 3. Results

### 3.1 First impressions on reading through the data set

The following features stand out most in the new descriptions of critical moments provided by coaches and their coachees:

1   Both coachees and coaches found it easy to come up with critical or key moments. Contrary to earlier research into the experiences of clients of coaching (De Haan et al., 2010a), there were no "no" responses. In fact, there was at least one critical-moment description from every interview, and the total amount of key-moment descriptions volunteered by coachees exactly equals the number of those volunteered by coaches (43, i.e. on average 2.05 key moment descriptions per interview). There is, however, one coachee who says 'There's nothing really that sticks out, obviously it's always a very casual conversation – I think that the biggest thing is that it's always very thought provoking, it makes you look at yourself quite a lot', but he then continues to volunteer one key moment.

2   There was a clear and sustained focus on the coachee throughout the descriptions: only one of the 43 coach descriptions referred exclusively to the coach's internal process (this one description still referred three times briefly to the coachee, by name) and only one of the coachees described exclusively what the coach was doing. Fifty-three per cent of coaches' descriptions referred to themselves and their interventions, and 44% of coachees' descriptions referred explicitly to the coach and to what the coach had done.

3   The coding of the content of the critical moments with 30 codes similar to those in De Haan et al. (2010a) showed that the most prevalent codes were again those about personal realisations (both about issues and about self) and those that are about specific behaviours of the coach (both directive and facilitative interventions). Together these four of the 30 codes make up almost 50% of the coded content. When coachee and coach descriptions are compared, there are two clusters of codes which are strongly skewed towards the coach critical-moment descriptions:

    1   the coach's emotional reactions which made up five codes but only 6% of the content; and
    2   physiological reactions of the coachee (such as skin tone, agitation and breathing), a single code which covered 2% of the content.

4   A lot of coachees and coaches comment on the same moment or situation, and they talk about those moments and situations in similar terms. In fact, 46 of the 86 critical-moment descriptions (53%) were clearly about the same moment or event cited by the other partner (examples are the pairs 9–10 and 51–52 in Appendix D.1).

5   The descriptions are narrative in nature and seemed to all four authors less exciting or engaging compared with the previous research. They seem to be of lower risk and less immediate impact. At the same time, they can be seen as an illustration of the straightforward, helpful and practice-based character of our own experience of 'everyday coaching'.

6    The nature of the descriptions is broadly positive and constructive; there was only one moment approximating a rupture in the relationship (see critical moment 4co13 in Appendix D.1, and compare with Day et al., 2008, which found evidence of ruptures in the relationship in *most* critical-moment descriptions). There seems to be an absence of tension, struggle and strong emotion in the new data set. There are only three occasions where coachees express interest in their coaches, see, for example, critical moment 8cl30 in Appendix D.1. We assumed this was partly because of an implicit psychological contract between the participants, and between the participants and us, to be appreciative and gentle towards one another, which, in turn, may be due to the preselection and the ongoing nature of all relationships.

7    The only differences initially found between coachees' and coaches' accounts were that coaches place more emphasis on their own actions and they use more jargon and psychological terms to describe what went on compared with their coachees. This reminded us of Yalom's (Yalom & Elkin, 1974, p. 79) statement that his own observations seemed more "sophomoric" than his client's writing.

8    There were a large number of references by coaches (17 out of 43 moments) to coachees' physiological responses (frowning, posture, note taking, agitation, breathing, etc.), see, for example, vignettes 3co9 and 5co17 in Appendix D.1, while coachees never referred to these matters.

### 3.2  Content analysis of the critical moments

All critical-moment descriptions were coded to identify recurrent themes, with similar codes as in our previous research (see, e.g., De Haan et al., 2010a). The coding did not show a large or consistent difference between coach and coachee moment descriptions, and it showed less consistency among markers than before (Cohen's Kappa was only 0.34 on average), which can be explained by the fact that the fragments are longer (on average 316 words per description), so there is more information conveyed in every critical-moment description. Because of the failure of the existing set of codes to divulge distinctive patterns in the data set, and because of the striking differences with some of the earlier data sets, a new more succinct set of codes was drawn up and tested, which would capture all critical aspects across all five data sets. There were four broad categories in these 12 codes: a moment of learning (codes 1 and 2), a moment of relational change (codes 3 and 4), a moment of significant action (codes 5 and 6) and a moment of significant emotional experience (codes 7–12). To provide help with the emotional codes (7–12), a table with the full range of emotions based on a tree structure built on six primary emotions (three positive and three negative) by Parrot (2001) was provided to the coders. For brief descriptions of the 12 codes, see Table 5.1.

Two of the authors (EH and CB) and one colleague who was not an executive coach (AC) coded the full data set of 352 critical moments with these codes. All codes were used at least three times by every coder, though there were four codes that were used for less than 3% of the data set: 6, 7, 8 and 11. We had anticipated this when drawing up the set of 12 codes, but we maintained these codes to keep a balanced and structurally complete set. Figure 5.1 shows the frequency of use of the codes, for all three observers and the full data set of 352 moments.

*Table 5.1* The 12 codes that have been used to analyse all five data sets in Chapters 2–5

| Code number | Short description of the code |
| --- | --- |
| 1 | A moment of learning: a moment in which new insight was created for coach and – particularly – coachee. |
| 2 | A moment of learning: a moment of working through, reflecting, gaining new perspectives and/or making sense of existing material. |
| 3 | A change in the relationship in the moment (positive). |
| 4 | A change in the relationship in the moment (negative). |
| 5 | Significant action in the moment (coach-led): applying oneself to a unique scripted process such as drawing, visualisation, role play, GROW (Goal, Reality, Options, Will) etc. |
| 6 | Significant action in the moment (coachee-led): organising future sessions, negotiating the session, taking away action points, making notes, etc. |
| 7 | Significant emotional experience in the moment: joy (coachee); heightened positive emotion. |
| 8 | Significant emotional experience in the moment: joy (coach); heightened positive emotion. |
| 9 | Significant emotional experience in the moment: anxiety (coachee); heightened positive emotion. |
| 10 | Significant emotional experience in the moment: anxiety (coach); heightened positive emotion. |
| 11 | Significant emotional experience in the moment: doubt (coachee); fundamental not-knowing, often a starting point for reflection. |
| 12 | Significant emotional experience in the moment: doubt (coach); fundamental not-knowing, often a starting point for reflection. |

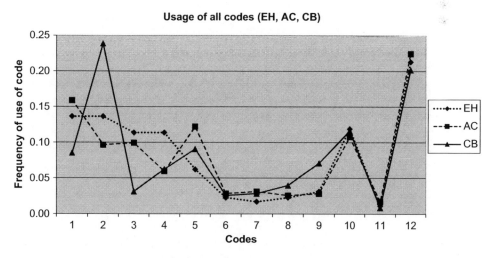

**Usage of all codes (EH, AC, CB)**

*Figure 5.1* An overview of the frequency of the use of all codes by all three coders, for the full data set of 352 critical-moment descriptions from coaching conversations. For the definition of the 12 codes, see Table 5.1.

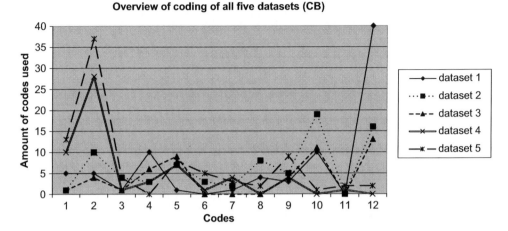

*Figure 5.2* Distribution of codes selected by coder CB for all five data sets. 1: less experienced coaches; 2: experienced coaches; 3: very experienced coaches (phone
interviews); 4: clients of coaching; 5: coaches' and coachees' direct comparison
(interviews). For the definition of the 12 codes, see Table 5.1.

To determine inter-rater reliability, Cohen's Kappa (Cohen, 1960) was computed
between all coders and found an average Kappa of 0.44, which seems a reasonable
figure given the number of codes: it is more than 30 times chance level. In any case,
the coding of individual moment descriptions will not be reported: all conclusions
will be based only on the totals of codes used for each of five data sets. These sets of
totals correlate 0.77 on average between the three coders. High reliability between
raters of 'helpful events' was also reported in psychotherapy research (Elliott et al.,
1985; Llewelyn, 1988).

Biases between the three coders were small (see Figure 5.1). EH codes more negative
changes in the relationship (code 4; 40 in total against 21/22 for the other coders),
and AC codes more coach-led significance in doing (code 5; 43 in total against 22 for
EH), while CB codes more anxieties of coachees (code 9; 25 in total against 10/11
for the other coders). The only boundary between codes which seems to have been
interpreted differently is the one between codes 1 and 2, which are both 'moments of
learning' – code 1 describes a sudden realisation and code 2 a more reflective working
through. In truth, these forms of learning probably do not have a sharp boundary
anyway. All coders use codes 1 and 2 in just over a quarter of their coding (mainly
in data sets 4 and 5), but AC uses code 1 in 62% of those and CB uses code 1 in only
26% of those, with EH in the middle: 50%.

Figure 5.2 shows an overview of the coding of all data sets, by one of the coders
(CB). From the figure, the following conclusions are immediately apparent:

• Data set 1 (critical moments of less experienced coaches) contains a dispropor-
tionate amount of 'doubts of coaches' (code 12) and 'negative changes in the relationship' (code 4). This confirms the main conclusions of Chapter 2 (De Haan,
2008c).

- Data sets 2 and 3 (critical moments of experienced coaches) share with Data set 1 a high proportion of 'anxieties of coaches' (code 10), while they contain significantly less 'doubts of coaches'. This confirms the main conclusions of Chapter 3 (Day et al., 2008; De Haan, 2008d).
- Data set 4 (critical moments of clients of coaching) shows an altogether different profile, with a much higher proportion of 'moments of learning' (codes 1 and 2). This confirms the main conclusions of Chapter 4 (De Haan et al., 2010a).
- Data set 5 (critical moments of coaches and coachees, directly compared) is overall much more similar to Data set 4 than to any of the three earlier data sets of executive coaches.
- From Data sets 1–4, one can observe that both coachees and coaches report more on their own emotions and sensations than on their counterparts' emotions and sensations, that is, descriptions from coaches (Data sets 1, 2 and 3) lead to more perceived codes 8, 10 and 12 (coaches' emotions and doubts) than the equivalent 7, 9 and 11 (coachees' emotions and doubts), and this is reversed in the coachees' descriptions (Data set 4). This was also reported in De Haan et al. (2010a).

A more in-depth comparison between the five data sets, distinguishing between the 43 'coachee moments' and the 43 'coach moments' in Data set 5, yields the following:

- The coachees' critical-moment descriptions in Data set 4 and the new coachees' critical-moment descriptions in Data set 5 follow a very similar pattern (see Figure 5.3 in the case of coder AC), both having a very high proportion of 'moments of learning' (codes 1 and 2). On average, the correlation between the coding of Data set 4 and of the coachee moments in Data set 5 of AC, CB and EH was 0.92, which is remarkably high and gives a strong confirmation of the conclusions from a rather disparate set of coachee moment descriptions in De Haan et al. (2010a). In other words, the fact that this new set of coachee descriptions shows the same patterns as the previous set given by completely different coachees (and obtained, moreover, in an entirely different way) means that the analysis of patterns in coachee descriptions in De Haan et al. (2010a) remains tenable for this new data set.
- Surprisingly, there is also a high correlation between Data set 4 and the coach moments in Data set 5 (see again Figure 5.3, for coder AC). On average, this correlation is 0.58 among the three coders, whereas the correlation between Data sets 1, 2 and 3 and the coach moments in Data set 5 is 0.003: negligible. We will come back to this surprising finding in the next section.
- The coders found an absence of negative changes in the relationship (code 4) in Data set 5, confirming what was concluded more informally at the beginning of the Results section, above, namely that descriptions in the new data set seem positive and constructive, as if celebrating or protecting the ongoing relationships.
- Remarkably in Data set 5 we have for the first time a higher occurrence of one's partner's emotions than one's own: coaches in Data set 5 come up with more anxieties of the coachee (code 9; see Figure 5.3 for coder AC) than of themselves (code 10).
- Coaches still report a significant number of doubts (code 12), consistent with earlier research (Day et al., 2008; De Haan, 2008c, 2008d).

These conclusions are true for all three coders.

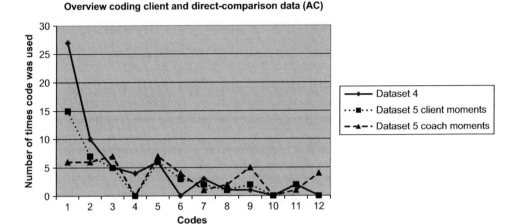

*Figure 5.3* Distribution of codes selected by coder AC for Data set 4 and for the coaches' and coachees' descriptions of critical moments in the comparison study, separately. For the definition of the 12 codes, see Table 5.1.

Finally, having this rather unique Data set 5, which allows a direct comparison of coaches' and their coachees' views on the same coaching conversation, also affords the analysis of those descriptions where coach and coachee seem to be speaking about the very same moment or event within the coaching conversation. Surprisingly, 46 critical-moment descriptions, more than half of the data set, are clearly mirrored in the partner's data, that is, relate to an event which the other person also selects as 'critical' or 'important'. Bear in mind that the duration of these conversations was about two hours on average, so this is an astonishingly high score.

The usage of codes on these particular descriptions was analysed by computing Cohen's Kappa (Cohen, 1960) for this new data set, Kappa being the standard measure for correlations between independent coding processes. Cohen's Kappas were computed for the coder's choice of code for the 'coach moment' compared with the coder's choice of code for the corresponding 'coachee moment'. It is a relatively small data set of only 23 measurements, but Kappas can be reliably computed. Cohen's Kappas were: 0.29 (AC), 0.38 (CB) and 0.47 (EH), each much higher than chance levels which are around 0.02. With the caveat that this conclusion is based only on a small data set of 46 codes, we can provisionally conclude that these coaches and coachees did not only agree in more than 50% of key moments on the particular *event* or subject matter they described, but they also seem to agree on the *nature* of those events, which seems a strong agreement between the two partners, particularly if one takes into account the low agreement sometimes reported in psychotherapy (e.g. Tallman & Bohart, 1999; however, Weiss, Rabinowitz, & Spiro, 1996, report variability in the agreement between coachees' and therapists' qualitative reports). Simon Machin (2010), in his phenomenological research among internal coachees and coaches, also found a surprising similarity in the stories they told about their shared sessions, and also contrasted this with the findings in psychotherapy.

## 4. Discussion

In summary, the direct-comparison data contributed by coaches and clients of coaching (Data set 5) suggest the following:

- Coachees' and coaches' experiences of coaching conversations are not as different as would have been thought, based on the earlier studies, neither in the *nature* of selected events (coaches' and coachees' descriptions are coded in similar distributions across a fixed set of 12 codes) nor in their specific *choice* of events (46 of 86 descriptions refer to an event also described by the partner in conversation), nor even in the *emphases* within their event descriptions (those 46 'shared event' descriptions were coded in a manner correlating about 20 times chance level, for all three observers).
- Coachees and coaches use similar language, and apart from one reported rupture in the relationship, all 86 descriptions were broadly positive and indicated learning, progress and accomplishment. Partly this may be due to the fact that, for 14 of the 21 sessions, the coachee and conversation was chosen by the coach and they will have chosen positive coachee relationships as they had to invite their coachee to the research.

Comparing this data set explicitly with all of the earlier data sets of coachees' and coaches' descriptions of critical moments of executive coaching led to the following results:

- Overall a strong endorsement of the main conclusions in the earlier articles. Although the new data set correlates strongly only with Data set 4, the new data set does also replicate some of the trends found in the other previous data sets. Sixty-two per cent of coachees' moments in Data set 5 were coded as 1 or 2 ('moments of learning'), while only 40% of coaches' moments were coded as such; in Data sets 1–4, these numbers had been 59% for coachees' moments and 9% for coaches' moments. Another interesting example is the relatively high occurrence of coaches' doubts: 56% for inexperienced coaches (Data set 1), 18%/27% for experienced coaches (Data set 2/Data set 3, respectively), and 5% for coaches in Data set 5 – all figures clearly higher than the 0% for clients of coaching in both Data set 4 and Data set 5.
- A high correlation between the coding of these direct-comparison coachee data and the earlier coachee critical-moment data set (Data set 4, correlations consistently over 0.90).
- No correlation at all between the coding of the new data set (Data set 5) and the earlier coach data (Data sets 1, 2 and 3), to the extent that the average correlation between the coaches' descriptions from Data sets 1–3 and from Data set 5 was exactly zero.

We think that these findings can be understood best from the realisation that this direct-comparison study contains a fair representation of straightforward, 'run-of-the-mill', successful and everyday executive coaching, with coachee and coach being in broad agreement, not only about the goals and outcomes of their sessions, but also about their coaching process and coaching relationship. We can assume that this type of 'run-of-the-mill' coaching is exactly what the coachees in Data set 4 also reported on, as many studies have shown executive coaching to be satisfactory and successful in most cases (see, e.g., De Haan et al., 2011; McGovern et al., 2001). On the other hand, Data sets 1, 2 and 3 were drawn from a much broader and deeper experience of executive coaching and have probably included rarer and more extreme examples of transformation, resistance or ruptures in the working alliance. In other words, while Data sets 4 and 5 focus on the everyday learning that takes place in generally positive coaching relationships, Data sets 1, 2 and 3 take their inspiration from special occurrences in coaching, moments and events that may occur only a few times in the lifetime of an executive coach – and, in particular, at the beginning of a coach's career when there are still great insecurities and doubts (De Haan, 2008d).

We cannot rule out the possibility that there are other qualitative differences between what coaches and coachees associate with the term 'critical moment' when it applies to the session they have just had today (Data set 5), as compared to when 'critical moment' applies to a whole coaching relationship (Data set 4) or to a career of coaching experience, however short in some cases (Data sets 1, 2 and 3). It may well be that the term 'critical moment' does not apply in the same way to the past hour as to a lifetime of work.

Both run-of-the-mill and exceptional circumstances are part of coaching practice, so all various data sets have something to teach executive coaching practitioners. Studies like these can provide crucial information for the training and development of executive coaches, while they may also help to inform and manage the expectations of clients of executive coaching. Here is a short summary of what we believe these data can teach us:

- Data sets 1, 2 and 3 give an indication that, in the careers of most executive coaches, there are such things as exceptional moments where the relationship is tested or ruptured and where coaches experience strong doubts and anxieties. Generally, the levels of anxiety of coaches in such events remain high, while the degree of doubting abates over time (De Haan, 2008d).
- Data sets 4 and 5 give an indication that what coachees are most looking for in coaching conversations are moments of realisation and emerging insight, that is, learning of some form that they can bring to use in their own practice. Data set 5 shows that coaches can and do work in such a way that they seem in agreement with their coachees about which are the events that matter and the nature of those events. Under exceptional circumstances, a different picture may emerge, where disruptions to the relationship between coach and coachee become more figural, and then we are back in the realm of Data sets 1, 2 and 3.

In summary, more agreement than disagreement was found between coachees and coaches:

- Out of 86 moments or events, 46 were selected by both coachees and coaches (53%);
- The critical-moment descriptions from coachees and coaches were similar (see Figure 5.3), and they use similar language apart from a few occurrences of jargon in the language of the executive coaches;
- Coachees and coaches place similar emphases within their description of those events, witnessed by the substantial correlations between the coding of these pairs of moments;
- For the first time, one can even notice that the anxieties that both partners in the conversation attend to are in a way similar: they are predominantly the anxieties of the coachee (see Figure 5.3), as one would hope in executive coaching.

In psychotherapy research, there are some indications that patients and therapists are reporting quite different events and moments, and that they have incommensurate memories of the sessions themselves (Elliott, 1983; Elliott & Shapiro, 1992; Llewelyn, Elliott, Shapiro, Hardy, & Firth-Cozens, 1988; Rennie, 1990; Tallman & Bohart, 1999). But Martin and Stelmaczonek (1988) also find a strong overlap between 111 critical-moment descriptions by counsellors and 94 critical-moment descriptions by their clients, even if slightly lower (33%) than what we find here (53%), and they find new understanding and insight likewise as the most important category of coding. However, one review study investigating all publications to date on agreement between clients and therapists found a high variability (Weiss et al., 1996). One interpretation worth noting is that therapists will address perceived weaknesses more than coaches, and will therefore have more emphasis on challenging, disruptive and even corrective interventions, which may result in less agreement between therapist and client than between coach and coachee.

## 5. Conclusion

This direct-comparison study of coaches' and coachees' critical-moment descriptions that were gathered straight after mutual executive coaching conversations has produced both a confirmation of earlier conclusions when studying critical moments in executive coaching and a linkage between the various disparate studies hitherto undertaken. We think we now understand better why coachees' and coaches' descriptions in earlier studies were so different, and we are beginning to understand how descriptions from coachees and coaches coming out of coaching sessions can also be extremely similar, as was the case here.

Interestingly, the results of this direct-comparison study connect with an old debate in psychotherapy process research (Mintz, Auerbach, Luborsky, & Johnson, 1973), which seeks to clarify to what degree the experiences and accounts of both parties in helping conversations are similar versus different. On the one hand, coach and coachee are essentially similar, both being 21st-century professionals with an interest in leadership and development. Moreover, during the conversation, they attend to the same 'reality' of the conversation as it emerges between them. On the other hand, one can argue they take up entirely different and complementary roles in the same conversation, with one focussing on own issues and the other focussing on the progress and development of the partner in conversation. So clearly, in the accounts of coaching, one would expect *both* a reasonable consensus *and* the 'Rashomon experience' named after Akira Kurosawa's classic 1950 Japanese movie *Rashomon*, where four participants retell a single event and come up with equally plausible but totally different and incompatible accounts. Most process research in psychotherapy has confirmed the 'Rashomon-side' of the debate, showing that clients and therapists do indeed place an entirely different emphasis in recall, selection and interpretation of significant events of therapy (Mintz et al., 1973; Weiss et al., 1996). Here is how Yalom (Yalom & Elkin, 1974; p. 222) formulates that side of the argument:

> I am struck by (...) the obvious discrepancies in perspective between Ginny and me. Often she values one part of the hour, I another. I press home an interpretation with much determination and pride. To humour me and to hasten our move to more important areas she 'accepts' the interpretation. To permit us to move to 'work areas', I on the other hand humour her by granting her silent requests for advice, suggestions, exhortations, or admonitions. I value my thoughtful clarifications; with one masterful stroke I make sense out of a number of disparate, seemingly unrelated facts. She rarely ever acknowledges, much less values my labours, and instead seems to profit from my simple human acts: I chuckle at her satire, I notice her clothes, I call her buxom, I tease her when we role play.

The other side of the debate about whether or not the experiences and accounts of both parties in helping conversations match seems to be reflected in the results of the present study. There seems to be a surprising degree of overlap between coach and coachee accounts, both in their recall and selection of events and in their emphasis and interpretation. However, given the originality of the design and the limited scope of the data set, it may be too early to argue that coach–coachee pairs have more in common than therapist-patient pairs.

From the point of view of education and professional development for coaches, the following recommendations can be drawn from this research:

1   Coaches need to be prepared for quite different circumstances in run-of-the-mill coaching and in the presence of real dramatic moments and ruptures. In ordinary coaching, they need to keep the focus on what coachees are interested in most: realisations, emerging insight and reflection. In extraordinary conversations, they need to be able to deal with their own substantive doubt and anxiety, and also with strong emotions in their coachees.

2   More effort can be put into preparing coaches for what they can expect in ordinary, successful conversations. The results of this enquiry have shown that coaches need to help coachees to look beyond their current solutions and mindset, to achieve new realisations and insight. They need to remain focussed on new learning and how they can support their coachees to achieve that. Epiphanies are

not necessarily what is needed. Sometimes it is enough to create a sense of support and reflection for the coachee. As concluded before (De Haan et al., 2010a), coaches need awareness of the fact that coachees seem to be focussed on changing their thoughts and reflections – rather than on pure space for reflection, reassurance or new actions. Coaches should ensure they have the skills to facilitate the emergence of new learning, reflection, realisation and insight.

3   Education should not just focus on the main findings of research into the outcomes of executive coaching (e.g. the "*common factors*" that in psychotherapy have been shown to be significantly related to outcome: factors such as the relationship, expectations and personalities; De Haan, 2008a). It is also important to consider what research into sub-outcomes (Rice & Greenberg, 1984) can teach us about, for example, the doubts and anxieties that executive coaches should bear in mind in their work, or coachees' expectations of session-by-session learning outcomes (realisations, changing perspectives, new insight, etc.).

When aspects such as the above find their way into coach training and development programmes, this would help in making a more clear-cut case for executive coaching for the benefit of purchasers of coaching, including more information on expected benefits and limitations of working with an executive coach.

We would suggest there is a great need for further investigation in this area, particularly in the following domains:

1   Critical-moment research, if only to assemble larger data sets upon which firmer conclusions can be based. A larger data set can also be used to (dis-)confirm the more tentative conclusions in both this and earlier chapters.
2   Direct-comparison studies such as the present one should be extended into longitudinal studies of coach-coachee relationships, which could study the progress of the intervention through the evolving reported critical moments. See the next part of this chapter for a first example of such research.
3   We would be most interested in finding out about critical moments and the coaching process from the perspective of the oft-neglected (indirect) clients and sponsors of coaching, which are the direct colleagues, managers and reports of the coaching client within the organisation of the coachee. It will be fascinating to investigate what they believe were the critical moments of their colleague's coaching journey (for an initial example of this type of research, see Chapter 6).

### 6. Introduction: research into critical moments in the process of a single case study

We believed that an answer to our question about the extent of different perspectives on the same conversation and the same coaching relationship could also be found on the basis of complete case studies. Other helping professions, such as psychotherapy, have a long history of analysing case studies, starting with Breuer and Freud (1895; short cases of 10–60 pages each) and Freud (1905; for the first time, an entire book on a single case study). Accounts of therapeutic relationships from both therapist and client date back to Yalom and Elgin (1974), who described their therapeutic encounters separately and published these descriptions jointly. One of the first studies to examine the degree of congruence between therapists, patients and observers regarding a therapy session was that by Mintz et al. (1973). This study found that there was always a reasonable degree of consensus regarding the patient's state of mind, but much less consensus on the assessment of the therapeutic relationship and the outcome of the session. After decades of research into the similarities or differences between therapist and patient perceptions of therapy, Weiss et al. (1996) published an overview of the relevant literature, including the findings of 41 such studies. This overview revealed a great deal of variation between these studies in the extent to which therapists and clients agreed on their assessment of the problem the therapy was intended to solve, the process followed during the therapy and its outcomes. For a more recent example of a case study described separately by both therapist and client, and then analysed by an independent researcher, see Mackrill (2011). For a brief summary of previous case studies in the coaching literature, see Chapter 1 of this book.

In recent years, research into the therapeutic process and critical moments in that process has been given a new impetus by the discovery of "sudden gains" in around 40% of patients receiving psychotherapy once a week and the strong indications that these patients with sudden gains have lower rates of relapse than other patients (see, e.g., Tang & DeRubeis, 1999). Sudden gains, or major improvements with regard to a symptom from one session to the next, have now been demonstrated in cognitive behavioural therapy, supportive-expressive therapy and psychodynamic therapy and for various disorders (see Present et al., 2008; Tang et al. 2007). If these sudden gains or major improvements are indeed as relevant to the longer-term outcomes as they now appear to be, then it becomes even more important to study individual sessions and the experience of clients in these sessions.

Although there is considerable research literature on therapists' and clients' perceptions of the therapeutic process, we have only found a dozen or so case study reports (Blattner, 2005; Day, 2010; Diedrich, 1996; Peterson & Millier, 2005; Fahy, 2007; Freedman & Perry, 2010; Kiel, Rimmer, Williams, & Doyle, 1996; Levenson, 2009; Mansi, 2007; Schnell, 2005; Tobias, 1996; Winum, 1995) in the coaching literature and almost all of these were written by coaches. To the best of our knowledge, the present study is the only complete case study by a coach and a coachee together based on their descriptions of their critical moments (although Peterson & Millier, 2005, and Freedman & Perry, 2010, have also reported on their joint coaching case together). It supplements the critical moments described by many coaches and coachees just after their coaching session in the first part of this chapter. This study has not been described as a single continuous account, that is, not as an ordinary case study, precisely because we wanted to compare the individual considerations of coachee and coach. For this reason, coach and coachee independently made notes immediately after the sessions (or at least on the same day), similar to the method used by Yalom and Elgin (1974). Only after the complete series of ten sessions did coach and coachee have the opportunity to read each other's descriptions. After that, each wrote a response to the other person's descriptions (see Appendix D.2 for the complete case study). It was only when this material was available that they decided to write the article jointly in order to give an honest and practical description of one specific coaching relationship as it developed. Certain personal details about coach and coachee have been omitted from the accounts; otherwise, the quotes in Appendix D.2 are faithful representations of the critical moments encountered individually by coach and coachee in their shared sessions.

This study therefore combines both traditions in the field of process research in the coaching literature: a study of critical moments and a case study analysis. In this way, we hope to contribute to a better understanding of the sub-outcomes and of the one specific factor that we know (from previous research) to be an excellent predictor of the outcome of coaching, namely the coaching relationship. In our formal analysis of critical-moment descriptions of a coach or coachee derived from a coaching assignment that they have gone through together, we test the following hypotheses, which we base on previous publications in this field:

H1.  Coach and coachee will refer to the same moment with a frequency that is significantly above chance. De Haan et al. (2010b) showed that in their data set, 53% of the paired descriptions referred to demonstrably the same moment or the same interaction in the conversation, which is much higher than chance. This differs from what is often (but not exclusively!) reported in research into psychotherapy, namely that psychotherapist and patient rarely mention the same moments from their shared sessions (see, e.g., Tallman & Bohart, 1999).

H2.  The coding of coach or coachee descriptions by independent raters will generally be comparable with the coding by independent raters in previous studies of coach descriptions (De Haan, 2008d) and coachee descriptions (Day et al., 2008). In particular, the coding will consistently show certain general differences, such as:

H2a.  Coaches are more focussed on their own anxieties and doubts;
H2b.  Coachees are more focussed on new insights and reflections.

H3.  Depending on the degree and importance of relational "ruptures" in the case study, the descriptions should contain indications of the two types of coaching that are distinguished in De Haan et al. (2010b), namely routine, "run of the mill" or "everyday" coaching versus coaching under "exceptionally strong anxiety".

H4.  Longitudinal development analysis will show that the conversations have a different effect throughout the course of the coaching, in a way that corresponds to the dose-effect relationship in psychotherapy (see, e.g., Howard, Kopta, Krause, & Orlinski, 1986). Based on this research into the outcomes of psychotherapy, we would expect coachee outcomes, such as new insight, to decrease from the first session onwards.

For a case study, it is important to have a theoretical framework at the outset, comprising the research questions, hypotheses, units of analysis, the reasoning according to which the data are linked to the propositions and criteria for interpreting the findings, including the potential for generalisation (Yin, 1994). For this purpose, one of us (EH) conducted two pilot case studies with two different coachees, consisting of ten sessions each. The hypotheses set out above were formulated partly on the basis of these analyses.

## 7. Method

The data for the present case study were collected in ten coaching sessions between the executive coach and the coachee.

## 7.1 Setting

In a preliminary meeting that took place at the coachee's request, coach and coachee agreed to hold a total of ten 90-minute coaching sessions over a period of six months. The first three sessions took place face to face in the United Kingdom; the remaining seven were conducted by telephone as the coach was UK-based and the coachee was in the Netherlands. The sessions were held in English, a second language for both coachee and coach, with an interval of approximately three weeks between each session. After the initial agreement, none of the dates had to be changed. Sessions always took place at the scheduled times, except on two occasions: once the coach phoned in late (fifth session) and once the coach had forgotten the UK/Netherlands time difference and had to be reminded of the starting time (seventh session). In the latter case, the session began an hour late, but still went ahead for the agreed 90 minutes. The coaching fee was reduced to £50 per session, to be paid to a non-governmental humanitarian organisation chosen by the coach. A reduced fee seemed reasonable because the coachee – like the coach – was engaged in collecting data.

## 7.2 Procedure

At the end of each session, coach and coachee individually wrote down the critical moments from their conversation, using the following definition of "critical moment": "an exciting, tense or significant moment from the duration of the coaching session". They always did this on the day of the session itself.

The coachee was told that the study would consist of analyses of the different critical-moment descriptions and comparisons of the coachee's and coach's descriptions from the successive sessions, and that the analysis would not be done until after all ten sessions. Both parties' consent to any future publication was obtained before the start of the coaching process.

This procedure resulted in 32 critical-moment descriptions, 14 from the coachee and 18 from the coach, which were then presented to four independent raters (persons other than the authors). The raters were given the same 12 codes to classify the critical moments as were developed in the previous study, that is, all of these codes had been used successfully for the previous data sets (e.g. De Haan et al., 2010b; see Table 3.1 for the codes). Once all of the critical-moment descriptions had been collected and the decision taken to describe the coaching intervention as a case study, the coachee and coach worked together on a phenomenological analysis of the critical-moment descriptions from each of the ten sessions (see Appendix D.2).

## 7.3 Participants

The executive coach was an accredited coach in his late forties with 15 years' experience in this field; the coachee was an MSc student of Theoretical Psychology in her mid-twenties. During the course of the coaching process, the coachee gained her MSc degree in the Netherlands and became a PhD student at a research school in Germany. The coachee had no previous experience of executive coaching. Outside of the coaching sessions, coach and coachee did not discuss (either verbally or in writing) the material from the sessions, nor the conversations themselves.

## 7.4 Analysis of the coaching process

In the first month, coach and coachee had two meetings about the research project that were clearly separate from the coaching conversations. Apart from the coaching sessions, there was no other contact between the pair until the week prior to the tenth session, when they had another meeting about the research project. In other words, for most of the seven months of the coaching process, they had no contact with each other apart from that via the coaching. After the first coaching session, the coach drew up a formal, written contract for the ten-session coaching assignment, setting out the following two goals:

1 *'You – the coachee – would like to use our sessions to think about your Master's thesis, which you are currently working on and which seems to be an interesting challenge.*
2 *You are looking for guidance in discovering – or want to get clear for yourself – how you can shape your personal development and career in the longer term. You mentioned four possible "career paths" you could choose from, and would like a better understanding of those options, your own self and your choices before actually choosing one or more of these options'.*

The coach wrote the goals down in this form, and the coachee agreed to them in the second session without requesting any changes. The sessions focussed largely on the question of how to find your way in a competitive and ambitious academic environment, how to stay afloat in such an environment and how to develop to the next "level" while at the same time pursuing other more commercial interests.

## 8. Results

Hypothesis 1 asked whether coach and client referred to broadly the same moments as being critical in the coaching conversation. To give one example, if one looks at the critical moments in the eighth session (see Appendix D.2) one can conclude that coach and client were clearly referring to the same moment as being critical in this (the eighth) session, namely the discussion about running out of steam and the sense of having completed the contract already.

Of the 32 critical-moment descriptions, 15 pairs (47%) clearly refer to the same moment in the session (see, e.g., the two moments in session 8). To be specific: there was a "common critical moment" in each session from session 3 to session 9 (i.e. seven sessions in total) and a second match with the same moment in session 6. This result supports the finding (De Haan et al., 2010b) that on the whole, coach and coachee experience the same moments in the coaching conversations as "critical".

Hypothesis 2 implied that the independent coders would assign the critical moments to the defined categories in more or less the same way. Cohen's Kappas were calculated to determine the degree of congruence between the four coders, resulting in a minimum of 0.25 and a maximum of 0.31, indicating reasonable congruence between the coders (Landis & Koch, 1977). Figure 5.4 shows how often the 12 codes were assigned, both for the entire data set and for the data sets with critical-moment descriptions by coachee or coach separately. Codes 1, 3 and 10 were the most common, although their relative allocation was very different for the data provided by coachee

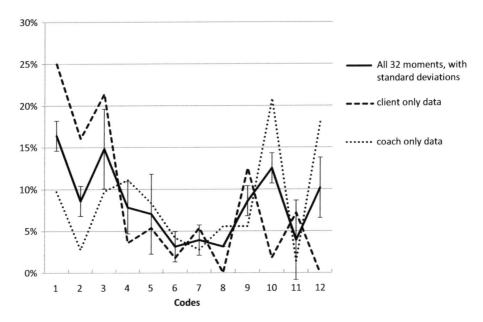

*Figure 5.4* Frequency of use of the 12 codes by all four coders, for (a) the complete data set, (b) the descriptions of critical moments by the coachee and (c) the descriptions of critical moments by the coach.

and coach, respectively. Moreover, the codings for the data originating from the coachee and those from the coach correlate negatively *(r* = –0.44), which differs from the other data set in which critical-moment descriptions were recorded immediately after the coaching session (see earlier in this chapter, or De Haan et al., 2010b) and in which the same correlation was *r* = +0.69. It therefore seems most appropriate here to analyse the coachee and coach data separately, as also stated in Hypotheses 2a and 2b.

Hypothesis 2a implied that the coach's critical moments would substantially be about uncertainty and doubt. This was confirmed by a distribution-free Wilcoxon test with confidence *p* < 0.01. According to Hypothesis 2b, the coachee's critical moments, on the other hand, would mainly concern new insights and reflections. This too was confirmed by a distribution-free Wilcoxon test with confidence *p* < 0.01. From these tests of hypotheses 2a and 2b, we conclude that the coach and coachee in this case study did indeed experience different aspects of the coaching sessions as critical: while the coach's critical moments were about uncertainty and doubt, the coachee experienced new insights as particularly critical (see also Figure 5.4).

Regarding Hypothesis 3, we observed that the data sets of both coachee and coach in this study contained moments of rupture or near-rupture in sessions 5, 6 and 7, as a result of which there was no clear distinction in this data set between "everyday" coaching and coaching under "exceptional circumstances" (see De Haan et al., 2010b). We suspect that this data set is a mixture of both during the course of this coaching process, which would provide support for Hypothesis 3 regarding the different data sets for different types of coaching.

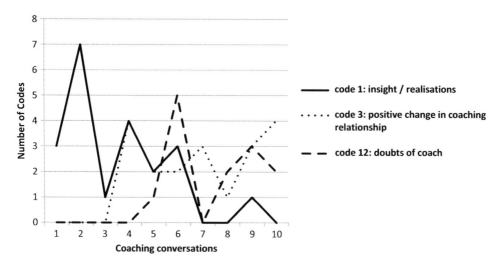

*Figure 5.5* Frequency of codes 1, 3 and 12 (see *Table 5.1*) during the course of the coaching process, for all coders.

We were especially interested in the development of critical moments during the series of ten coaching sessions (Hypothesis 4). We mapped the frequency with which codes were assigned in successive sessions using regression analyses, testing the hypothesis for one direction only, since Hypothesis 4 did not specify in which direction an effect was expected. Each of the 12 codes was regressed on the session numbers to provide an estimate for a significant change in the allocation of codes as the sessions progressed. The results indicate that codes 1 and 3 show significant increases and decreases, respectively ($p < 0.05$), over the course of the series of sessions (see Figure 5.5), and that code 12 shows an almost-significant increase ($p < 0.10$). The other codes show no significant increase or decrease. Based on these results, the following conclusions appear warranted:

- (code 1) Most of the new learning in the critical moments occurred in the first few sessions, after which the number of new insights gradually decreased.
- (code 3) Within the critical moments, the coaching relationship gradually developed in a positive direction; from this, it can be concluded that coach and coachee built up a stronger relationship and bond of trust with each other during the process.
- (code 12) Within the coach, the amount of doubt within the critical-moment descriptions seems to gradually increase.

## 9. Discussion

This case study relates to a fairly customary series of ten 90-minute coaching sessions held approximately every three weeks. Many aspects of this case study can also be found in other executive coaching processes: a written contract with two goals that were revised over time, a rupture in the relationship in sessions 5 and 6, signs of recovery from the rupture in session 7 and the emergence of a few core "themes", which are an in-depth reflection within the coachee of challenges that she faces, both inside and outside the sessions. This is the story of a properly contracted, time-limited coaching relationship with clear goals and positive outcomes (in terms of career decisions, self-confidence and self-awareness), a story that could just as easily be about many other coaching relationships.

## 9.1 Agreement with previous research into critical moments

Since this case study follows on from earlier research into critical moments in executive coaching, its findings can be compared with those from the earlier research.

### 9.1.1 CORRESPONDENCE IN PERCEPTION OF CRITICAL MOMENTS

The percentage (47%) of common critical moments observed in this study was very close to the 53% described earlier in this chapter and also in De Haan et al. (2010b) about an independent data set. Assuming that each coaching conversation consists of hundreds of "moments", based on Stern's definition (2004) that a "moment" in a conversation lasts two to eight seconds, then the chance of the same moment being chosen for the same pair of descriptions is well below 1%. However, there is inevitably a great deal of repetition, elaboration and deepening in the moments in a coaching session. Nevertheless, a correspondence of 47% (and 53% in De Haan et al., 2010b) is a remarkable result and provides strong support for Hypothesis 1.

### 9.1.2 CORRELATION IN CODING BETWEEN DATA SETS

Since only one coder (AC) coded all six data sets in the six studies, we can only report correlation coefficients for distributions of the 12 codes in the coding by AC (although correlations between the different coders yield comparable scores). An exploratory analysis tested whether the frequency of codes assigned by this one coder correlated between the different data sets. The present data set appeared to correlate best *as a whole* with the data set of descriptions by experienced coaches in De Haan (2008d) ($r = 0.57$, $p < 0.05$). The data sets of coachee and coach *individually* correlate better with certain earlier data sets. The coachee data correlated ($r = 0.56$; $p < 0.05$) with the coachee data in De Haan et al. (2010a) and also ($r = 0.67$; $p < 0.05$) with the coachee data in De Haan et al. (2010b). The coach data correlated ($0.75 < r < 0.78$, $p < 0.01$) with the three data sets of coach descriptions in De Haan (2008c, 2008d) and Day et al. (2008). Strikingly, these coach data show no correlation with the coach data in De Haan et al. (2010b), which appeared to correlate closely with the coachee data in both that study and the earlier one (De Haan et al., 2010a, 2010b). We believe this is because the data sets of both coachee and coach in the present study contain moments of rupture or near-rupture in sessions 5–7 (as described above), so that the choice between coaching under "everyday" or "exceptional circumstances" (see De Haan et al., 2010b) in this data set is not clear. We suspect that the data set in the present study is therefore a mixture of both over the course of time.

### 9.1.3 DIFFERENCES BETWEEN CRITICAL MOMENTS OF COACH AND COACHEE

In this study, coach critical moments were most frequently categorised with codes 10 and 12 (Table 5.1), that is, coach's uncertainty and doubt. Coachee critical moments, on the other hand, were most frequently classified with three codes (1, 2 and 3; see Figure 5.4), indicating moments of learning and a positive change in the coaching relationship. These results are very similar to those of previous studies. While coaches usually mention their own uncertainty and doubt in critical moments (De Haan, 2008c, 2008d), coachees usually report moments in which they learn something new as being the most critical moments in their coaching experience (De Haan et al., 2010a). Moreover, it is striking in Figure 5.4 that the coding of coach and coachee critical moments is mirrored exactly for codes 7 and 8; 9 and 10; and 11 and 12, respectively (see Table 5.1 for brief descriptions of the codes). As in previous studies, both coach and coachee focus more on their own emotions and doubts than on those of their conversational partner.

### 9.1.4 COMMON CRITICAL MOMENTS

As observed above, 15 of the 32 critical moments refer to the same moments in a session. This 47% frequency of "common critical moments" is very similar to that in the other comparative study, where the descriptions of coaches' and coachees' critical moments were recorded independently in interviews immediately after the session (see earlier in this chapter and De Haan et al., 2010b), and where common critical moments accounted for 53% of the total. As mentioned earlier, the present study found an average of almost one common critical moment per session; there were no common critical moments in either the first two sessions or the last one. In De Haan et al. (2010b), all sessions in which common critical moments were recorded fell between the start and end of the series (i.e. they were neither opening nor closing sessions); perhaps the slight decrease in the occurrence of common critical moments in the present study is therefore connected with those first and last sessions, where coach and coachee are still adjusting to the conversations or are already going their own way in their thinking.

## 9.2 Limitations and avenues for further research

We are aware that the present study covers only one coaching assignment and that, in view of certain aspects of the study, its results may not be generally valid. After all, this was not executive coaching in the strict sense: the coachee did not have a leading position in an organisation, but was an occupational psychologist, which will have influenced her perspective on and expectations of coaching. In addition, the goals set out in the original contract seem to be more relevant to career guidance than to executive coaching. In terms of content and dynamics, however, the series of sessions does bear a strong similarity with executive coaching. Moreover, we believe that what happened in the relationship including the critical moments is representative enough of executive coaching to state that the results of the study are relevant to other executive coaching relationships. This is supported by the high degree of correspondence found with other studies on executive coaching relationships (e.g. De Haan, 2010a, 2010b), which worked with a different set of coaches and coachees. We therefore believe that the research process used in this study is a good model for more systematic research into critical moments in coaching processes, in order to gain a better understanding of how change and learning occur in coaching sessions.

Both experienced and inexperienced coaches need more cases from the full spectrum of executive coaching, and not simply sketches of purely positive or purely negative case studies (e.g. Berglas, 2002 & Levenson, 2009 respectively). We believe that analysis of critical moments is a useful way to study individual coaching relationships and to compare the results per moment and per session between different studies by means of samples. We hope that more researchers will use this or a similar method to investigate other series of ten or more coaching sessions for critical moments of coachee and coach. If this is done, we will be able to gather more evidence for both the dynamics during the course of the relationship and the outcomes that can be expected from executive coaching sessions. In addition, more phenomenological analysis based on published case studies is needed to map patterns and to study certain general areas of concern, such as – as was the case in this study – coaching in a second (or third, etc.) language or in different cultural contexts. To these ends, it is useful to have a model for studying the process of executive coaching that has already been applied in the analysis of many hundreds of critical-moment descriptions and has been shown to lend itself to very diverse situations and different participants in coaching processes (De Haan, 2010b).

In conclusion, this study shows a higher degree of correspondence than would have been expected based on chance in the critical moments that coach and coachee chose independently of each other (Hypothesis 1). Second, it demonstrated significant differences between the coachee's and coach's descriptions (Hypothesis 2), even though they often considered more or less the same moments to be critical (Hypothesis 1). Third, we observed different patterns in the coaching sessions around ruptures (Hypothesis 3) and, for the first time, other longitudinal patterns as well, such as patterns showing similarities with the dose-effect relationships demonstrated in psychotherapy (Howard et al., 1986; Hypothesis 4). This confirms the importance of recognising that the coachee's experience of coaching differs from that of the coach, and that the beginning, middle and end of a coaching process can have different characteristics.

Our most encouraging finding was the similarity between the experience of the two participants (Hypotheses 1 and 3), which refutes the "*Rashomon* conjecture" of completely different memories in helping relationships (Mintz et al., 1973). This finding indicates that truly empathetic understanding, compassion, learning from each other and partnership are possible, and that coach and coachee can have a shared perspective on the outcomes of a coaching process after the event. These are essential conditions for the effectiveness of a coaching assignment and will need to be demonstrated clearly and objectively in order to validate executive coaching.

## SUMMARY OF CHAPTER 5: "TWO VERSIONS OF THE SAME CONVERSATION"

In this fourth phase of the research into critical moments in coaching, two separate projects were set up to investigate, by means of field research, the differences previously found between coach's and coachee descriptions of critical moments in coaching:

1    Twenty-one coachees and coaches were interviewed immediately after one of their coaching sessions. This project yielded 43 coachee descriptions and 43 coach descriptions of critical moments.
2    A single ten-session coaching process was followed from start to finish as a case study: coach and coachee were asked to describe one or more critical moments within the same day after each coaching session. This project yielded 14 coachee descriptions and 18 coach descriptions of critical moments.

The new collection of critical-moment descriptions given by coaches and coachees immediately after shared sessions appeared to show largely the same patterns as the coachee descriptions we examined in Chapter 4:

1    In almost every description, the focus was clearly on the coachee (in only one coach description and one coachee description was the focus more on the coach).
2    New insight is again the most common essence of the critical-moment descriptions.
3    In as many as 53% of cases in the first project and 47% in the second project, coachees and coaches describe the same moment or the same situation, and in similar terms.
4    The only differences initially found between coachees' and coaches' accounts were that coaches place more emphasis on their own actions and use more jargon and psychological terms to describe what went on compared with their coachees.
5    There were a large number of references by coaches (17 out of 43 moments in the first project, and also once in the second project) to coachees' physiological responses (frowning, blushing, posture, note taking, agitation, breathing, etc.), whereas coachees never referred to these matters.
6    In both projects, we were able to demonstrate more doubt and anxiety in the coach than in the coachee.

Based on this research, we devised a universal coding of all critical moments in which a single unique code could be selected for each description:

•    Moments of learning (code 1 "New insight" and code 2 "New connection / perspective");
•    Moments of relational change in the coaching relationship (code 3 "Positive change in the relationship" and code 4 "Negative change in the relationship");

(*Continued*)

- Moments of significant action (code 5 "Significance in doing in the moment, coach-led" and code 6 "Significance in doing in the moment, coachee-led"); and
- Moments of significant emotional experience (code 7 "Joy, coachee", code 8 "Joy, coach", code 9 "Anxiety, coachee", code 10 "Anxiety, coach", code 11 "Doubt, coachee" and code 12 "Doubt, coach").

Based on this model, we found that the scored codes for moments as recorded by coachees and coaches immediately after coaching sessions (the first project) correlate with those of the coachees in Chapter 4 with an average of 0.92. Even the coach descriptions of critical moments still correlate with 0.58. In the case study, where there were more doubts and anxieties, especially in the coach, we saw that the coachee data had a correlation of approximately 0.56–0.67 with other coachee data, and the coding of the coach descriptions correlated only with that of coach descriptions from the first two chapters (0.75–0.78).

In the second project, where we monitored the effects of coaching over time within a single coaching relationship, we were able to show that (1) most new learning in the critical moments occurred in the first few sessions, after which the number of new insights gradually decreased; (2) the coaching relationship gradually developed in a positive direction with regard to critical moments, from which we can conclude that coach and coachee built up a stronger relationship and bond of trust with each other during the process and (3) in the coach, doubt in the critical moments seems gradually to increase.

All in all, it seems that the critical-moment descriptions in this chapter relate mainly to the "everyday" learning that takes place in generally positive coaching relationships, whereas Chapters 2 and 3 identified coaching moments and events that may occur only a few times in the lifetime of an executive coach – and especially at the beginning of a career when the coach is still struggling with insecurities and doubts about coaching.

# Chapter 6

# Critical moments in coaching

## What coaching sponsors have to say

### A. Anecdote

Once, quite near the start of my career as an executive coach, I coached the number two board member of a telecoms multinational for four years. The coachee approached me following a referral from one of my mentors, who was retiring. I was actually a bit young for the assignment, especially because the coachee was a very experienced director and I felt there was quite a gulf between us in terms of status and cultural diversity. I had never visited his native country before and he had little experience of mine. But the recommendation was warm and Mario enjoyed working with me. Our sessions always followed the same pattern: with a healthy dose of optimism, he went through various organisational dynamics and weighty decisions with me, while I mostly remained silent. Very occasionally, I would summarise along the lines of 'So today you're mainly dealing with...' or 'It seems you've run into this or that'. He listened kindly and attentively, confirmed what I had said and continued speaking without much noticeable change. Internally, I struggled quite a bit with my role and wondered if I was actually contributing anything. Indeed, I checked this with him, but he said he was satisfied and every year he signed up for six more sessions. There was no sponsor in this process although, as with any coaching assignment, his boss was often brought in as a topic for conversation. I only contracted directly with Mario and never got to know anyone else in the organisation. After four years or so, he thought that was enough and moved on to evaluate and conclude the coaching. I am curious to know where he's working now, is he still working, or maybe already living his dream of a lakeside country estate in the mountains....

Nowadays, I do consider it worthwhile to speak to the sponsor as well, certainly at the start of an assignment. It need not be the sponsor or manager her- or himself – it could simply be the "manager in the mind of the coachee" in which case I would encourage the coachee to have a conversation with his boss about the coaching and tell me what her or his boss advised. So, during contracting I increasingly ask, 'And what would your manager expect from our work?' or 'And how will that make a difference to others in your organisation, how will your boss be able to tell, say, that our coaching sessions are effective?' and so on. I find this kind of organisational anchoring important, partly because I find that executive coaching is really an organisational-development intervention and has noticeable consequences for those around the coachee. Moreover, the organisation is paying – quite rightly – for the coaching. But even if none of that is the case and the coachee really is speaking just for himself, like Mario above, the organisational perspective is still a very fruitful one.

Simply because a coach can base so many astute challenges on questions such as 'how will others in the organisation respond to that?' or 'what do your boss and colleagues think of it?'. Such questions invite us to rethink and reconsider what we are developing, thus promoting a new perspective and independent reflection.

Nowadays, therefore, my coaching work is much more "embedded" in organisations. To cite an example, here is a critical moment from the review of a recent coaching assignment, as described by my coachee:

> For me, a critical moment was when I sought my coach's help to prepare for a meeting with a board member in my organisation who is also responsible for the HR department. I was holding the meeting in order to defend and retain one of my team members, someone he was planning to fire. Because I was well prepared and understood how my "opponent" might react and what he might argue, the meeting went very well. Though we disagreed on important aspects, I was able to make my point and propose a solution that was humane, fair, and incorporated both his perspective and that of others in the organisation. For myself, the outcome was that respect for me increased. I had come across as a valid, equal partner who has to be reckoned with and is not afraid to fight for something. What helped during the coaching was that the coach had his own view, and that it differed from mine. He managed to outline a more hopeful and more global picture of the situation, which in a sense sharpened my own arguments. The discussion expanded my horizons and encouraged me to include my board member's vision in my thinking. Coaching also helped me gain a better understanding of other people's image of me. And last but not least, it broke down some internal barriers that had previously stopped me acting in the way I wanted to.

This excerpt illustrates nicely the embeddedness of coaching within the organisation, how complex issues in the organisation run through the coachee's mind and how coaching is especially valued as a way to increase personal insight and understanding of a situation (see also the other "coachee critical moments" as discussed in the previous two chapters).

## B.  Essences

Previous (quantitative) studies on the effectiveness of coaching have focussed on the views of coachees, coaches and coachees' colleagues on the outcomes of coaching in general. In this chapter, we also look at the mindsets of these three key players in coaching assignments, but this time not in the form of generalised (numerical) outcomes. In this process research, we look more closely at the impact of specific "moments" in their coaching assignments.

In this follow-up to previous studies of critical moments in executive coaching (see the previous four chapters), critical moments in coaching conversations were analysed from three perspectives, namely those of executive coaching clients, their coaches and their sponsors. In this way, we hoped to find out more about how coaching conversations are experienced in the broadest sense. The purpose of this research was again to find out more about "sub-outcomes" of coaching: "mini-outcomes" as they arise within the coaching process and as a result of that process.

Our research extends previous studies in two ways: first, we take a process-oriented, qualitative approach by investigating which events are regarded as critical by coachees and coaches within their coaching contracts to date. Second, we consider the perspective of sponsors of coaching who refer to the same coaching assignments as coachees and coaches have done.

In total, 177 critical-moment descriptions were collected (49 from coachees, 49 from coaches and 79 from sponsors of coaching), of which 147 could be matched between coach, coachee and sponsor working on the same assignment. The moments from the same coaching processes were collected as part of a longer, quantitative study of coaching outcomes (see De Haan, Grant, Burger, & Eriksson, 2016) using a single "open question" about critical moments (a form of "mixed methods research", see Chapter 1). More than 4,000 coachees, coaches and sponsors participated in that major study, but only in 49 cases did all three parties answer the open question at the end of the form. The descriptions were coded with an existing and a new coding scheme and analysed with reference to a larger data set comprising 561 critical-moment descriptions from executive coaching assignments.

The present study therefore looked mainly at critical moments of coaching cited by coachees, coaches and sponsors in relation to shared coaching processes. We found that coachees and coaches showed much greater alignment in what they regard as critical in their coaching assignments, much more so than with the sponsors, even when all three were referring to the same coaching process. More specifically, we found that coachees and coaches mainly describe as "critical" moments where they gained new realisations and insight (as we saw earlier in Chapters 4 and 5) or where the coach initiated significant action. Coachees and coaches also frequently cited changes in the inner layers of the metaphorical "onion" of personality, ranging from communication, through attitude, to creativity, knowledge and self-awareness, and referred to the same critical moments in almost half of their descriptions. Sponsors, on the other hand, mainly point to positive changes in the relationship with the coachee, and moments when the coachee initiated significant action. In general, the sponsors' descriptions turned out to be very positive, which explains why no description was given the code for "negative change in the relationship" (code 4; see Figure 6.3). This may be the result of self-selection, because a high proportion of the sponsors in the large-scale research project had chosen not to answer the open question about critical moments. In terms of the "onion" model, sponsors also observed more frequent changes in the outer "layers", such as coachees' communication and interpersonal skills. Finally, coaches and coachees seemed to be more aligned (41% agreement) in their choice of critical moments than either sponsors and coachees or sponsors and coaches (26% and 23% agreement, respectively).

The present study extends previous research by also including sponsors' critical-moment descriptions. Figure 6.6 embeds the sponsors' critical-moment descriptions obtained in the present study into previous research conducted with coachees, coaches and coach-coachee dyads. The figure shows that more than a quarter of the critical-moment descriptions from sponsors have been categorised as containing significant action initiated by the coachee (code 6), a code which was rarely used in the earlier chapters, for any coachee or coach critical-moment descriptions. This is some first evidence that organisational sponsors and managers do attribute behavioural changes in their employees to coaching assignments undertaken, and that they do so differently to coaches and coachees.

Together with the earlier qualitative research into critical moments in real, contracted, executive coaching assignments, this study offers empirical support for the presence of tangible change within and as a result of coaching conversations. We believe that we now have ample evidence that coachees and coaches by and large agree on the kind of momentary changes that occur through coaching, except in or near the presence of significant ruptures in the relationship where coaches report significantly more emotions in the form of anxiety and doubt (see Chapter 5 and De Haan, Bertie, Day, & Sills, 2010b).

Finally, we have found further evidence that also sponsors can recognise significant change coming out of coaching conversations. However, sponsors draw attention to a different aspect of these changes, namely the actions that the coachees initiate as a result of coaching conversations. At this stage of research, by analysing critical moments experienced by third parties, we are beginning to see meaningful evidence of organisations' experience of coaching conversations, and of the organisational consequences of those conversations. This kind of scrutiny of critical moments in coaching conversations gives some idea of the differences in mindsets engendered by the three roles taken in and around coaching sessions, those of coachee, coach and sponsor. These differences in mindsets are well described by the "window on coaching" model put forward by Clutterbuck (1985) and De Haan and Burger (2005; see also Figure 6.1):

1   Coachees and coaches conducting normal coaching conversations seem to have an "insight-focussed" ideology where significant moments are those of new learning: new perspectives and new insights related to self and coaching objectives and themes;

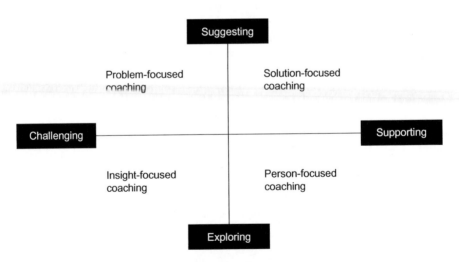

*Figure 6.1* Various models or philosophies of executive coaching, as introduced by De Haan and Burger (2005). These four different models are based on dominant activities within coaching, such as *exploring* the issue, *confronting* the issue with other ways of looking at it, *suggesting* advice around the issue and *supporting* the person raising the issue.

2   Coaches when in the presence of rare ruptures or dramatic events in coaching conversations seem to have a "person-focussed" ideology, where the orientation is much more towards highly personal anxieties, emotions and doubts;

3   Organisational sponsors of coaching seem to have more of a "problem-focussed" or "solution-focussed" mindset, which is more action-, behaviour- and future-oriented.

It is interesting that within these overall differences, sponsors do mention deeper layers of personality, such as self-awareness, attitude, confidence and authenticity (see Figure 6.4), even as much as the coaches and coachees are doing. The sponsors may be more interested in changes in their relationship with their colleagues (Figure 6.3), yet they still define those relationships as multilayered and not just superficially in terms of communication and behaviour (Figure 6.4).

Knowing more about the ideology of the various partners that come to build the coaching relationship can be extremely helpful. Coaches can adapt their contracting to what the other parties find most critical in this helping relationship – and they can also adapt their style in the presence of misunderstandings and ruptures. All in all, communication between the various parties working together in this essentially triangular endeavour can be improved by a deeper knowledge of likely default ideologies, such as their orientations towards emotions, problems, solutions and insights. Finally, we may be discovering how change from executive coaching is being retranslated and refined through the various stakeholders involved: coaches may be focussing a lot on their own anxieties and doubts, yet at the same time translating this sensitivity into new insight for coachees (by, e.g., free association and making use of countertransference, as in insight-focussed approaches – De Haan & Burger, 2005). Coachees may then be able to translate new insight into new behaviour and a changed outlook within their organisations, translating their new learning into observable relational change with their sponsors and other counterparts (adapting to work environments which may be more action- and problem-oriented than coaching conversations), as well as, conversely, retranslating new organisational experiences into requests for new insight from coaching, etc. The substantive and measurable emerging changes from executive coaching conversations that are beginning to come to light in coaching outcome studies (De Haan & Duckworth, 2013 or Jones, Woods, & Guillaume, 2015) are well captured by the following words from Mahatma Gandhi:

> Carefully watch your thoughts, for they become your words. Manage and watch your words, for they will become your actions. Consider and judge your actions, for they have become your habits. Acknowledge and watch your habits, for they shall become your values. Understand and embrace your values, for they become your destiny.

It is as if a coaching conversation creates a "ripple" in the mind, which propagates, first between coachee and coach, and then in the form of new action into and within the organisational context of the coaching client.

## C. Research into critical moments experienced by coachees, coaches and sponsors of coaching

### 1. Introduction: research among sponsors

Although the term "executive coaching" refers to a diverse range of interventions relying on different paradigms and methodologies, most researchers and practitioners would probably agree that clients of coaching enter the process with learning and development goals, to increase their performance within their organisation, or to reflect upon their own behaviour (De Haan & Burger, 2005; Downey, 1999; Parsloe & Wray, 2000; Zeus & Skiffington, 2002). Most professionals would also agree that executive coaching is an organisational intervention, designed to benefit an organisation through working with a single individual (Smither, London, Flautt, Vargas, Kucine, 2003). When clients are asked to evaluate coaching outcomes, they have been found to report higher goal attainment (Grant, 2003), greater self-efficacy (e.g. Baron & Morin, 2010; Evers, Brouwers, & Tomic, 2006), improved social skills (Spence & Grant, 2005; Wasylyshyn, 2003) and better team performance (Sue-Chan & Latham, 2004) in response to coaching interventions. Although some of the coaching outcome studies have used feedback data from peers and managers (Peterson, 1993; Smither et al., 2003; Thach, 2002), what remains largely unexplored is the question of whether and how those positive outcomes are also visible to others in the organisation. With organisations spending billions of dollars on coaching interventions globally (Sherman & Freas, 2004), we need research that establishes whether those investments pay off not just for the client of coaching, but particularly for others with whom the coachee interacts at work. The present study therefore aims to extend previous research by examining the coaching process not only from the perspective of coachees and coaches, but also from that of their sponsors in the organisation, who were the coachees' direct line managers, partners or HR directors.

Making use of a qualitative methodology, we first aim to replicate existing findings on the critical moments of change that coachees and their coaches attribute to their coaching assignments (see the previous chapters). Second, we build on those previous studies by including critical moments that organisational sponsors notice in response to those same coaching assignments. For this purpose, we are imagining that in executive coaching, there are two processes running concurrently: the coaching process with all its twists and turns, and indeed with critical moments as observed by the two partners; and the organisational processes where coachees collaborate with and work towards requirements of their colleagues, clients and sponsors. In this research, we are comparing the critical moments in this second process to the critical moments from within the coaching process. Our coding of such qualitative data will allow us to identify and quantify similarities and differences in coachees', coaches' and sponsors' perceptions of critical moments both within and as a consequence of executive coaching conversations.

### 1.1 Coachees' and coaches' critical moments in coaching

Despite the popularity of coaching interventions in organisations (Sherman & Freas, 2004), rigorous empirical studies on the outcomes of coaching are rather scarce. The research that has been conducted has generally focussed on the coachees' and partly on the coaches' perspectives concerning the beneficial outcomes that coaching entails (De Haan & Duckworth, 2013). Although we recognise the value of such quantitative outcome studies, we start with more qualitative data in this study. By analysing the qualitative data rigorously, we aim to shed more light on the question of what happens *within* the coaching process; in other words, we focus more on *sub-outcomes* than on overall outcomes. Rice & Greenberg (1984) define sub-outcomes as outcomes achieved within the process, from moment to moment, as distinct from outcomes which are generally the result of the process, that is, which can be measured after completing the full coaching assignment.

Several previous research projects have already investigated critical moments in coaching assignments for coachees and coaches. More specifically, they have asked coachees and coaches the following question: 'Describe briefly one critical moment (an exciting, tense, or significant moment) with your coach / coachee. Think about what was critical in the coaching journey, or a moment when you did not quite know what to do'. Study participants were inexperienced coaches (De Haan, 2008c), experienced coaches (Day, De Haan, Sills, Bertie, & Blass, 2008; De Haan, 2008d), coaching clients (De Haan, Bertie, Day, & Sills, 2010a), dyads of coaches and coachees that were interviewed directly after their sessions together (De Haan, Bertie, Day, & Sills, 2010b), and, in a case study, a single dyad of coachee and coach (De Haan & Nieß, 2012). Collecting such descriptions of what had been experienced as significant, tense, anxiety-provoking, exciting or pivotal in some way confirmed that such descriptions of "critical moments" tend to refer to major events in the coaching relationship and can therefore be defined as "sub-outcomes" of that relationship: important outcomes or events on a moment-by-moment or session-by-session basis (Rice & Greenberg, 1984).

The critical-moment descriptions collected in those studies were coded by independent coders using the coding scheme displayed in Table 6.1, which is described in more detail in De Haan et al. (2010b). Broadly, the coding scheme uses 12 codes and refers to four categories:

1   Moments of learning (code 1 "New insight" and code 2 "New connection/ perspective");
2   Moments of relational change in the coaching relationship (code 3 "Positive change in the relationship" and code 4 "Negative change in the relationship");
3   Moments of significant action (code 5 "Significance in doing in the moment, coach-led" and code 6 "Significance in doing in the moment, coachee-led") and
4   Moments of significant emotional experience (code 7 "Joy, coachee", code 8 "Joy, coach", code 9 "Anxiety, coachee", code 10 "Anxiety, coach", code 11 "Doubt, coachee" and code 12 "Doubt, coach").

The main findings of those previous studies into critical moments of coaching suggest very broadly that, while inexperienced coaches express mainly their own doubts as critical moments (De Haan, 2008c), more experienced coaches tend to refer to critical moments as sources of anxiety (De Haan, 2008d). It is important to note, however, that those coaches were asked for a critical moment with one of their coachees, which they could well have interpreted as the most significant moment of their whole portfolio of work. It is therefore not surprising that these two groups of participants are

*Table 6.1* Critical-moment coding scheme as found in De Haan et al. (2010b), equal to Table 5.1 in Chapter 5. This coding was used for the data set in this chapter and also (retrospectively) for all earlier data sets of descriptions of critical moments in coaching conversations

| Code number | Short description of the code |
|---|---|
| 1 | A moment of learning: a moment in which new insight was created for coach and – particularly – coachee |
| 2 | A moment of learning: a moment of working through, reflecting, gaining new perspectives and/or making sense of existing material |
| 3 | A change in the relationship in the moment (positive) |
| 4 | A change in the relationship in the moment (negative) |
| 5 | Significant action in the moment (coach-led): applying oneself to a unique scripted process such as drawing, visualisation, role-play, GROW (Goal, Reality, Options, Will) etc. |
| 6 | Significant action in the moment (coachee-led): organising future sessions, negotiating the session, taking away action points, making notes, etc. |
| 7 | Significant emotional experience in the moment: joy (coachee); heightened positive emotion |
| 8 | Significant emotional experience in the moment: joy (coach); heightened positive emotion |
| 9 | Significant emotional experience in the moment: anxiety (coachee); heightened positive emotion |
| 10 | Significant emotional experience in the moment: anxiety (coach); heightened positive emotion |
| 11 | Significant emotional experience in the moment: doubt (coachee); fundamental not-knowing, often a starting point for reflection |
| 12 | Significant emotional experience in the moment: doubt (coach); fundamental not-knowing, often a starting point for reflection |

biased towards reporting particularly dramatic and emotional moments. When, on the other hand, clients of coaching were asked for their critical moments of coaching (with the help of the same question above), they instead reported moments of new realisations and insights as particularly critical. Similar results are obtained when dyads of coaches and coachees were interviewed independently after a joint coaching session: *both* parties had a tendency to report new realisations and insights as most critical to the session, and they were in substantial agreement in terms of which moments they selected as being critical in the session they had just completed.

These are important findings and worth testing with a new and wider data set. The finding that coachees are frequently referring to new realisations and insight in their critical-moment descriptions, in combination with the fact that they are mostly selecting positive experiences of coaching (De Haan et al., 2010a), may indicate that coaching clients are particularly helped by acquiring new insight and learning. In other words, it is possible that on a within-session, moment-by-moment level coachees prefer to be served by insight-focussed interventions and less by the other three main contributions in executive coaching: problem-focussed, person-focussed and solution-focussed approaches (De Haan & Burger, 2005; see Figure 6.1). It is important, however, to hold such an interpretation of the earlier findings lightly, because growing coachee insight will be common to all successful approaches and may therefore be one of many "common factors" (De Haan, 2008a) in professional coaching approaches. Nevertheless, our growing understanding of how coachees describe their most critical moments in the coaching relationship may inform extensive debates in the coaching literature around which method or approach to offer to coachees. Since the present study looks into critical-moment descriptions each from a single coaching assignment (rather than taken from a whole portfolio of client work), we would expect to replicate this finding; more specifically, we suggest:

- *Hypothesis 1:* Coachees and coaches mostly refer to moments of insight and learning (Codes 1 and 2 in Table 6.1) in their critical-moment descriptions of coaching.

### 1.2 Sponsors' critical moments in coaching

While rigorous studies concerning the outcomes of coaching interventions from the perspective of coachees and coaches are limited to less than 20 (De Haan & Duckworth, 2013), even fewer studies have investigated whether *sponsors* notice any positive outcomes that they attribute to the effectiveness of coaching. Nevertheless, preliminary evidence suggests that the beneficial effects of executive coaching are also visible to others in the organisation. Studies which estimate the changes caused by executive coaching in terms of 360° feedback show that managers who worked with an executive coach receive better evaluations on the second 360° feedback instrument compared to those who did not work with an executive coach (Smither et al., 2003). Similarly, Thach (2002) found that leaders who were coached for an average of six months received more favourable evaluations through 360° feedback. Managers and HR partners of coaching clients have been found to report more effective leadership behaviours and better interpersonal skills among participants of a commissioned coaching programme (Wasylyshyn, Gronsky, & Haas, 2006). Olivero, Bane and Kopelman (1997) found that managers who participated in a management development programme with additional coaching received higher ratings of productivity (an 88% increase) compared to managers who participated in the management development programme alone (only a 22% increase in productivity).

In sum, there are a few empirical studies which suggest that coaching interventions provide some benefits that are also visible to others in the organisation. The second aim of the present study is to extend this line of research by inquiring more deeply into the experience of line managers and sponsors of coaching clients. More specifically, we aim to identify critical moments for sponsors of coaching and to compare triads of coachees, coaches and sponsors in terms of what critical moments they notice in shared coaching assignments. To the best of our knowledge, only two published studies so far have also included coachees', coaches' and sponsors' perceptions of coaching outcomes separately, albeit that, in the second study, they did not necessarily stem from the same assignments. Peterson (1993) studied $N = 370$ leaders from various organisations at three points in time (pre-coaching, post-coaching and follow-up) with outcome defined by their own coaching objectives and five standard "control" items, rated by at least themselves, their manager and their coach (multi-source ratings). The coaching programme was intensive and long-term, with typically 50+ hours of individual coaching with a professional coach over at least a year. Peterson found that coachees, on average, achieved significant improvement on all measures of outcome related to coaching objectives (effect sizes $d > 1.5$). Schlosser, Steinbrenner, Kumata and Hunt (2006) invited triads of coachees, coaches and the coachees' managers to report outcomes they attributed to coaching engagements. These participants were asked to select from a list of 25 outcomes the ones that they believed had improved as a result of the coaching engagement. While only $N = 14$ managers responded to the authors' request, results indicated that all three groups (coachees, coaches and managers) regarded employee "engagement" and "promotability" as the main outcomes of coaching. Managers, however, rated the effectiveness of coaching significantly lower than coachees and coaches did.

The present study extends these quantitative approaches by looking at the "sub-outcome" level (Rice & Greenberg, 1984) for the first time, on the basis of critical-moment descriptions of triads of coachees, coaches and sponsors working together on the *same* coaching assignment. While we hypothesised that coachees and coaches would refer primarily to moments of new insight and learning (codes 1 and 2; see Hypothesis 1), we would argue that such moments of new insight or realisation will be less relevant for the sponsors of those assignments who are only indirectly involved (or only involved directly at the contracting and review stages). For this reason, we suggest that sponsors mainly report critical moments which refer to more readily observable moments of *change* (codes 3 and 4) and to *new actions* taken by coachees (code 6). If this is confirmed, we would have some preliminary evidence for sponsors operating more from a "problem-focussed" understanding of executive coaching (De Haan & Burger, 2005; Figure 6.1).

- *Hypothesis 2:* Sponsors mostly refer to moments of change in the relationship and significant action taken by the coachee (codes 3, 4 and 6) as critical ones.

The coding scheme which Hypotheses 1 and 2 refer to (see Table 6.1) was originally developed inductively for classifying many hundreds of coachees' and coaches' critical moments of executive coaching. Several codes therefore refer to critical moments that are likely to arise within coaching sessions, which may be less observable for sponsors of coaching, such as the codes referring to emotional states of coaches and coachees (codes 7–12). Although we expect these codes of the earlier scheme to be less relevant here, we have chosen to retain the scheme as a whole as a first coding system, to allow a direct comparison with the earlier studies.

However, we also felt the need for a second more tailor-made coding scheme, which could test this particular hypothesis. For this reason, we adopted a grounded theory approach (Glaser, 1992; Strauss & Corbin, 1990) to develop a second coding scheme. The grounded theory approach made use of 41 sponsors' critical-moment descriptions collected at an earlier date. In this inductive way, we arrived at another scheme for classifying critical moments of change particularly from the sponsor perspective, but usable for all three parties (coachees, coaches and sponsors). We noticed that our scheme turned out similar to Schein's (1985) conceptualisation of the "onion" of organisational culture. This coding scheme, which is depicted in Figure 6.2, suggests that while "outer layers" such as changes in behaviour and communication of coaching are visible to outsiders, "inner layers" refer to invisible learning or personal change in, for example, attitudes and knowledge. While coachees and coaches directly involved in the coaching assignment may thus notice more of the inner levels of the onion model, those inner layers may be less visible to sponsors of coaching.

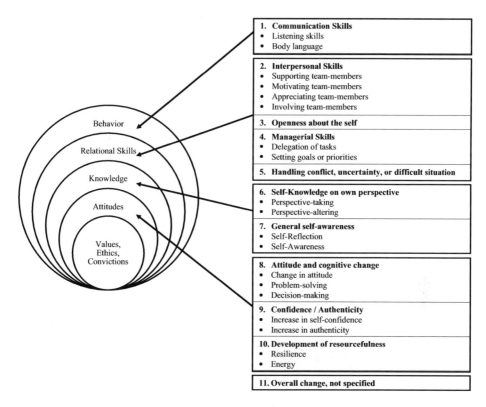

*Figure 6.2* Second critical moments coding scheme based on Schein's (1985) "onion" model.

If coding would confirm that sponsors are more occupied with the "outer layers" of the model, this would give support to the idea that sponsors describe their critical moments more from a "problem-focussed" perspective and less from an "insight-focussed" perspective (see De Haan & Burger, 2005), which we know from earlier research (see Chapter 5 and De Haan et al., 2010b) has been more the perspective of coachees and coaches in regular coaching sessions (i.e. coaching sessions without dramatic events). We therefore propose:

- *Hypothesis 3:* Sponsors refer significantly more than others to moments of communication or change that are visible on the outer layers of the onion model (codes 1, 2, 3, 4 and 5), as critical ones.

### 1.3 Congruence between coachees, coaches and sponsors

Hypotheses 1, 2 and 3 are concerned with the nature of the moments that coachees, coaches and sponsors refer to as critical with regard to the shared endeavour of the executive coaching work. What however remains unexplored so far is the extent to which those three parties actually refer to the *same* moments as being critical to them. More particularly, we were interested in finding out how often triplets of coachees, coaches and sponsors refer to the same moment of change that they notice during or as a result of coaching. This would be important as another way to understand the level of agreement between various participants in the coaching assignment, and also as a way to study the "*Rashomon* conjecture" proposed and much debated by psychotherapists (Johnson, 1973; Mintz, Auerbach, Luborsky, & Johnson, 1973; Weiss, Rabinowitz, & Spiro, 1996).

Previous research has consistently shown that coachees and coaches refer to the same moments as critical significantly above chance level, and thus that there is not much of a "*Rashomon* effect" in executive coaching, which would be the case when participants in a coaching conversation leave the session with different, incommensurable accounts of their experience together (based on Kurosawa's movie *Rashomon* where a single event is recounted very differently from four different perspectives). De Haan et al. (2010b) showed that in a coachee-coach direct comparison study, coachees and coaches referred to the same moment in 53% of the descriptions, while in a longitudinal investigation where coachee and coach wrote down their critical moments after each coaching session they referred to the same moment in 47% of the descriptions (De Haan & Nieß, 2012; see also Chapter 5). Not only did coachees and coaches refer to the same incidents at a frequency much higher than chance, but they also tended to agree in their descriptions of their critical moments (De Haan et al., 2010b), thereby disconfirming the *Rashomon* conjecture.

In those two studies, coachees and coaches were asked for their critical moments straight after shared coaching sessions, while participants in the present study referred to one coaching assignment consisting of many sessions and they did not normally answer straight after mutual sessions. For this reason, we expect the amount of congruence between coachees and coaches to be smaller than in those two previous studies reported in Chapter 5, yet we suggest that they are still above chance. Since sponsors are not directly involved in the coaching assignments, we expect congruence between coachees/coaches and sponsors to be smaller than between coachees and coaches.

- *Hypothesis 4a:* The incidence of shared critical moments between coachees and coaches, that is, the percentage of cases in which they both refer to the same shared incident, will again be well above chance level (under 1%), but also significantly below the level found in earlier studies into a single coaching session (47–53%).
- *Hypothesis 4b:* The number of times that sponsors and coachees (and also sponsors and coaches) refer to the same moments as being critical is significantly smaller than the number of times that coaches and coachees refer to the same critical moments.

## 2. Method

### 2.1 Sample

Participants of the present study ($N = 177$) were recruited through two different sources. First, potential sponsors of coaching were approached at a Business School in Great Britain and as part of another study (Clutterbuck, De Haan, Wels, Lucas, & Winter, 2009), resulting in an initial sample from sponsors of $N = 30$. Second, we made use of a large-scale online survey using a single open question on critical moments (i.e. a mixed method design, see Chapter 1) to recruit coachees, coaches and sponsors of coaching who were involved in the same coaching assignment (De Haan et al., 2016), adding $N = 49$ coachees, $N = 49$ coaches and $N = 49$ sponsors of coaching from matching assignments. Sponsors were nominated by the coachees as those work colleagues who sponsored their assignment, so they were mainly their line managers, though in some cases they were HR Directors or more senior partners in professional services firms. In total, 130 sponsors completed the overall research questionnaire (a response rate of around 20%) and 49 of their answers to the open question could be matched with answers by coaches and coachees (38%). Participants were drawn from 22 different countries with the help of a wide network of 366 executive coaches who participated in this worldwide large coaching outcome study. Coachees and sponsors had an almost equal gender split, while coaches had an average experience of 13.31 years ($SD = 7.19$), 67% were female and 86% were external coaches (with the remainder internal mainly in large public-sector organisations), mostly conducting stand-alone executive coaching assignments.

## 2.2 Materials

Data for this study were obtained by asking participants whether they have 'experienced something that felt like a "critical" moment (an exciting, tense, or significant moment) where they noticed a difference and to describe briefly one (or more) such critical moments'; in the case of coachees, we added 'during coaching'; in the case of coaches we added 'in your work with this coachee' and in the case of sponsors of coaching we added: 'with your colleague, where you were directly aware of the impact of executive coaching'. We highlighted direct awareness of executive coaching because we are looking for experiences which they somehow relate to the coaching work. We chose the word "impact" here because it was the most general term we could think of: it could be interpreted as the sponsor wished without limiting the range of their answers. Coachees, coaches and sponsors were thus asked essentially the same question with small modifications, which was also the same as the core research question in all earlier research programmes.

## 2.3 Procedure

After the 49 coachees', 49 coaches' and 79 sponsors' critical-moment descriptions had been collected, they were coded three times blindly and independently by four independent coders out of a group of eight coders. In the first two of these coding procedures, critical-moment descriptions were drawn randomly and blindly from all three sources: coachees, coaches and sponsors; in the third coding round, the source of the critical-moment description had to be revealed to the coder, by definition:

1   *First coding* – The descriptions were coded based on the original coding scheme that has already been used in previous studies (see Table 6.1). For this first coding, a forced-choice design was employed, forcing the coders to only attach one code to each critical-moment description. We knew from the earlier studies that coders had never asked for more categories. This was replicated in this study, so forced choice with these 12 codes was straightforward.

2   *Second coding* – The second way of coding was developed inductively from moments collected from sponsors of coaching, by using a grounded theory approach

which on second iteration could be linked with Schein's (1985) "onion" model, see Figure 6.2. According to this model, organisational culture can be regarded as a metaphorical onion, where visible organisational *behaviours* are located on the outer layers of the onion, while organisational knowledge refers to less visible, middle layers, and underlying *assumptions* of the organisation are found in the inner layers. More specifically, 11 codes (see Figure 6.2) evolved from the sponsors' critical-moment descriptions collected prior to the present study, which naturally fitted into an "onion" model similar to the one proposed by Schein (1985). Code 1, namely changes in communication, such as listening skills or body language, refers to changes in behaviour (first layer of the "onion" model).

Codes 2–5 refer to changes in relational skills (second layer of the "onion" model). They include interpersonal skills (code 2), such as supporting, motivating, appreciating and involving members of the team, openness about self (code 3), managerial skills (code 4) such as delegating tasks and setting goals and priorities, and handling conflict, uncertainty or difficult situations (code 5).

Codes 6 (self-knowledge, such as perspective-taking and perspective-altering) and 7 (general self-awareness and self-reflection) represent the middle layer of the "onion" model, namely knowledge.

Changes in attitude (fourth layer of the "onion" model) are described by codes 8–10. Code 8 implies changes in attitude and cognitive change, such as problem-solving and decision-making, while code 9 describes changes in self-confidence and authenticity. Code 10 refers to a development of resourcefulness, such as energy or resilience.

Code 11 (overall change, not specified) was developed to fit the descriptions that did not mention a specific change.

No code was developed to refer to the core of the "onion" model (basic assumptions, ethics and convictions), as none of the critical-moment descriptions referred to changes on that level.

For the coding based on this second coding scheme, we again employed a forced-choice design in which coders were asked to only administer one code per critical-moment description – however, in this case, the final code is a "remainder" category (see Figure 6.2).

3 *Third coding* – For the third way of coding, we asked the coders to indicate whether the critical-moment descriptions from the same assignment (i.e. triplets of coachee, coach and sponsor; $N = 49$) were congruent in that they were referring to the *same* moment or incident as being critical. More specifically, we asked them to indicate whether they thought there was a correspondence with regard to content between the coachee and the coach, between the coachee and the sponsor, between the coach and the sponsor, and between all three critical-moment descriptions that came from the same coaching assignment.

To estimate the degree of agreement between coders, Cohen's Kappa was calculated for each of the three ways of coding. For the first coding scheme, which includes 12 codes, we found a Cohen's Kappa of $\kappa = 0.240$. For the second coding scheme, using 11 codes, Cohen's Kappa was slightly higher at $\kappa = 0.318$. Finally, for the third way of coding (congruence), which has five codes, Cohen's Kappa was $\kappa = 0.282$. All codings thus indicate fair agreement between coders (Landis & Koch, 1977). We averaged the codings by adding up the times each code was assigned to the critical-moment descriptions by each coder and dividing through the number of coders and critical moments. This procedure ensured that none of the coders' assessments were lost.

## 2.4 Range of critical-moment descriptions

In order to help the reader gain a basic understanding of the critical-moment descriptions collected from coachees, coaches and sponsors of coaching, we have chosen a number of short but representative vignettes; see Appendix E. Those data show the range of critical moments that were mentioned by the participants of this study as well as the range of congruence (which is increasing towards the bottom of the table in Appendix E) between the three different parties.

## 3. Results

### 3.1 Coachees' and coaches' critical moments in coaching

Hypothesis 1 suggests that coachees and coaches mostly refer to moments of insight or learning (codes 1 and 2) as critical ones. It was tested based on the first coding scheme that was also used in previous studies. Figure 6.3 displays the proportion of codes

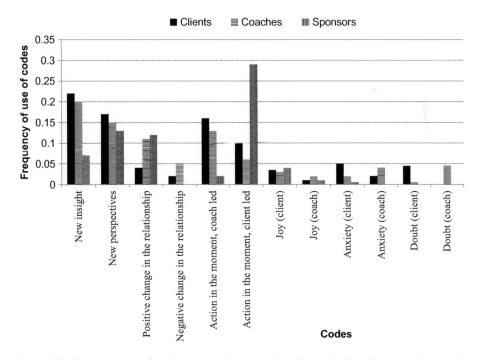

*Figure 6.3* Proportions of codes assigned to coachees', coaches' and sponsors' critical-moment descriptions in this new study, within the first coding scheme consisting of 12 categories of "critical moments".

assigned to coachees', coaches' and sponsors' critical-moment descriptions based on this coding scheme. This graphical representation of the data shows that codes 1 and 2 were indeed used most frequently for coding both coachees' and coaches' critical-moment descriptions. Paired sample t-tests were conducted to investigate whether this difference compared with the other codes was statistically significant. The tests showed that codes 1 and 2 were indeed used significantly more often than all the other codes at $p < 0.001$, except for code 5 where the difference was not significant. The results were thus mainly supportive of Hypothesis 1.

### 3.2 Results for sponsors' critical moments in coaching

Hypothesis 2 states that with respect to the same, original coding scheme, sponsors refer to moments of change and coachee-led action (codes 3, 4 and 6) as critical ones. Again, Figure 6.3 includes the graphical representation of the data based on this coding scheme. It shows that sponsors of coaching differ substantially from coachees and coaches with respect to their critical-moment descriptions: coachees and coaches seem to be more aligned in their critical-moment descriptions when compared to sponsors (a similar alignment between coachees and coaches straight after shared coaching conversations was also found in De Haan et al., 2010b, and De Haan & Nieß, 2012).

In order to statistically test Hypothesis 2, we again made use of paired sample t-tests, comparing the frequencies of codes 3, 4 and 6 to the frequencies of the other codes. Results indicated that codes 3 and 6 were indeed used significantly more often at a $p < 0.01$ level than any of the other codes (except for code 2, where the difference to code 3 was not significant). Code 4 was, however, not used at all for coding of sponsors' critical moments, possibly because sponsors only reported positive changes as a result of coaching. The results offer strong but partial support for Hypothesis 2: while code 3 (positive change in the relationship) and code 6 (significance in doing in the moment, coachee-led) were indeed used significantly more to describe sponsors' critical moments, this was not the case for code 4 (negative change in the relationship).

Based on the second coding scheme grounded in the "onion" model of organisational change, Hypothesis 3 states that sponsors mainly refer to moments of change that are visible as they are on the outer layers of the coaches' onion model (codes 1, 2, 3, 4 and 5) as critical ones. Figure 6.4 displays the proportions of codes from the second coding scheme assigned by coders to the critical-moment descriptions for coachees, coaches, and sponsors of coaching. The graphical representation of the results suggests that codes 1 (communication skills) and 2 (interpersonal skills) were used very frequently for coding sponsors' critical-moment descriptions, especially when compared to the ratings for coachees' and coaches' critical-moment descriptions. Codes 8 (attitude and cognitive change) and 9 (confidence/authenticity) were, however, also used frequently for coding sponsors' critical-moment descriptions. Paired sample t-tests were again conducted to test whether the differences in the frequencies of codes 1, 2, 3, 4 and 5 in comparison to the other codes were statistically significant. The results indicated that code 1 was only used significantly more frequently for coding sponsors' critical moments than code 6, but not more frequently than any of the other codes. Code 2 was used more frequently than codes 6, 10 and 11, but there was no difference to the other codes. Codes 3 and 4 were not used significantly more frequently than any of the other codes. Code 5 was used significantly more often than

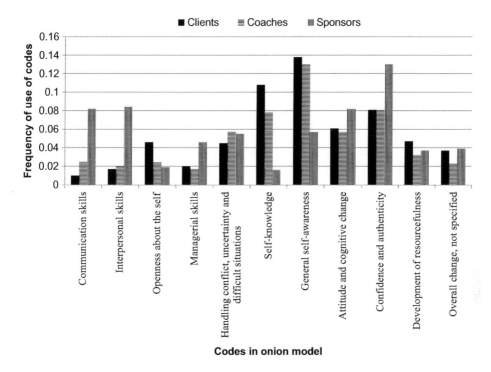

*Figure 6.4* Proportions of codes assigned to coachees', coaches' and sponsors' critical-moment descriptions in this new study, within the second coding scheme based on Schein's (1985) "onion" model.

code 6 only. In sum, the results suggest that codes 1 (communication skills) and 2 (interpersonal skills) were indeed used more frequently than some of the other codes, offering only limited support for Hypothesis 3. However, some of the codes on the inner layers of the onion model, such as codes 7 (general self-awareness), 8 (attitude or cognitive change) and 9 (confidence/authenticity) were not used significantly less frequently for coding sponsors' critical-moment descriptions.

The results of both coding schemes thus suggest that coachees and coaches are more aligned in what they regard as critical moments in their coaching assignments than sponsors are. With respect to the first, original coding scheme, we tested that finding with paired sample t-tests and our results indicate that sponsors of coaching reported fewer moments of new insights (code 1) and coach-led significance in doing in the moment (code 5) than coachees and coaches did. Instead they reported more critical moments that were coded as coachee-led significance in doing in the moment (code 6) when compared to both coachees and coaches. With respect to the second, newly developed coding scheme, we found that sponsors of coaching referred to significantly more critical moments of communication skills (code 1) than coachees, but the difference to coaches was only marginally significant. Sponsors furthermore referred significantly more often to critical moments that were coded as interpersonal skills (code 2) than coachees and coaches. Sponsors, however, referred to significantly fewer critical moments that were coded as self-knowledge on own perspective (code 6) or general self-awareness (code 7). Sponsors thus refer to more changes in the outer layers of the "onion" model (codes 1 and 2), while coachees and coaches refer more frequently to changes on the inner layers of the "onion" (codes 6 and 7).

### 3.3 Results for congruence between coachees, coaches and sponsors

We were also interested in the degree of congruence between triplets of coachees', coaches' and sponsors' critical-moment descriptions, as they were referring to the *same* coaching assignments. More specifically, we suggest that the degree to which both coachees and coaches refer to the same moments as critical is above chance (Hypothesis 4a) and that the degree to which both sponsors and coachees refer to the same moments as critical is smaller than the degree to which both coaches and coachees refer to the same moments as critical (Hypothesis 4b). A graphical representation of the results pertaining to those two hypotheses can be found in Figure 6.5. It shows that in 41% of these triplets, there is no congruence between any of the three parties in what moments they refer to as critical ones. Put differently, in 41% of the critical-moment descriptions, none of the coders recognised a congruence. In around the same number of cases (41%), coachees and coaches, however, refer to the same critical moments of their coaching assignments. Given that these coaching assignments had lasted for an average of nearly eight sessions (a median of seven sessions), which would be more than ten hours of coaching on average, this amounts to a correspondence which was well above chance and offers strong support for Hypothesis 4a. Figure 6.5 also shows that correspondence between coachees and sponsors (26%) as well as between coaches and sponsors (23%) was considerably smaller, thus offering support for Hypothesis 4b.

However, as this is narrative research, we need to be careful with our interpretations: here, we seem to have found congruence between all three parties, and particularly between coaches and coachees, a degree of congruence which is clearly

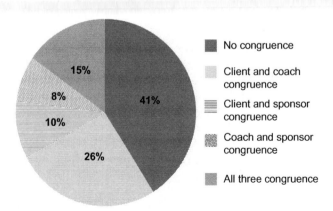

*Figure 6.5* Congruence between coachees, coaches and sponsors referring to the same coaching assignments.

above chance. On the other hand, any congruence we found is not – and can never be – *full* congruence, because the critical-moment descriptions are by design independent and therefore different. They have only been recognised by coders as belonging to similar instances of the coaching work. Moreover, in 41% of all critical-moment descriptions, the coders report *no* congruence across coachee, coach or sponsor perspectives. We do not know if in those descriptions completely incommensurable narratives were told, or rather narratives which other parties would easily recognise as well, simply because we have no means to test this retrospectively. So, despite the surprisingly high agreement in both selection and nature of description of critical moments (compare Figure 6.5) between coachees and coaches, we cannot rule out significant remaining "*Rashomon*" phenomena where both parties tell very different stories indeed.

## 4. Discussion

The results of this research show that there is considerably more agreement between coachees and coaches about the critical moments in their coaching relationship than between them and the sponsors. In the main, coachees and coaches described as "critical" those moments in which new insights were gained or an attitude or cognitive change occurred. The sponsors, for their part, emphasised behavioural change among clients of coaching, such as in their communication skills.

As found in previous research, there were indications that coachees and coaches holding normal coaching sessions mainly describe as "critical" the moments in which new knowledge, perspectives and insights are gained, and in doing so they cite the same moments to an extent that goes beyond pure chance. Sponsors, for their part, appear to attach more importance to new initiatives and changes initiated by the coaching client.

These findings become more convincing if they are compared directly with the original data sets of earlier studies, as we have done in Figure 6.6 where we took out the data set from the case study as those data were slightly more messy. This comparison shows that blind coding of six data sets of critical-moment descriptions (a total of 529 critical-moment descriptions each coded by at least three coders of which one, AC, coded every data set) collected from inexperienced coaches, experienced coaches (two data sets), clients of coaching, coachees and coaches together after a shared session, and sponsors of coaching assignments, are actually very distinct:

1   Critical moments from inexperienced coaches over their whole coaching experience are classified as "doubts of the coach" (code 12; see also Figure 6.6) in more than half of cases. The coach's anxieties (code 10) are also prominent.
2   Critical moments from experienced coaches over their whole coaching experience peak at both "doubts" and "anxieties" of the coach (codes 10 and 12 in equal measure).
3   Critical moments from coaches and coachees straight after sessions contain mainly new insights (code 1) and new perspectives (code 2).
4   Critical moments from sponsors of coaching (this research) are coded as "significant action led by the coachee" (code 6) in almost a third of cases.

Compared with those earlier findings, the data from the coaches as collected this time (shown in Figure 6.3) are a mixture of the earlier patterns as one would expect. This data set contains mostly experienced coaches, but we have not excluded inexperienced coaches, and is based on assignments that have just started as well as assignments that have gone on for many hours (where, on average, coachee and coach had already spent more than seven sessions together). In Figure 6.3, we can see that the coach data in fact contain a significant amount of anxiety and doubt, features we would expect if either coaches were very inexperienced or if they are reporting the most significant moments of their careers (which was the case in Day et al., 2008 and De Haan, 2008c, 2008d). This may also contribute to the fact that the overlap between coachee moments and coach moments (41% in this study) is marginally smaller than in the earlier studies (De Haan et al., 2010b, and De Haan & Nieß, 2012, where this degree of overlap was 53% and 47%, respectively). We would still consider that the fact that almost half of critical-moment selections overlap between coachee and coach

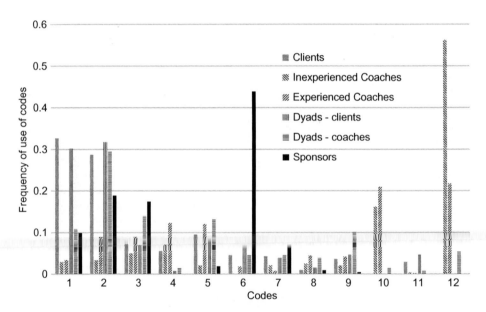

*Figure 6.6* Comparison of sponsors' critical moments with earlier research findings from all data sets in Chapters 2–6 except for the case study data, that is, 529 critical moments in total. The frequency scores are averages for three coders (AC, CB and EH) and are standardised at a total of 1. The following conclusions are clear from this figure: (1) coachee data peaks in the first two codes that are related to new insight and new learning; (2) coachee and coach data from "dyads", that is, recorded directly after coaching conversations, are very similar; (3) general coach data peaks in codes 10 and 12, that is, "anxiety, coach" and "doubt, coach", with inexperienced coaches experiencing more doubts; (4) sponsor data peaks in code 6, that is, action initiated by the coachee. There are also two other codes, codes 3 ("positive change in the relationship") and 7 ("joy, coachee"), where the sponsors' moment descriptions are the most frequent ones. For the definition of all codes, see Table 6.1.

is remarkable particularly as we know that they had an average of some eight sessions together before answering the questionnaire. Taken together, these findings mean that all earlier conclusions from critical moments in coaching studies that we could test are supported in this study.

## 5. Limitations of this study

The limitations of the present study are:

- First, that the sponsor data set (like the data sets for the other parties in the previous chapters) is still quite limited (only 79 sponsors' critical-moment descriptions of which 49 could be matched to both coachees' and coaches' descriptions), despite our having access to a very large-scale research programme, which has yielded more than 4,000 questionnaires (De Haan et al., 2016). We think that because of their more detached and supervisory role, it is harder to collect usable data from organisational sponsors. A larger data set would allow us to dig more deeply into the perceptions that organisational colleagues tend to develop towards coaching clients, in their roles of sponsors of executive coaching.
- Second, that the degrees of agreement between coders are still relatively small (Cohen's Kappa around $\kappa = 0.3$). Kappas are similar to those in previous studies and they are probably small because coders are collapsing whole narratives into single code descriptors. In our view both larger data sets and finer coding systems will need to be developed if we really want to understand what makes a difference in coaching conversations, particularly if we want to do that for each party to those conversations.
- Third, and following from the previous point, coding in narrative research and the social sciences is bound to suffer from considerable overlap between coding categories and from differences in interpretation of the meaning of both the narratives (the critical-moment descriptions) and the coding categories. Such fuzziness around meaning is hard to avoid without losing the richness of the original experiences, but will further degrade agreement between coders.

### 5.1 Further research

Critical-moment descriptions have convincingly been shown to be a promising area of coaching process research, and we can only hope that more studies will appear in the future, so that our understanding of "critical incidents", "sub-outcomes" or "momentary changes" in coaching assignments deepens and expands further. In particular, it seems important to explore more deeply the area of (non-)congruence of critical-moment descriptions, by not just collecting descriptions of critical moments of coaching, but also asking coachees, coaches and perhaps even sponsors to which degree they can recognise the narratives of the other parties in the common endeavour. Such research should be able to shine more light on the *Rashomon* conjecture, the question whether participants in shared sessions develop essentially similar or different narratives of their time spent together.

## SUMMARY OF CHAPTER 6: "THE EXPERIENCE OF SPONSORS"

In this fifth phase of the research into critical moments in coaching, we obtained 79 descriptions of critical moments by sponsors, plus 49 each for coachees and coaches – referring to the same 49 coaching relationships in which the three parties worked together (i.e. 177 descriptions in total).

Whereas the previous patterns in coach and coachee descriptions relating to the same coaching relationship were confirmed (this time, coach and coachee described the same moment or situation in 41% of cases), sponsors' descriptions of critical moments clearly behaved differently:

1   Sponsors' descriptions focussed mainly on new actions initiated by the coachee and on positive changes in their relationship with the coachee (i.e. not on new insight and new perspectives, like the other two parties in the coaching relationship).
2   Sponsors' descriptions agreed with coachee descriptions in only 26% of cases, and with coach descriptions in only 23%.
3   Sponsors pointed significantly more often to critical moments involving communication skills and interpersonal skills than did coachees and coaches, so the descriptions are about a more visible and "outside" level of potential organisational and personal development.

Looking generally at all 561 critical moments studied in this book, we can conclude that coachees, coaches and sponsors do show many similarities in their choices of critical moments, but at the same time have a different underlying philosophy when it comes to coaching conversations:

4   Coachees and coaches conducting normal coaching conversations seem to have a more "insight-focussed" ideology, where significant moments are those of new learning: new perspectives and new insights related to self and coaching objectives and themes;
5   Coaches when in the presence of rare ruptures or dramatic events in coaching conversations seem to have a "person-focussed" ideology, where the orientation is much more towards highly personal anxieties, emotions and doubts;
6   Organisational sponsors of coaching seem to have more of a "problem-focussed" or "solution-focussed" mindset, which is more oriented towards "actions" and "solutions", that is, the specific benefits for the organisation.

# Chapter 7

# Lessons to apply in practice

## A. Anecdote

The end of a coaching process is often different from the rest of coaching and it is useful to bear in mind a range of possibilities, from gratitude to non-attendance, from disappointment to deep pain and anger at saying goodbye. The last session is the one that is most often cancelled and, together with the very first session, the fullest one. This is because several different tasks vie for attention: normal ongoing coaching, evaluating and reviewing, and celebrating and saying goodbye. Endings touch us all deeply, and unconsciously evoke memories of the many other times in our lives when we had no choice but to say goodbye to significant comforts, customs and people (such as "being born", "weaning", and "starting school"). For us as coaches, therefore, it is crucial not to add any new pain to the pain that already exists around endings, no matter how much people try deliberately not to feel or recognise that pain. There are many different potential responses to a significant ending. Sometimes we attempt to shrug our shoulders and casually carry on, sometimes – to make things easier – we conveniently forget it's the end and focus on the future, sometimes we'll say "see you later" rather than "farewell", sometimes we try to schedule follow-up appointments to make the ending more bearable. Sometimes, in intensive processes, multiple occasions during many sessions are needed to reflect on the impact of the impending end, even if only to prevent a relapse that could undo most of the coaching achievements in what was, up to that point, a successful partnership.

I usually remind my coachee that the final session is approaching by mentioning this in the penultimate session. And I usually take our original learning goals with me to the last meeting, so we can review them. Often these old learning goals have long since given way to new ones, but it can still be refreshing to look back at them. It can even yield unexpected inspiration, as happened recently with Carol who started her own business during the coaching contract. Our sessions usually focussed on a number of business decisions she was facing, and then generated lists of homework she wrote down for herself. As is often the case with a final session, she arrived looking slightly depressed, contrasting sharply with our other sessions. She said she was tired and had not been able to do much of her homework. She wanted to use the session to put everything back on the rails. When she did that, it turned out that her progress was not all that bad; it was more that she had done activities other than strictly the homework she had set herself. Most of our time in this session was again devoted to feedback on activities and formulating new ones, alongside some summaries and hypotheses on my part. When the flow started to dry up towards the end of the session, I picked up our contract again. It contained two learning goals. The first was mainly about the more meaningful, creative new businesses she was setting up. The second was that she wanted to become more of a "silent rebel" again; this was how she had perceived herself in earlier years and something she felt had fallen by the wayside in adulthood. She forced a wry smile when I reminded her of the second learning goal and for a moment fell silent, literally a silent rebel. 'Thank you', she said, 'now I know what to do'. I am not sure what she meant by that, but it had conviction. This vignette shows in my view how simply recalling a memory or an intention from the start of a coaching process can sometimes counteract the slight dip or feeling of melancholy on saying goodbye and can help the coachee to leave the process with a more autonomous intention.

I do not believe in dependence in coaching or "interminable" coaching relationships. Coaching sessions are not all that many in number and they are not usually very frequent. But at the same time I can see that a coach who becomes entangled with a company, for example, by developing other significant coaching relationships in the same leadership team, or by being not only a partner in reflection but also, say, a provider of substantive management advice or other recommendations, ultimately does more harm than good. We also need to take care that coaching contracts are not automatically renewed and begin to resemble endless lunches that transition imperceptibly into dinner and continue into the dark night. On the other hand, we cannot really set clear boundaries for when coaching ceases to be effective. Sometimes a leader can choose to see his or her coach from time to time over several years. At a low frequency of around four sessions a year, this can be beneficial for some time, although I often notice that after four years or so some of the tension and creativity disappears from such relationships, and that a calm warmth and mutual affirmation start to come more to the fore. For me, there are a number of good ways both to restore creative tension and to end the relationship in a way that does not feel like rejection. For example, you could renew inspiration by holding another round of interviews with your coachee's direct colleagues, or you could coach the leader's team for a session to round off the coaching. The latter happened with Mario, who was mentioned in the previous chapter. We had been working together for around four years, holding five or six sessions a year. We agreed that I would attend a meeting chaired by him, that I would give back as openly as possible what I noticed in that meeting, and that we would then hold two more individual coaching sessions to finish off. The team was curious and happy to agree. There were times in these meeting when I did not recognise Mario from the coaching sessions. In some respects, he radiated far less self-confidence than I had seen on an ongoing basis in the coaching. My observations during and after the session were more about the team, about how it behaved, how it used the time, how it arrived at decisions and when things seemed to stall, and what issues might have been lurking under the surface. I shared some of my more personal observations about Mario with him in our next coaching session, resulting in new development goals. Nevertheless, we rounded things off quite soon afterwards; no doubt he continued to work with his own people and perhaps other coaches in order to achieve the new targets.

## B. Essences

What is the essence of all of the qualitative research in this book? What can we conclude from this hotchpotch of creative coaching research and the two or three longer research programmes in this field? I will give my answer here but realise that it is highly subjective. You can look at qualitative studies in very different ways, and to an extent you are stuck in a "hermeneutical circle", in which you mainly consider what you already thought about the topic of investigation before. Nevertheless, it is useful to read these studies with some regularity and to allow other voices to get through to you, so that your own prejudices and certainties are undermined and contradicted and you can begin to allow different perspectives to emerge.

I believe that all of the qualitative research in this book helps us above all to see how important it is to deal with paradoxes and contradictions and to transcend them. Very often, coaching clients raise dilemmas that pitch two options or actions against each other. Just as often, a little conversation reveals that there is a third option, or the possibility of implementing neither option, or both options at the same time – and, more importantly, that it is possible to choose a fundamentally different perspective, one from which the whole earlier contradiction no longer exists or no longer matters. This is a general observation about coaching that holds true surprisingly often amidst the insoluble dilemmas, ingrained conflicts, mutual incompatibilities and intractable problems posed.

As argued in previous work (De Haan & Burger, 2005) and in many other places, the coachee usually enters the coaching process with at least one "basic change paradox". In every coaching assignment, we can recognise forms of ambivalence that can often be summed up as "change me, but without changing me". The coachee is keen to learn and change and to achieve the goals of the contract, but, at the same time, she or he wants to remain the same person they are, and to preserve what has already been achieved. Or, to put this phenomenon differently, a coachee presents with straightforward 'learning objectives' but at the same time conveys at a deeper level very contradictory tendencies and objectives. The hidden 'needs' are often quite different from the more overt 'wants'. Gradually during successful coaching it emerges that both are indeed possible: in other words, you can change something fundamental to your own attitude and behaviour and then integrate it into existing personality structures and into successful existing leadership behaviour. However, at the start of a process, this is often far from clear. From the new perspective that slowly emerges during coaching, you can indeed "change without changing" and say "yes" to your initial paradox.

We see a similar problem and a similar solution in the development of coaches. As coaches, we find that we need to develop both a thick skin to deal robustly with a variety of customers and emotions, and a "thin skin" to pick up on fine shifts in sessions, vague signals and subtle sensitivities. So we want to work on developing a thinner and thicker skin at the same time, to become more sensitive while also toughening up. And this turns out to be indeed possible; however, we learn it only very slowly. In this way, we learn to develop strength and thus offer "containment" (Bion, 1963) for coachees, while at the same time becoming more open, vulnerable and flexible during our coaching conversations. To borrow Harrison's metaphor, we offer both a safe, robust castle and a sensitive, risky battlefield for learning something new (Harrison, 1963).

To coaches, this initially seems very difficult to learn, but with ongoing supervision, it is often entirely possible to become both more sensitive and more robust (see also De Haan, 2008b).

I am increasingly convinced that the transformation of an initial contradiction or polarity is a very characteristic phenomenon, not only of coaching assignments, not only of the development of coaches, but also of the coaching dyad itself and of many of the leadership dilemmas that coachees bring to coaching. To begin with the latter, we all bring very different personalities to our work, leading us to face all sorts of highly personal, ideosyncratic successes, anxieties and defeats. We notice on a daily basis that we do things very differently from colleagues, and possibly much better, but we notice just as often that we are impressed by (or envious of) the unique achievements of those same colleagues, that we could never emulate or match. It is by now well known that leaders face their own personal shadows and each develop completely unique patterns of derailment, hubris, pride and overdrive that coaching is ideally suited to help with (see De Haan & Kasozi, 2014). And yet the same leaders who are so different are also intimately acquainted with precisely the same set of basic emotions that we all experience. In that respect, we are all the same again. So, in our most personal, deepest and most intimate selves, we are all precisely and entirely the *same* ("the most personal is the most universal", as Carl Rogers put it – Rogers, 1961), while at the same time we are also extremely and highly personally *different* in that deepest area. Once again, it is mainly a question of perspective: we all seem to have the same Lego blocks that we each put together differently. Yet these building blocks are universal and the same set of blocks applies to all of us. In other words, you can imagine both organisation and personality as a mix of similar and unique components:

- (external aspects that we can choose ourselves over the course of our career:) political association, job type, work location, work content, seniority, roles, connections, etc.
- (more internal aspects that are much harder to change if at all:) our religion, habitat (climate and ecology), education, appearance, life experience, hobbies, marital status, etc.
- (even more internal, immutable aspects:) gender, sexuality, age, body, race, ethnicity, parenthood, etc.
- (yet deeper internal aspects related to personality:) intro/extraversion, emotional stability, openness, optimism, altruism, personality structure, dark sides and vulnerabilities, etc.
- (even deeper aspects having to do with universal feelings:) love, jealousy, anger, sorrow, fear, courage, etc.

We all share these aspects in our own unique way, that is, in different combinations, but at the same time, we also share them with everyone else. So, at the same time, we are deeply different from and deeply the same as others. Another paradox.

I interpret the results of all of the qualitative research in this book in this light: every article, every finding in the articles is both radically unique and unrepeatable (in contrast with more regular quantitative, statistically driven research, where experiments can be replicated and results verified or falsified) and, at the same time, very recognisable to every coach who reads the research.

To my mind, the following are striking examples of paradoxes from the research in this book:

1   *Rashomon* and non-*Rashomon*
    As we saw in Chapter 5, there is a great deal of agreement between the ways in which coachee and coach look back on their shared conversations, but there are also striking differences: differences in choices of critical moments, differences in what is observed during those moments and differences in perception of the outcomes. We had expected these differences, certainly following the research in previous chapters. But what we did not expect is that there are also so many similarities: in around 50% of the critical moments cited by coach and coachee, there is a significant overlap in terms of both the choice of moment and the theme in the moment. Moreover, coaches and coachees appear to identify mostly the same kind of moments, namely those involving important realisations on the part of the coachee.

2   What you see is not the only reality
    Qualitative research shows in a subtle way that, even when you think you see or understand something clearly, there are still many other ways to look at it. Your coachee may see something completely different and you yourself may see it differently when you look at it again, and so on. There is no single 'reality' in coaching and there is no single cause to a specific problem, nor is there a single potential solution to a specific coaching question.
    Coaches often look at coaching in terms of their interventions: directing or following, supporting or confronting. But coachees may look through a completely different lens, for example, that of new action versus new insight and new tools versus a new attitude or new approach (see the "coachee model of coaching" in Chapter 4).
    That coachees and coaches develop different ideas about the encounter and the shared assignment is already clear from case studies (see, e.g., the jointly written case studies in Freedman & Perry, 2010 and Chapter 5), and it is also readily confirmed by other research. In our studies of descriptions of critical moments, we found that coaches and coachees show considerable overlap in the choice of moments they experience as critical and also in terms of what makes those moments critical for them (i.e. finding new insight and new perspectives). But at the same time, we also see many differences: time and again, coaches are more concerned with their own doubts and anxieties, and thus with the conversation and the relationship itself, as they develop in the here and now in interaction with their coachees. They also seem to look at physiological responses of the coachee more; in other words, they look at "how" an issue is introduced and not just at the "what" of that issue.
    There is no single view on the coaching relationship; there are at least two. Working alliance aspects are normally scored very differently by coachee and coach, and also differently by observers on the basis of video recordings (see De Haan, 2008a). Only for the coachee and observer scores do there appear to be correlations with the outcomes of coaching (Gessnitzer & Kauffeld, 2015). Coaches' self-perceptions of their own empathy were found not to agree with their coachees' perceptions of the same, and it was only the perception by coachees

that correlated with empathetic coaching behaviour (namely paraphrasing) (Will, Gessnitzer, & Kauffeld, 2016). Similar to empathy, the coach's behaviour is perceived very differently by coaches and their coachees, as shown by quantitative research (De Haan & Nilsson, 2017).

And yet, despite all of these differing perceptions, it is entirely possible to coach by phone and in a second or third language (Cox, 2012). Information loss therefore places hardly any limitations on coaching. What happens on a deeper level of psychological space, safety and understanding seems to be much more important than language and means of communication (see, e.g., Machin, 2010).

3   The customer is a king who does not always know what s/he wants

Given that there are differences between the ways in which the coachee views his own issues before and after coaching, often involving different perspectives at the same time (due to "ambivalence"), and that there are differences between the ways in which coachees, coaches and other stakeholders such as sponsors view these issues, it seems wise to regard the coachee's wishes with a degree of curiosity and reservation or caution, because there are often a multitude of (conflicting) wishes and needs at play, for example, in the matching process. Extensive research has been carried out into matching (see, e.g., Boyce, Jackson, & Neal, 2010), showing that coachees often want to reduce diversity, and sometimes choose on the basis of appearance or other spurious reasons (Gray & Goregoakar, 2010), but at the same time, also seek psychological depth in order to make coaching meaningful (Machin, 2010). These findings have led me to my belief that it is probably best to offer coachees a higher rather than a lower diversity in the coaching relationship if there is a choice: high diversity can make the relationship more productive, if only for the increased potential of fresh insight, something that indeed coachees seem to be looking for in their coaching conversations (see Chapter 4).

For coaches, three types of lesson can be learned from these three patterns in the qualitative research.

1   Practise looking from multiple perspectives (Kauffman & Hodgetts, 2016) and, as regards coaching itself, practise looking from the other person's perspective, that is, that of the coachee and also the sponsor. Allow the other person as much initiative as possible and summarise as clearly as you can, so your empathy is not just registered by you, but actually experienced by the coachee (Will et al., 2016). Gradually you will discover ambivalences which give rise to paradoxes, dilemmas and contradictions, where "stagnation" or a "rupture" or a "problem" may be experienced. It is only when these come into view that we can begin to transcend and transform these same contradictions. As we saw in previous chapters, it might well be that coachees and sponsors have different ideas from you about the potential benefits of coaching, for example, in the form of new perspectives and insights (mainly coachees, see Chapter 4) or new behaviour and actions (mainly sponsors, see Chapter 6).

2   Practise confidence (Alvey & Barclay, 2007) and courage in adopting a dominant-friendly attitude (Ianiro, Schermuly, & Kauffeld, 2012), provided you continue to allow the coachee the initiative (Gessnitzer & Kauffeld, 2015).

Overcoming contradictions and dilemmas requires safety and patience above all, which may give the courage to view problems from a meta-perspective and no longer as "either/or" choices. Coaches therefore need to offer a high degree of safety, calm and trust, within which the grip of a paradox is no longer experienced as paralysing but ever more as creative. And crises can be experienced as invitations to see things in a new way and gain new insight.

3   Practise avoiding the "same" in order to include the "other" in the coaching relationship. All too often I meet coaches who understand their coachee in terms of themselves: 'Ah, I've experienced that too', 'I've been there too', 'I recognise that problem', 'I struggled with that years ago' and so on. This is the beginning of empathy: recognising yourself in the other person (and because the most personal is the most universal, this always holds true in some sense and there is always something to discover that we can recognise). But true empathy goes much further: it means recognising the *other* in the other person, and that calls for something more.

Taking all the evidence together, I am convinced that for coaching conversations in the midst of dilemmas, contradictions, ambivalence and paradox (which contrary to common belief is more the rule than the exception), we need to generate and apply *love* above everything else. The coach needs to bring acceptance, understanding and respect to both sides of the dilemma, and also to a third or a fourth or a fifth (etcetera) position that may emerge and may, for example, consist of the current positions of the coachee's line manager, client or opponent. From this loving and respectful understanding, we can begin to invite the coachee to transcend her own paradox and discover a new perspective which might afford integration or acceptance of the entire dilemma including one's own shadows, gremlins, derailers, opponents and hubris. And when it comes to love, even 'too much' is not enough, as Figaro says in the quote at the beginning of this book. So we as coaches can safely assume that we can develop further in this particular area and enhance our care, love and respect for our coachees' struggles.

## C. More qualitative research on the journey to coaching mastery

In the training, supervision and accreditation of coaches, they are asked to carry out qualitative research into their own practice in order to learn from their own coaching conversations. This often involves writing case studies, recording conversations and producing transcripts with a running commentary. In this final chapter, I would like to give an example of such qualitative research by analysing my own recent fragment for re-accreditation as a coach. The analysis is based on the first 15 minutes of the conversation with a manager in a production company who is working on a major new product launch.

In the transcript, brief responses from the conversational partner are in square brackets. My running commentary is written in at various parts of the dialogue, and my own subsequent thoughts about what I am doing in this conversation are in italics. Because I sometimes have assessors in mind, this is a way of looking at the same material from multiple perspectives.

| Erik | Yes. OK. So... Hello Greg [hello] and happy for this session to be recorded and this is our third session. [Yep] So, where would you like to begin today? | 1:02 |
| Greg | Erm, I've got my list of things that we wrote last time [I see] and I would quite like to update you on my progress, because I have made some progress, but I haven't done everything which is what I predicted. | 1:14 |
| Erik | Ok, good. | 1:28 |
| Greg | Erm, So, I've done the – so on my list was the designing the things that I wanted to be able to sell, erm, and I feel like that I can tick those things off. I haven't managed to make everything because there's, I've, erm, I made quite a few mistakes the first time round, so I know how to correct them. It just took longer. [Mm] The second thing on the list was trying to work out prices – realistic prices and I've got a big question mark next to that one because that erm, I'm struggling with and I'm not sure how to – erm, that might be something that I can talk to you today about, maybe. | 1:30 |
| Erik | I see, Yes. | 2:16 |
| Greg | Ern, I'm kind of – there's the bit that's about packaging, labelling and presentation and logos and things. [Yes] And, I think I've made progress with that, and again, I feel like I know what I need to do to finish that job off now and that's not a hard job. That's something [Ah] that I'm [Wow] happy to get on with. [Yes] Erm, and the other things are the setting up a website which I've started doing but I haven't finished doing. I haven't set up a website, I've set up a new webshop, but I haven't [I see] put anything on it yet. [Ah, yes, yes]. | 2:18 |
| Erik | Yes... well thank you... that's an overview......... What would you really like to come away with after this session? | 2:55 |

He comes in enthusiastically. What a torrent of words. I only have to ask, 'Where would you like to begin today?', and it all bursts forth. Now I have to be seen to do some contracting for this session, although I also want him to keep the initiative.

*For me, a conversation is not a coaching conversation unless it has been made clear somewhere what its purpose is, what the intention is. But I know that other people, more "insight-focussed" coaches, think differently about this and favour "free association", that is, responding spontaneously and in the moment to what the other person brings in, wherever the coachee goes.*

After a few minutes of listening and humming, I say, 'What would you really like to come away with after this session?'. That keeps the initiative with him, and gives us something to measure the conversation by. I am pleased with myself that I have now started the contracting.

| Greg | I think I'd like to feel like err, like I'm doing – I'm – I know it's never going to be done, cos that's not the nature of it, but I'd like to have a list of all my finalising jobs [Aha] so that maybe the next time that I see you there is something up and running and I could have even sold something, if you know what I mean. | 3:04 |
| Erik | I see. I see. So, you – are you saying you would like to come away again with a list? [Yeah] Erm, a list which might help you then for next time to be up and running, as you call it, yeah? [Yeah, yeah] Ok, so that sounds like a very specific, very clear request. Could you say anything – could you say a bit more about what that entails because you also said, erm, that you are aiming for a particular feeling today about some – some kind of a motivation which you'd like to achieve today, as well as the list. | 3:29 |

I take as the core of our contract his statement of 'A list of all my finalising jobs, that maybe the next time that I see you there is something up and running and I could have even sold something...'.

I summarise this and I also pick up the word 'feeling', which was one of his first words after my first contracting question. So I ask about the feeling or motivation he wants to come away with. I am glad I've picked up that he wants to come away with a particular feeling as well, perhaps a little more of the same enthusiasm he came in with.

In my summary, I say 'a list *again*' and 'that sounds like a very specific, very clear request', and to me when I relisten something of my disappointment comes through, that he has come to coaching to make a list.... To me, frankly, it sounds a bit like a boring learning goal. And I then criticise myself for reacting so judgementally to what my coachee is coming up with, and for not fully willing to help where help is asked.

| Greg | Erm, maybe a bit of – I'd like to feel a bit more confident that it's just a job that needs doing. I'd like to take my emotions out of it a little bit and be a bit more like – like I've got the big question mark next to the like how much things are gonna cost and how much [Yes] I want to charge for things [Yes] and I think I spoke to you last time about that kind of goes back to that feeling of, oh it's not good enough and stuff like that [Yes] and I'd like to be able to just do it and not consider those things and just think, like, a bit coldly about it. So, [Mm] yeah, I'd like to feel a bit more confident that I don't – no second guessing – I just need to want to get it done. | 4:17 |

In answer to my question about the sort of feeling he wants to come away with, he says he is mainly looking for more confidence.

*When he says, that he no longer wants to be feeling that what he is doing is not good enough, I could have probed deeper and I regret that retrospectively. He also adds that he wants 'to think a bit coldly' about this launch. And that he wants to come away with the feeling that he 'just needs to want to get it done'. On second reading, these comments seem to give away something about an underlying, warmer and more self-critical feeling, that I would like to have explored.*

| Erik | I see, yeah. Ok, so there's also an objective here around confidence [Mm] and it sounds like the confidence is really linked very much with the financials; with being certain about the cost and clear about the cost as well. [Yeah] Or prices, should I say. | 5:05 |
| Greg | Like it should be worth something to somebody else. | |

He says that the price is the first step, and I summarise that he wants more confidence about the price and more certainty about the right pricing. He agrees, and says 'yes, it should be worth something to somebody else'. He sounds as if he himself only partly believes in this and that he is still rather self-critical.

| Erik | Yes, OK. OK, well let's work on that. Where do you think we – we'd best begin within that? | 5:25 |
|---|---|---|
| Greg | Erm. Erm, like I keep – I keep thinking, cos people like it, I've given them away – like I've said before, I've given them away as presents and I've given them to people who've shown an interest who've said "Oh that's nice." If we've won new customers, I've given them just as a little present for people. [Mm mm] And, I – you know, we're all too shy – I've said – they've said, "Well you should sell it." And I say, "Oh I don't know." And, then I don't and then I sort of, maybe, broach the subject, I don't know how much, I really, genuinely don't know how much I'd sell them for – and I'd really like somebody at that point to say, "Well, I feel like I would pay this much for it." without trying to be kind to me. I really, genuinely want to know what they think it's worth [Ah] without even taking me out of the equation. So, I sort of want to – and like none of the people – all of the people that I give them to are direct colleagues, clients or like family, or people who've, you know, been – there's been a couple of people who've shown – I've got an Instagram page and there's a couple of people that have asked me to give – you know, sell them something on Instagram. There's two people who I think might not be worried about, erm, offending me cos [I see] they have connections to us. So [Yes] I did ask them, but I made them things before I feel like we've refined it, but I want an objective opinion and like a range of objective opinions about how much they'd sell – their worth. [pause] | 5:37 |
| Greg contd. | [So] Or, [Yes] it would be that alternatively I'd just put a price on it, and if nobody buys it I lower the price. Or – | 7:11 |
| Erik | Ah yes. OK. OK, so, you'd like to either ask objective people that you know through Instagram? [Yeah]] Or, you would yourself come out with the price [Mm] but you feel that you may have to lower it if you come out with the price yourself. | 7:17 |

First I try to give him back the initiative: 'OK, well let's work on that. Where do you think we – we'd best begin within that?' He then explains how much the new products are already appreciated within the organisation and outside, but that he has no idea what to sell them for on the market. When he asks his friends, he feels they name a high price to encourage him or to say something nice about it, not because they mean it. So he'd like the opinion of someone who is more objective, someone who is objective and knows the market. And he's also considering going to the market to test out prices: 'It would be that alternatively I'd just put a price on it, and if nobody buys it I lower the price', he says hesitantly. I summarise.

| Greg | Yeah, Yeah, but that's OK, I don't mind, I don't mind that, I just don't want to feel embarrassed or feel like I've failed if that happens. | 7:34 |
|---|---|---|
| Erik | Exactly. That would then also have an impact on your confidence [Yeah] if it goes like that [Yeah] if you were – it's interesting that you are saying that if you do put a price on it then it will go almost then – almost it will go down. So, is not the other, you know, the other way also a possibility? That it might go up? | 7.42 |

And then he says more personally, 'I just don't want to feel embarrassed or feel like I've failed if that happens...'.

I respond by saying it's interesting that he says that if you do put a price on it, the price could go down. Couldn't the price also rise as a result of the market's reaction?

*Here I believe I am doing an interpretation for the first time and actively participating with sense-making. Perhaps this won't be taken so well by my assessors, because I am giving my own opinion on the coaching issue. I realise that similar to Greg who wants to sell his products at the right price, I am also concerned about 'selling' my coaching style, warts and all, and that I am quite fearful that it be assessed at a low "price point".*

*Here what I am trying out is a specific, "insight-focussed" way of coaching. After-wards I have the slight feeling as if I am failing here in the eyes of other coaches, a parallel with the feeling of failure in my coachee. What I refer to here as a "hypothesis" might be described by another coach as a "closed question" and even an attempt to lead the coa-chee in a specific direction, that is, not really a coaching intervention. Interpretations are tricky: on the one hand, they are perhaps the most helpful thing we can offer as coaches (see, e.g., the evidence in Chapter 4 of this book); on the other hand, they can amount to a possibly coercive steering of our coachee in a particular direction... And now I myself have ended up in an either/or dilemma during my study of this session....*

| Greg | Yeah, that could happen, I suppose. Yes. | 8:04 |
|------|------------------------------------------|------|
| Erik | Is that something about your confidence, as well, that if you were to put a price on that really, it's worth less; it would kind of erode that price? | 8:08 |
| Greg | Yea, Yea, I think so. Hm. Yeah, I think I'd find it easier. One of the things that makes that a bit easier is that I've changed the name of it now, so I've got – one of the things was on my objectives was giving it a brand that didn't include my name and I've chosen the name and it makes it a bit more anonymous, so I could – I could put prices on things without feeling like I'd know that they were attached to me but not necessarily anybody else would know that they were attached to me, and I think [Ah, Yes] that might help me. | 8:15 |
| Erik | Yes. So, would that help you in both scenarios that you discussed? | 9:07 |
| Greg | Yeah. | 9:10 |
| Erik | Yeah, you could present it as something that's out there and even though you are intimately linked with it, they wouldn't know that; the people who formulate the price wouldn't know that. | 9:14 |
| Greg | Yeah. Yeah, I could like disassociate myself from it, a little bit. | 9:23 |
| Erik | Yeah. Yeah. So, it really – it really sounds that it's very hard for you, erm, to err, erm, because this association sounds really hard for you to come up with a price [Yes] and then stay with it or give yourself a price. So, it's better left to others [Yeah] to the market and to others then. [Yeah, Yeah]. And are you confident in that, cos you're saying that in a kind of a cautious way as well? | 9:27 |
| Greg | Yeah with reservations. | |
| Erik | But are you confident in the market then to do that for you, to get to the right pricing? | 10:01 |
| Greg | I think I am. I think I'm more confident that that. I think they would know this is like such an un erm – an unfamiliar territory to me. I've never, ever done anything like this before. I've got no idea how much some things are worth apart from like what I've paid for myself. [Yeah] Yes, so I haven't got any experience in – I can't justify it in any way. [I see] If I could say this is like – maybe that's another way of doing it, is work how much materials are [Aha] and – | 10:06 |

My coachee agrees with my hypothesis that he unconsciously introduces a downward trend in the pricing, so I ask about his confidence; does this say something about his confidence?

*And it strikes me that I use a chain of four different questions, a true barrage of questions, something I always discourage other coaches from doing – and now it is happening to me. Again, something my assessors won't view positively. Moreover, I have the feeling again that I am interpreting between the lines and that this won't look good, depending on which perspective on coaching you choose.*

Yes, he says and goes on to say that he has changed the product's name so that it's not so easily associated with his online reputation or company. Then the rejection might be easier to bear. He says he's going to leave it to the market to come up with a price, and that is the best way for him.

But I notice he says this in a cautious way, so I reflect this back to him as something that strikes me. He agrees and says he does indeed feel "reservations".

*I am always happy when I've done something "in the moment", like I have now. So, I lean back a bit in this part of the conversation, I notice. It's funny how a reflection that you find worthwhile brings you peace in one way or another.*

He continues talking about how little expertise he has with this sort of thing, that it really is the first time he has had to set a price, that he himself likes to estimate prices of others and would have an opinion about competitors' prices, and he wonders if he should perhaps reason more from the cost price of the product.

*It strikes me he is clearly deliberating here, and that he is beginning to enter into a kind of either/or dilemma, namely the decision on which to base pricing: the "market" or the "price of the materials"?*

| Erik | Yes, you work with a margin. [Yeah] So you put up a margin over and above the price of the materials. [Yeah] Ah, but then again, it's the same question, how much is the margin, how much the materials. [Yeah] [pause] | 10:42 |
| Erik contd. | You say you're a little bit more confident if you buy it yourself. Are you really, erm, yeah, do you have a view on other peoples' products and what they are worth? [Yeah] Do you have a strong view on that? | 10:54 |
| Greg | No. I've got a probably like a little bit of a benchmark in my head that I wouldn't go above [Aha] and if like if it's something really special [Yes] I've got like I know what I would pay for something similar from somebody else. [OK] | 11:12 |

Implicitly, I tell him that his either/or dilemma is neither here nor there, and that he is only raising the same issue or goal in a different formulation, in my view. Then I move back to what he said about confidence before and summarise. I give back that he seems more confident when talking about estimating the value of other people's products. I ask if he has a strong view on that? Yes, he says, 'I've got a probably like a little bit of a benchmark in my head that I wouldn't go above'.

| Erik | Could that be a starting point for you? | 11:29 |
| Greg | Yeah, I think that's probably the most, the best compromise isn't it? The like. | 11:32 |
| Erik | What would be the compromise? | 11:36 |

I respond to this growing confidence and say, 'could that be a starting point for you?' 'Yes, that is a good compromise', he says.

*In the session I did not understand where the word "compromise" came from, although now I can see it in the transcript: he was still looking at an either/or dilemma between market forces and cost price, and now sees a compromise or a third way.*

But because I do not immediately follow that, I ask, 'what would be the compromise?' to find out what he means by this word. And later I say more explicitly that I was puzzled for a moment when he said "compromise".

| Greg | Well, then I'd be – I'd be thinking about what everybody else does and I wouldn't have to make it something, you know, that doesn't have to be anything to do with me. This is like this is how much this kind of fashion costs. That's what it costs everywhere else so that's what it costs here as well and that makes it more like [Yeah] I dunno, more reasonable or something. | 11:39 |
|------|-----|-----|
| Erik | OK, so that would make you formulate a price based on your own experience as a buyer? [Yeah] And independent from the fact that you're also, you know, intimately attached to, [Yeah] to it or that it is the price on you, almost. [Yeah] | 12:01 |
| Greg | Yeah, yeah, and it's not – and it takes it away from being a price of me. | 12:18 |
| Erik | Yeah. And, how would that work for you? And, does that open up a third way or is that – is? | 12:23 |
| Greg | No, I think that's the middle way. I like that. | 12:29 |
| Erik | OK. Ah, that's why you say compromise, yeah. I was puzzled for a moment when you said compromise. | 12:36 |

'A middle way', he says, that is, not just an estimate from the market place, nor something based on the materials of the product. He seems to consider going to actively look into the marketplace himself to see what the prices are, and make a kind of average. He adds, 'That's what it costs everywhere else so that's what it costs here as well and that makes more like, I dunno, more reasonable or something'.

*I realise why I do not initially pick up what is meant by the word compromise. I think that is because I had already moved on from the dilemma; I had not accepted it as a real contradiction. I had said 'deciding on the margin is still deciding on the price, so it is essentially the same thing'. For me, that meant discussion over. When he then in his own time, and without taking my argument on board, finds a way out of his dilemma by positing a 'third way', I am no longer with him, and I have no idea why he talks about a compromise. It is interesting how coachee and coach can drift apart in this way, by the coach doing his own thinking for the coachee and voicing a challenge to the coachee's thinking, but not taking the coachee with him.*

I remember feeling a little proud here because I was daring to be open about my own not understanding. It would have been easy to go with the flow and be happy with Greg about his 'middle way', and not worry about my lack of understanding for how this can be a compromise and a third, middle way. It is always good to check these things, so that you can then begin to register within yourself what you as a coach make of this solution or compromise, independently.

| Greg | Yeah. It feels like the right choice. | 12:36 |
|---|---|---|
| Erik | OK. Can we talk that through, because that's important maybe if you've found a right choice? How does that look? | 12:40 |
| Greg | Well, it's like it's – do you mean in detail about the costings or do you mean – ? [pause] | 12:47 |
| Erik | Yes, how would you do that? How would that look? So, what would be the steps? Would you involve others with it or not, cos it's somewhere in the middle between involving others – the Instagram, the – | 12:52 |
| Greg | They don't need to know that they're being involved. I could just look up various different websites of handmade fashion items that are similarly finished [Yeah] and work – like write down all of the prices of similar things and then add it all up and then divide it by the amount of people who want it (laughter) and do it as simply as that. | 13:06 |
| Erik | And, taking into account your own experiences as a buyer, you said, I think. [Yeah] So, so you would, in some other case you would say "No, no, no, that's over my own maximum. I wouldn't pay that for it." [Yeah] So you would adjust, maybe – | 13:23 |
| Greg | Yeah, leave those ones out, or something. Yeah, I'd be working – yeah, I'd use myself as the customer and. [Yes] think about how – yeah. | 13:38 |
| Erik | You do sound a little bit more confident when you say it that way. | 13:48 |
| Greg | Yeah. I think I feel more confident about it like that. | 13:51 |
| Erik | Yeah. So, do you – can you actually envisage yourself doing it that way? | 13:57 |
| Greg. | Yeah. Yeah, I think I can and I like what you said about being aware of things that I wouldn't pay for, as well. So, sort of like using that as part of the telling me, that doesn't, you know, that just because it's that price, it doesn't mean that the market – that means that mine – I want to make mine that price as well. I can choose. I don't have to [Yeah] – | 13:59 |

Still somewhat on the back foot, I ask him to talk me through the 'right choice' that he now says he has found. I see that as helpful, because I give him an opportunity to double check if it is really the right choice and he has reached his original goal in this matter. I get him to explain the "middle way" again in its entirety, mainly to help him achieve clarity, and then say, 'it sounds that you're more confident about that when you say it that way'. He agrees. I ask another check question, 'Can you envisage yourself doing it that way?' He agrees again. Now I feel like a helpful coach again, and my confidence goes up again, at the same time as his, is my impression.

Because of this growing confidence, I see my chance to give my interpretation again, so I say that if he does it this way, by taking out some "high" prices, it would still be a lowering movement of pricing. That it still feels like he is adjusting his own prices downwards even before the launch.

| Erik | I still notice that if you do it that way, you're still in a kind of, erm, process where you start out with some high prices, some lower prices and you would take out, so you would still – it would still be a lowering movement of pricing. So, it still feels a little bit, in that sense, 'depressing' if you start out with certain prices which are around and you say, "Oh those are far too high, so I won't take them into account." Or yeah, readjust them downward so, in a way but now in a more roundabout way, you're still adjusting your own prices downwards, it feels like. | 14:22 |

| Greg | Yeah, Yeah. I don't know. I think it's safer. It just feels safer to me. It feels like it's more likely that things will sell, [Yeah] If it means that it's less likely to not work I think that I've got it in my head that if you're going to succeed or fail and there's not much middle ground and if it fails then that's it, and it's all gone and there was no point in any of it in the first place, whereas, if it succeeds I can build on that success and like, maybe, at some point put prices up, if they can be put up and stuff like that. [OK. Yep] I think that's how I'm thinking of it in my mind that [Yep] like, I guess maybe that I'm thinking that if they don't sell that's not really an option. They've got to because I really, really want to do something different and I really want it to work. | 14:59 |

Now he defends himself as I come up with my interpretation for a second time, now on the basis of a different pricing strategy.

*For me that slight defensiveness is a sign that I have gone too far in restating my hypothesis, and must be careful not to get overly attached to it because otherwise I too will end up in black-and-white, either/or thinking.*

He actually says: 'I think it's safer. It just feels safer to me. It feels like it's more likely that things will sell'. He adds that

> I've got it in my head that you're going to succeed or fail and there's not much middle ground and if it fails then that's it, and it's all gone and there was no point in any of it in the first place, whereas, if it succeeds I can build on that success and like, maybe, at some point put prices up.

There is a robustness in his defense so I back off and acknowledge his newly found confidence again. In retrospect, the challenging hypothesis may have helped him realise how 'safe' he is, on the one hand, and how deeply motivated, on the other.

*Here we seem to be presented with another typical coaching dilemma, although I only realise this afterwards, when studying the conversation. The coachee is considering a product launch that will lead to either success or failure, and is trying to avoid the second, lesser option. So the coachee puts himself face to face with a contradiction between only two options that on second thought he might be able to transcend.*

| Erik | I see. Yeah. Yeah. Well, it sounds that you're confident about that. So, tell me where to go next then in this conversation. | 15:44 |
| Greg | Can we make something like revisit the list that we wrote last time? [Yes] And, add things to my this time list and add on the costing thing in more specific detail? | 15:59 |
| Erik | Yes, sure we can. Yeah. So, you were saying four areas. The first area you did really well. [Yeah] Second area was the pricing. So where would you like to begin, erm, on [Erm] that? | 16:13 |
| Greg | Erm, find examples of comparable products [Yes] and just basically write a list of the different prices. | 16:30 |
| Erik | Yes, yes, so you're building on your list that you had, I think. [Yeah] Yes, excellent. | 16:49 |

After a reflective silence I ask him where he wants to go next in this conversation and we recontract for the future. He goes back to the request for a list to come away with from the conversation and identifies four areas around the product launch that he wants to discuss. I compliment him on what he has already achieved in the first of these four areas. We use the rest of this conversation to discuss and plan the other three areas which are essential for the product launch later this year.

*Looking back on the conversation from a distance, I see two critical moments for the coach: when I do an interpretation that hits home, namely that he has gained in confidence, and later, when I repeat another interpretation because I thought it was related to the overarching theme of 'confidence', and he still does not go along with it the second time. Before I really start to doubt my contribution as a coach, he fortunately moves on to state how confident he has now become.*

*There also seem to be important moments for the coachee, for example, when he starts talking about a "compromise" and a "middle way": this seems to represent a particular form of progressive insight, and afterwards he seems to know what to do. Or perhaps later, when he has to defend himself against a repeated interpretation on my part which implies that a certain lack of confidence is making him adjust the price of his new product downwards in advance.*

*It is nice to see that even a 15-minute fragment at the start of a random coaching session can easily give rise to one or more critical moments.*

---

### SUMMARY OF CHAPTER 7: "LESSONS TO APPLY IN PRACTICE"

A brief summary of the actual benefits of all the qualitative coaching research is provided in this book. First, we are invited to think again about our profession. Then our preconceived ideas about it are contradicted, and we learn about practices and "discoveries" other than the ones we already knew. Next, we learn how important it is to confront and transcend paradoxes and contradictions.

We learn to handle the fundamental "change paradox" better, with more respect and love for those who are changing.

We learn that the *Rashomon* assumption is both true and false: there are surprising similarities between the stories that coachees and coaches tell about a session they have experienced together, but there are also clear differences.

We learn that there are multiple perspectives on coaching, both from within ourselves as coaches if we allow it, as well as from our coachee and the sponsor. And we learn that the coachee often does not know, and does not always really know, what his or her real needs are.

So we learn that we need to be careful with quantitative measurements, with evaluations and scores, because there is still a whole underlying story, and even multiple stories, and that this is true even for relatively short sections of coaching such as the 15-minute example in this chapter. We learn to be more open to different stories about the same moment in coaching – and we learn that, despite these many different perspectives, there is still a surprising degree of convergence between ourselves, our coachees and the sponsors of the coaching contracts: if something truly worthwhile is achieved in the coaching, then (almost) everyone sees it, and we can rely on it.

Qualitative research can therefore give us more confidence that we can approach our work professionally in a variety of different ways, that we can view it from many different perspectives and that we then still can find an important degree of agreement.

An encouraging result, and one which itself is undoubtedly part of the (demonstrably powerful) effect of executive coaching.

# Appendices: Examples of critical moments

## Appendix A: Critical moments of inexperienced coaches

### Overview of the 80 critical moments of less experienced coaches

The following is a list of all 80 critical moments, to which I have made only minor changes in terms of style and spelling. The moments fall naturally under the headings that describe aspects of the coaching process, but they could also have been classified differently, and many critical moments can be categorised under a number of different headings in principle. I have already carried out an initial *interpretation*, therefore, by choosing this order and these headings.

### I. ALL MOMENTS ARE CRITICAL

i  'I can't describe one critical moment; all of my coaching sessions to date have been very critical. Especially the uncertainty about the course the proceedings will take, even though feedback shows time and again that the coachees view the sessions positively. They say they find tools they can use to make progress in their work.'

ii  'At the moment almost everything is still critical for me because this is the first time I've worked formally in the role of coach. So I'm still searching for my role and that of the coachee. Sometimes it's hard to find instruments: you could just talk, but the coachee needs tools or exercises as well.'

### 2. THE VERY BEGINNING – ACQUISITION

iii  'Taking on a coaching assignment: discussion with the main client in the organisation, which may or may not be in the presence of the coachee.'

iv  'I found it difficult to propose coaching to someone in the first place, to ask whether individual coaching by me might be a solution. How do I know, or sense, whether a potential coachee would appreciate a coach? I find

*(Continued)*

entering into a coaching relationship difficult, so I don't quite know how to approach it.'

v  'I find getting to know new coachees the most critical part, time after time, because you don't know how people will react. Perhaps they're not willing, or not open to coaching and it often turns out that those are the very people who need coaching.'

vi  'What was critical for me was that she responded eagerly to my coaching offer. I wasn't sure whether to continue with my offer because it has consequences for the relationship. At the same time, I am pretty sure certain that it will work out well for both of us.'

## 3. THE VERY BEGINNING – THE FIRST CONVERSATION

vii  'The first conversation with my coachee was my most critical moment. How do you prepare for it? How will he react to your approach? Will it all be over inside of half an hour? And so on.'

viii  'I had the first contact with my coachee this week. A first "rendez-vous" like that is always critical: what will she look like, how will she come across, what will she think of me?'

ix  'A woman I know quite well is referred to me for coaching. She comes straight to the point. Her current manager has said that she needs to find out why she keeps getting into conflict with people. She wants to figure that out with me. Almost immediately she starts explaining why she acted in this way or that way, saying that it's mainly down to the others. I ask some questions, which she answers in the same vein. When I want to move on after a while to talk about the coaching, goals, appointments, etc., she is not interested. She thanks me for "the good conversation", but doesn't think that talking further will solve very much; after all, I don't know either why everyone is against her. What I found most critical here was taking the lead in the conversation and positioning myself as a coach (with someone I knew, in this case). It was my intention to let her go for a while, to let her experience attention, and so on. But then I needed to discuss the coaching options with her and give her co-responsibility for the appointments. I let that slide. In hindsight, it was critical to ask whether this was indeed the right match and to make the topic of personal responsibility open to discussion.'

x  'Our first conversation went well until we started discussing the coaching plan. He suddenly made some very unpleasant remarks. My instinct was to get defensive, but I was able to avoid that. I asked him a question about his behaviour towards me. That made him think. At the end of the conversation he gave back that this had been his big learning moment during the conversation.'

## 4. THE VERY BEGINNING – BUILDING A RELATIONSHIP

xi 'Gaining the coachee's confidence so that essential problems can be discussed. She knew me as a member of the management team with a reputation for being demanding and straight-to-the-point. Now I was to be her coach. In the beginning she said her main problem was lack of time. That was true, but it was hiding something more important: the fact that she was facing burn-out and had come to a deadlock in her project and was unable to break through the impasse. So we had to develop a common idiom at the start and I had to discover where she was experiencing problems. The moment when she stated that she had a problem and that she trusted me was indeed a breakthrough in a sense. Now she is very happy with the coaching and gives me too much credit for it.'

xii 'I experienced a coaching situation with a colleague where it was difficult for me to connect with his way of thinking. This colleague was a self-made man in his profession and quite a few years older than me. He was struggling with assignments he had to carry out and wondering how to deal with them. He was doubting himself enormously. This coachee radiated strength to the outside world and a strong will of his own, but had serious doubts about himself. Because of his outward appearance, everyone assumed he knew how to handle all sorts of problems and like a magnet he attracted all kinds of issues and problems. Sometimes he got hopelessly bogged down in them. My problem in this coaching process was that my and my colleague's world views were so different that it was very difficult for me to gain an idea of his thinking and his standards. This made it difficult to mirror, confront or explore. When I gave back summaries in conversations, it usually turned out that I hadn't understood and as a result the conversation became a cascade of misunderstandings and incomprehension. So it was very frustrating to have to end this coaching after two sessions.'

xiii 'I was having a first conversation: an intake and initial exploration at the same time. The critical moment came when I asked about her private life. Did she want to trust me to that extent in this first conversation? Fortunately, she did, but I heard myself explaining and defending why I felt the need to do that.'

## 5. AM I GOOD ENOUGH?

xiv 'The fact that the coachee chose me gave me a lot of confidence and room to work. I do experience some pressure because she has a lot of experience of therapy and because she took a personal effectiveness training course recently.'

xv 'I find it difficult to coach senior people, who have so much more work experience than I do.'

## 6. AM I DOING IT WELL ENOUGH?

xvi 'What I find difficult as a coach is the fact that I sometimes attach too
much importance to knowledge. Whereas, if I know about something, I
also want to come up with solutions. Something else I find myself wrestling with as a coach is the question of whether you mainly go along with
the coachee's needs, or whether you can also give feedback off your own
bat, even if the coachee isn't expecting such feedback or is not yet "ready
for it".'

xvii 'My most critical moment was when I followed my coachee entirely in
what she was saying in a coaching conversation, and kept "playing back
her words". In the end, this left little scope for a solution to her problem.
I always had the feeling, up to and including the next conversation, that I
had forced something. And so I was afraid that my approach had disrupted
the coaching process towards her longer-term goal. My "not quite knowing what to do" left me at a crossroads: giving back what she said or bringing the conversation back to her original question. The latter didn't seem
like something a coach should do – I was afraid the conversation would
get bogged down. This example shows that, even if I don't know what to
do, I often decide just to do something. But perhaps I can still change that
during the conversation and then ask for feedback about my approach.'

xviii 'When I don't understand what the question is or how to tackle it. People
frequently confide their issues in collaborating with each other to me in
confidence and as yet I am not always effective enough in coming up with
tools to achieve a solution. The awareness of the problem and the potential contribution of the manager himself in that respect and the overriding
importance of bringing about further change and development within the
division in partnership. To put it briefly, the welding together of individual
experience and objectives to create a common interest of greater value.
A critical example was a direct request to contribute towards the team
coaching of a management team in the form of a workshop where, besides
the naming of individual and collective objectives, questions such as personal relationships and how to optimise such relationships also came into
play. I felt rather powerless in the face of such dilemmas.'

xix 'Not knowing what to do: the manager sent me an underperforming colleague, saying that his performance needed to improve within a given
period or he would be dismissed. I noticed that the manager didn't expect
anything from the coaching and had actually already drawn his conclusions. I just dived in, not actually knowing what to do. I hadn't discussed
the conditions for coaching further with the manager, nor any room for
manoeuvre. The employee was dismissed after six months. I was left with
a sense of failure.'

xx 'An IT specialist has been working on a project for a year. He is wondering whether his results will actually be used and says he has no understanding of how things work in his organisation. He is annoyed that
everything there works so irrationally. I try to broaden his understanding

of the context. I also explain, using examples, that "irrational behaviour" can indeed contain logic. He himself tends to explain a lot of technical matters to me. After a while I try to bring him back to his request for help. I have a strong feeling that I'm not helping him, but he doesn't really confirm or deny this.

After a few weeks he calls in sick due to "disruption in relationships". I can't understand this and ask for an explanation, but he can't substantiate it. I wonder if he is depressed. He himself doesn't rule that out; I now hear for the first time that he has had symptoms of depression in the past. The company doctor wants him to return to work gradually. My advice is to consider psychological help. In this case I failed to see a major underlying problem.'

xxi    'The critical moment for me was when my coachee received blunt criticism from a colleague and sought my opinion on it. I agreed with the essence of the colleague's comments, but saying this was a critical moment. It was critical because I was afraid he would hold it against me.'

xxii   'Talking to my coachee about the way she spoke and the abstract language she used, which did not connect with other people.'

xxiii  'Bringing up the stilted relationship, and getting out of it.'

xxiv   'Starting a conversation with a manager who was not happy about having me as his coach.'

## 7. THERE'S SOMETHING THERE...

xxv    'A critical moment is when I can tell there is something going on behind all of the information being communicated to me, but I can't yet put my finger on it. In that case I'm not quite sure what to do. In hindsight I think I should have reflected that fact back, but in the heat of the moment it didn't occur to me.'

xxvi   'Critical moments are moments when you have to be very open yourself in order to coax someone out of his shell. You point something out, such as an awkward response, and mention it directly which makes me feel like working on the edge.'

xxvii  'For me, a critical moment in the relationship with the coachee was the realisation that he had hired a consultant who might turn out to be a better manager for the office than the coachee himself. I haven't mentioned this as such. Not yet. I'm not sure how to handle this. I did ask how he plans to handle the fresh, useful insights of this new employee who is his intended right-hand man. And how do these new ideas affect him?'

xxviii 'A coaching session with someone who I think radiates dissatisfaction with her current job, but responds with denial to all attempts to bring this up, even if I confront her with the facts she has told me. Apparently it doesn't help to keep pressing this button harder and harder, but where is the button that does work?'

## 8. THERE'S NOTHING THERE...

xxix    'I find it difficult when I have absolutely nothing to go on, or when the question is very open.'

xxx     'A critical moment is when my coachee doesn't give an example, or not until late in the conversation.'

xxxi    'When there is a lot of talk that leads nowhere. Then I find it hard to coach in a valuable way. How do you structure the conversation and how do you help the coachee to focus and find insights?'

xxxii   'The people who see it as something compulsory are difficult.'

## 9. WHAT DO I UNLEASH?

xxxiii  'The impetus was my coachee's current inability and desire to learn how to set better boundaries, and to be more assertive in certain work and other situations, so that the effectiveness of her efforts would lead to improved results. During the conversation we acted out a sort of role-play where I reflected the potential feared reaction of the "adversary", as soon as she expressed her opinion openly. Gradually I unearthed all sorts of irrational, obstructive convictions that were deeply rooted (in her youth) and were imposing many restrictions on her, both at work and in her private life. This was a critical moment because I could see she was becoming very aware for the first time of her way of thinking, preserved for so many years, and seemed to be determined and inspired to change it. That this would directly affect her position in family relationships was inevitable. In the end things only improved, but I wondered whether and how I could find a balance, as a coach, between objectivity and responsibility.'

xxxiv   'I am currently coaching a woman who works as a consultant to a non-profit organisation. She was at home for a few months at the start of this year due to overwork. She has now returned to work and wants to get off to a good start. Objectives of the coaching are (1) to strengthen her understanding of her strong points, needs and stress factors, (2) to deepen her understanding of the sort of work that suits her best, and (3) to formulate an appropriate career strategy within the current organisation.

A critical moment for me was when we reached a sort of personal core after two sessions. On the one hand, I felt we were really getting to the root of her problems and that was great, but on the other hand I found it scary that I was getting into something that I did not know how to handle. And what then? Where does the coach end and the therapist begin?'

## 10. THE COACHEE'S EMOTIONS

xxxv    'The coachee in question was sent by his manager for coaching and for referral to a programme in the area of assertiveness. After a conversation with the coachee I told him that, on the basis of his story, I had a feeling that something else was the matter. The coachee began to shake all over and burst into tears, and then a whole story came out about the way he had been feeling in recent months. At that moment I didn't know what to do as the coach, apart from showing concern, and I asked the coachee if he was happy for me to refer him to the company doctor. In hindsight, that was a good decision. At the time, however, I was pretty nervous about it.'

xxxvi   'With one of my coachees I conducted a reintegration programme. It was only partly voluntary. In one of our sessions the man became very emotional. It was the first time I had seen that side of him, he is generally a very rational man. He threatened to stand up, walk out the door and never come back. I could feel I was getting pretty warmed up and quickly asked myself what that would mean for him and for the organisation. I asked him very calmly what would be the point of that, apart from getting him out of a difficult situation at that moment in time. That surprised him and he took time to think it over and reply. We both saw that moment as a turning point in our sessions. It gave him the space to return to the organisation in a new position. The course of sessions was completed successfully.'

xxxvii  'A new project worker in an organisation where job losses were likely felt threatened by a number of workers who were jealous because she did have a job. She was very distressed by this, and I didn't know how to advise her.'

xxxviii 'It's always critical for me when emotions get very high. For example, when my coachee is especially angry or upset due to incidents at work, such as other people's actions or behaviour. Because at moments like these you get so close to the core of the other person that I'm always afraid of saying or doing the wrong thing, which can ultimately have a huge influence on my coachee's development. I want to help and steer, but not in the wrong direction. Then I doubt if I'm doing the right thing.'

## 11. YOUR OWN EMOTIONS

xxxix   'Moments when I experience a degree of resistance or irritation in myself. For example, I remember a conversation with an internal coachee that took place in response to her desire for further personal development. In accordance with her wishes, she was given the opportunity to expand her range of duties and thus the responsibility to shape and interpret

*(Continued)*

those duties herself, with help from others. She made no initiatives to take ownership of those duties but waited until I asked how it was going and then reported that nothing had happened. She didn't feel responsible for her own development. That irritates me and I have to take care that my irritation doesn't form a barrier in subsequent conversations.'

xl    'A critical moment for me is often when I get annoyed at the other person's behaviour or attitude. For example, if the employee doesn't gain the insight and hence the conviction that they need to change, otherwise they won't make any progress. When do I say as the coach that we need to stop? Perhaps a dramatic turn of events, but that feeling sometimes creeps up on me when I have such conversations.'

xli    'The coachee had only been employed for a week and came back from our organisation's introduction days. During that time she had spoken at length with a former team-mate of mine about inclusion and exclusion in our team. The coachee told me she was very happy with these conversations and they had been good for her. This was a critical moment for me because I got such a good feeling about including the coachee in our team and took it personally that I hadn't thought in advance that inclusion and exclusion could be a topic. I wasn't prepared for it.'

## 12. YOUR OWN DOUBTS

xlii    'Sometimes I'm afraid I have communicated too much of my own doubts, for example about a situation raised in a conversation.'

xliii    'My coachee didn't know how to handle a particular situation. At that moment I couldn't give any good advice, because I had no experience of it myself and found it hard to put myself in his situation. Which coaching style should I use in a particular case?'

xliv    'Moments when I don't know what to do are when my coachee says he is faced with a delicate issue. I always ask him to describe the situation and then ask why it is a delicate issue for him. We then analyse the possible consequences of doing A or B and look at what he feels comfortable with. So far so good, but then he always asks what I would do. I never know to what extent I should share my own opinion, so as not to influence him. The factors I consider in reaching a decision might be completely different from his own and not necessarily any better or worse.

This coachee also says that I act as his "conscience". That is very flattering, but it also puts me on a pedestal, by which I mean that he expects his "conscience" to be infallible, and I am certainly not that. Plus you can only fall off a pedestal! So I don't know how to handle this situation.'

xlv    'When the manager receiving coaching makes me feel that I need to offer the solution: "Should I do A or B?"'

xlvi    'Situation of a novice manager. She has a lot of potential but knows that she needs a challenge from her environment in order to actually raise the bar. Her manager is not so demanding. Her words: "He doesn't ask how it's going, as long as nothing goes wrong it's all fine, I don't get any critical comments, he's always positive. So what's my actual use in this organisation?" My own idea is that she doesn't experience her own challenges as compelling enough to give her the impulse she needs. Her supervisor doesn't give her this either. Summary of the moment we got stuck:

MY QUESTION: Why do you need a critical environment?
HER: That's what I do it for, for my manager and staff.
MY QUESTION: What do you yourself want to achieve?
HER: If I perform better, those around me think it's good but they think it's good anyway, so never mind the extra effort.
MY QUESTION: Do you take your manager seriously?
HER: No, not really.

There you have it ... an impasse! I could only think it was time for a different environment, but that's easier said than done.'

## 13. DEFERRING YOUR OPINION

xlvii   'I can't cite one critical moment right away, but I do frequently experience tension between consulting and coaching. It is difficult not to offer an opinion but to allow the coachee to arrive at his own conclusion on how to handle the situation raised in the conversation. I also have trouble with objectifying situations presented by my coachees who are part of the same organisation. I notice that I have my own "opinion" on the situation. This is because, in many cases, I know the people and the organisational culture in question. Plus, my coachee often knows in advance what I think about it all. As a result of my consulting and judging, I am often afraid of coaching too much in one specific direction.'

xlviii  'A difficult point that frequently recurs is when I am discussing with someone how he could tackle something. Because I work in the same field, I often already have a clear idea of how things should be done or what the end result should be. However, the fact that someone else is working on a job means of course that the result is not always the same as if I were to do it myself (leaving aside the issue of whether they do it better or worse). I find it difficult to let go.'

xlix    'A coachee's direct question: do you think I'm suitable as a manager? That was difficult because I had doubts about it, but didn't want to hurt, discourage or demotivate him.'

*(Continued)*

l    'At a particular moment the coachee opted for a strategy that I person-
     ally did not support. I found it very difficult to remain objective and
     not to air my own opinion, for example by asking leading questions. I
     saw the solution in front of me but the coachee clearly couldn't see it, or
     not yet.'

li   'I've always known what to do. What is difficult, however, is to distin-
     guish between myself as a manager who has and wants to provide solu-
     tions, and as a coach who mainly has to focus on recognisability and the
     other person's problem-solving ability. Then you feel as if you have to
     settle for a second best solution from the other person. Sometimes I am
     explicitly asked what I would do. In that case, I sometimes illustrate my
     working method.'

lii  'When my coachee let off steam about a situation we both find very an-
     noying. Then I faced the pitfall of joining in the grumbling.'

liii 'My coachee is a trained psychologist and psychotherapist. She works for
     us as a policy adviser. She came to me in a period of burn-out. She said
     she had already gone through several coaching processes and was also
     seeing a psychologist, and so far she had not seen any benefit. She knew
     why she felt so bad, but didn't have the energy to break out of the vicious
     circle. While I was explaining how I planned to work with her and that
     we would work together to find her strengths, she looked at me very sus-
     piciously. I heard myself talk enthusiastically but in the meantime could
     well imagine that she wouldn't see much benefit in this process either.
     Nevertheless, she did begin the process. She was so disheartened that
     she badly needed some help. After a few sessions in which I detected an
     upwards trend, we had explored things and were making a plan to find
     her another job, she came up with some very unrealistic ambitions. Jobs
     that required a minimum of four years' study. Anything that was within
     her reach didn't appeal to her. Then I got the impression that all of our
     sessions up to that point had been in vain. I got a bit irritated about this.
     Later I understood that it was about flight behaviour and I discussed
     that with her.'

## 14. BREAKTHROUGHS

liv  'Critical moments are when someone's awareness is raised as the "penny
     drops".'

lv   'Seeing, hearing and feeling that the other person has suddenly arrived at
     an understanding, so that everything is different from that moment on.'

lvi  'There are many critical moments, especially in a positive sense. I mean
     the feeling of satisfaction when things are going well, and you have helped
     someone achieve what they wanted to achieve.'

## 15. DIRECTING THE CONVERSATION

lvii    'The moment when you feel you have to start to create structure in the conversation still gives me cause for doubt. What is a good comment or question? And questions arise such as: what will come out of this conversation? What should I offer, or should I offer nothing at all?'

lviii   'For me, critical moments are when I need to decide whether to follow a particular road or to turn off due to an intervention on my part.'

lix     'Individual coaching: striking a balance between business context and personal growth.'

lx      'When I confronted her with her behaviour for the first time. In our conversations we always went round in circles. A recurring argument was the pressure of work that she had to perform under. I couldn't break out of the circle until I confronted her with her behaviour: by continually raising the argument of work pressure, she didn't need to change her behaviour. The confrontation led us to go deeper and helped to break the circle. It was critical because I didn't know how she would view this and felt we were entering someone else's territory.'

lxi     'Coaching session with a colleague who is consulting me for career advice. The dilemma is whether to continue with all his current activities, including national presence, or take a step back but also lose some of the shine. In his enthusiasm, he explains how he invests his time in the national network. I think this is precisely where the dilemma lies and wonder about how to confront him with it. He is a very analytical and highly educated man, so I try a detour. I throw at him: "So you're leaving your employer and customers in the lurch." Him: '???' Me: "Your employer and customers deserve a well-rested employee, but you don't seem to take that seriously, because you just tire yourself out in your spare time."'

lxii    'The most critical and frustrating moment was the one when I didn't know what to do. I was coaching someone on how best to deal with a close colleague who was causing her a lot of stress. She had a number of learning questions, because she *seemed* to realise that she could not change her colleague. The sessions were about: "what can I do to handle this better?" Yet she kept coming back to the fact that her manager had to talk to her colleague and frustrations like that, instead of looking at her own behaviour. I often brought her back to the learning questions and confronted her with them, but that helped only temporarily. In the end, we identified a number of choices for her to change the current situation, but it took a lot of pulling and pushing on my part (I was often pushed into the expert control, that I usually stayed out of by throwing the questions back, but this didn't always work). In the end, I got tough and said: "The choice is yours, if you want to change anything you will have to take action yourself. If you don't do that, what else do you want to get out of these sessions?" Then she said she agreed, but she never took any action and the sessions came to an end.

*(Continued)*

I realise that in the end I didn't have a clear understanding of her learning question, that she mainly wanted me to listen and give her advice occasionally. I (and not she) thought it was necessary for her to realise that her own behaviour also played a role in the situation. She saw that in part, but really not enough.'

lxiii 'My coachee is a director of a support service. Our sessions are often about his management team, which doesn't function as a team. A critical situation was the moment when he said that he had given up his management team. They are good as individuals, but not as a team. He doesn't want to put any more energy into it. When he concludes this he is no longer open to reflection on his own behaviour and doesn't want to examine it any further. I don't manage to persevere, so he takes the reins into his hands and changes the subject.'

## 16. MATCHING COACH TO COACHEE

lxiv 'I am fairly extrovert myself. My coachee, on the other hand, is fairly introverted. Time and again, I find it exciting to be able to see during conversations whether or not my comments are hitting home, or whether or not he agrees with them. Usually I don't find out until later, when he comes back to it. I ask about it directly on a regular basis, but I still have the feeling that I don't know exactly what is going on in him and whether or not I am helping him.'

lxv 'A critical moment was a coaching session with an issue about introversion. The person in question was so shy that making contact with other people was beyond them. She also found it hard to make contact with me and at the end of an hour's coaching I was exhausted because *I* was working hard, not *her*.

Her presence was mainly physical and I was always speaking because she didn't venture anything, not even when long silences fell. In the end I chose to mirror her behaviour very closely (doodling during an answer, not making eye contact, not saying anything back), which forced her to choose a different role. It worked out well, but could also have been very counter-productive.'

lxvi 'When and how to make the transition from more substantive matters to personal matters. I find that particularly difficult with introverted coachees who have little, or very subtle, expression.'

lxvii 'Someone who didn't want to change or develop himself, or denied suggestions for development. Or someone who wanted something that I seriously doubted he could do. Or someone who wanted something I was sure was impossible.'

lxviii 'I'm coaching one director who, in my experience, can be blunt and sometimes a bit rude. You can hear his own interests in a lot of the things he says and he is often at odds with those around him. If you look at this case by case, he does make progress: he does realise things, but structurally nothing really changes. I haven't been working with him for very long. I'm trying to strike a balance between timing, i.e. when and how to say something, and building the relationship, i.e. when to let it go. I also wonder if he really wants to change. It benefits him a lot, or he wouldn't continue to display this behaviour.

From the outset he also rejects what he calls "psychobabble". "Pragmatic" is his buzzword. This isn't a bad thing in itself, of course, but it does close the door to him taking a more structural approach to things.'

## 17. LIMITS OF COACHING

lxix 'Coaching often goes unnoticed, and is not connected with a coaching contract or explicit coaching conversations. The disadvantage of this is that I sometimes don't realise until later that I'd have done better to have tackled it differently.'

lxx 'My coachee, who is also a colleague because I am an internal coach, was clearly in a jam in terms of workload. I wasn't sure whether to tip off his manager in order to support my coachee.'

lxxi 'I find it a challenge to learn how a coach can best handle the "professional distance" between coach and coachee. My most critical moment was when the coachee confessed that he had feelings for me. I didn't quite know how to handle that situation.'

lxxii 'Through my manager I heard that my coachee is getting a "bad name" in the organisation. He didn't want to say who the comments came from, but my coachee doesn't seem to be meeting expectations. I can't understand these comments at all. I only hear positive stories about my coachee. I also hear fairly positive stories about him from close colleagues and other people within the organisation. How do I bring this up? Moreover, his promotion is now in doubt and, in my opinion, this is unjustified.'

lxxiii 'Specifically, I find it hard to hear my coachee being criticised in the corridors and don't know how to communicate this to her. I don't know whether it is useful to say to her that there has been criticism behind her back. I *would* like to do something with the content of the criticism, but how do you raise that? Is it something she has to find out for herself? And how do you make the first move here?'

lxxiv 'At a given point during a review session, my internal coachee described her experiences with a manager. She had observed the manager in various situations and clearly exposed the plusses and minuses using a number of examples and situation sketches.

*(Continued)*

At the same time, my role as a senior member of staff led to a process in which the same manager's secondment was under discussion: whether to extend or terminate it? After a quick internal consideration, but without consulting my coachee properly, I used her information.

She rightly called me to account over this. Of course, I immediately apologised. I also considered it very annoying and a clear mistake on my part. I should have known better. However, we did straight away have a good discussion about mutual responsibility, mutual trust, how to handle information and when to disclose what. But it was still difficult for me to end that conversation in an amicable way. Various roles were mixed up on both sides: coach, coachee, manager, employee, colleague. In short, my opinion was that I had lost my grip.'

lxxv  'My coachee, a manager within the same organisation, is discussing his difficulties with a colleague and wants to raise this with her. He has put things down on paper, such as his experiences and his feelings. We have an extensive session on this, in which I commend him on how he has put it down on paper and how he intends to deal with it. He discusses the results of the session briefly with his manager and in the end decides to tackle it in his own way.

The critical thing about this story is that, after his chosen approach to the colleague escalated, I heard from my coachee's manager that he was hiding behind me. This was disappointing for me, because I felt I'd been used in the problem he had with his colleague.

At the time I didn't know what made most sense: give him feedback about my feelings, or leave it at that because he apparently didn't feel strong enough to speak on his own account.'

lxxvi  'Because I have different roles in my job and deal with many different levels of management, I often find myself in a situation where I have prior knowledge or background information that my coachee doesn't or shouldn't have. And in many cases it's not my job to share this knowledge with my coachee.

There can also be situations where I feel obliged to do something with the information I receive from the coachee towards higher management, such as send out a signal. At these moments I doubt what to do; until now I have been frank about such dilemmas with the coachee. In my view, I still run the risk of the coachee seeing it as a limitation that I sometimes represent several interests.

In other words, I often feel obstructed by the fact that I am an internal adviser and coaching is only one of my roles.'

lxxvii  'The feeling that I might lose my coachee due to "too many cooks", because another supervisor was already present. I wondered if I should raise this in the organisation, let it pass, and/or discuss it with the coachee.'

## 18. IMPACT OF THE ORGANISATION

lxxviii 'The most critical moment was when an employee, my internal coachee, broke off his training, stopped it after a year and then wondered where to go from there. It turned out that a traumatic experience within the organisation was his reason for stopping. As a result of the coaching conversation that helped him to handle that experience, he is now continuing his studies. I find it very difficult, when the organisation has laid down guidelines, to induce employees to set in train a development process themselves.'

lxxix 'Recently there was a "what next?" moment with a manager who is having problems with his department and the management of the company. While technically very capable, he frequently has angry outbursts that reduce his effectiveness. He is deeply affected by the fact that some people don't like him, and is keen to do something about it. During the sessions we look at how things could be different, with a bit of positive thinking, visualisation and NLP, but not long ago part of his department was transferred to another manager. So we're back to square one. I think that's a shame. A moment when I am not sure how to help him from here, and whether it makes sense generally.'

## 19. TEAM COACHING

lxxx 'Team coaching: bringing different interests in team conflict on to the table and making them workable.'

# Appendix B: Critical moments of experienced coaches

## B.1 Overview with a selection of 78 critical moments of experienced coaches

The following is a random selection of 36 of the original 78 critical moments, to which I have made only minor changes in terms of style and spelling. The moments fall naturally under the headings that describe aspects of the coaching process, but they could also have been classified differently, and many critical moments can be categorised under a number of different headings in principle. The headings have been chosen in such a way that more than one moment comes under each heading. I have already carried out an initial *interpretation*, therefore, by choosing this order and these headings. In making this selection of critical moments, I kept two moments per heading so as to give a good overview of the whole spectrum.

In the overview, the moments under headings 1, 5, 8, 15, 16 and 17 were in Dutch only and those under heading 12 in English only. The moments are therefore reasonably well mixed and different national cultures contribute to most of the headings. Interestingly, the Dutch have much more to say about counter-transference[1] (headings 15, 16 and 17). This might be due to the more direct and candid nature of Dutch culture. After all, counter-transference is something very personal and intimate, which perhaps not everyone writes about easily. I should add that it was a Dutch person (myself) who chose the headings.

There are in fact only three chapters in the following overview of critical moments:

1  Managing key conditions (headings 1–3),
2  Deepening the coaching conversation and the coaching relationship (headings 4–11), and
3  Handling what happens in the coaching conversation and the coaching relationship (headings 12–18).

## 1. MANAGING KEY CONDITIONS. CONTEXT OF THE COACHING CONVERSATION

i  'I have three meetings in a row with people from the same organisation. At my house, not at the company. I'm overrunning a bit, so the fifteen-minute break between appointments is always used up. So they see each other when they arrive and leave. They are very friendly and cheerful towards each other but I feel uncomfortable and think I'm not handling this right.'

iii  'At the start of a team coaching programme, very early on in the proceedings, you often get members putting demands on the table or quibbling over basic conditions. I find this annoying: you don't know the team yet, you barely know the team members, haven't yet formulated a common objective, either for the team or for the coaching, but you have to intervene immediately. You set the tone; you lay down your key conditions in a non-negotiable way: you can get off to a flying start or you can pack up and clear off. A tense moment.'

## 2. MANAGING KEY CONDITIONS: TRIANGULAR[2] CONTRACTS

iv   'It's exciting to see if the other person will let you connect with him, if trust will develop, particularly when someone feels coerced.'

viii  'One critical moment I remember is I had been asked by the MD of a company to do some "remedial" coaching with his deputy. They did not share the same management style. The MD had briefed the deputy and he was happy to be involved in the coaching process. I had clear success criteria from the MD – which were to work with the deputy to explore the areas the MD was not happy with and determine a way forward. On my first meeting with the deputy, he told me that he was actively looking for a new job and his aim was to leave the company at the earliest opportunity. His mind was made up (we explored this). He did not want the MD to know this. This posed an ethical dilemma for me. In working with the deputy, some of the issues I would have explored with him were: how far he was willing to change his style; how this impacted his own values; what other options did he have, etc. In other coaching situations I have worked with coachees to help them move on to new jobs. However in this case, I did not feel I could coach the deputy in leaving the organisation, though he would have liked me to. So we needed to terminate the coaching relationship before it had started – but with me unable to explain to the MD client why. We resolved this by my coaching the deputy to explore the best way to further his plan of leaving at the first opportunity, and him coming to the conclusion that it would be better if he were to tell his MD rather than hiding it from him. I suppose the critical bit was that for a while I really did not know how best to approach this – having loyalty to both clients.'

## 3. MANAGING KEY CONDITIONS: "READING" THE COACHEE

xiii  'Feeling disillusioned after five years with her present employer my coachee has handed in her notice and has found a new job. It's our first meeting; we have been working together for an hour. She's charming to work with, we have covered a lot of ground, yet it is tiring – energy-sapping even. I suggest a break and a cup of tea in a different location. Suddenly she has lots of energy and is talking about what she really wants to do. This is totally different. We return to the coaching room and I am puzzled by something I can't put my finger on, so I observe how her energy has risen and fallen away again. Something shifts. We agree that we need to hold onto the positive state of mind for thinking about her new job, rather than falling into the trap of feeling overwhelmed that characterised her last job. I also sense there is a risk of me putting too much into this relationship, and I do not want to disempower her. Instead, I suggest we agree some ground rules for working together which include us explicitly taking joint responsibility for monitoring energy levels and intervening when we feel them slipping.'

xiv  'I have a first meeting with a coachee and he says nothing for the first few minutes, with a lot of facial expressions. I have never experienced this, I find it unusual, but I don't say anything, just smile. I believe he will say something in the end, and he does.'

## 4. DEEPENING BY EXPLORING

xv  'I was the change and HR consultant, working with staff of a global Financial Services company on the implications of a potential sale of a global subsidiary. I was involved in all the negotiations. The sale was aborted twice – slightly complex in that it also had a third party involved. I had positioned myself with the MD of the subsidiary as his informal coach, so there was no explicit contract but we had regular one-to-one sessions. On one such occasion, we were talking about the second "abort" and I managed to start helping him to explore how he was feeling towards the whole situation. He opened up to me, was very open about what he wanted but then talked about his relationship with his boss. It became clear that he didn't know what was going to happen to himself after the sale so he was inadvertently putting "spanners in the works" in the negotiations. As a result of this session, he went to his boss and asked him explicitly about his own future. Another buyer came along and the MD was very upfront from the start that he was not part of the sale – the whole thing then went through smoothly.'

xvii  'One of my coachees, a finance director of a medium-sized company, had heard, just after his intake meeting with me, for a coaching programme, that the company was to be investigated. The operation of the management board was a central focus of the investigation. He was the last one in and knew that he had to change his communication style. Very soon, however, the Supervisory Board had reason to conduct an investigation into whether the composition of the board was correct. The coachee was well aware that his position was under discussion. Within a week, we went over his communication style, when it was appropriate and when not, and what he considered a suitable position in the investigation. It became clear during these sessions that he had to become much more conscious of the effect of his words. The combination of his strong drive in an environment where changes were viewed with a great deal of anxiety made his position very risky. In the end his interview with the consultancy firm took place the following week. It went very well. When it was over the firm rang him in the evening to say that, before the interview, they had been of the opinion that his position was no longer tenable. The good impression he made during the interview had caused them to change their minds. The meeting felt almost like an exam for the coachee. The fact that it went well meant he had "passed". This was the springboard for a successful coaching programme in which he was able to broaden his repertoire of behaviour permanently.'

## 5. DEEPENING BY CONTINUING TO ASK QUESTIONS

xviii    'One critical moment occurred during conflict coaching of two people in an escalated conflict, where the failure of the coaching would result in one of them being dismissed. The conflict coaching of the pair was the springboard for team coaching of the entire team in order to create responsibility for results among the team as a whole. Distrust played a major role and at one point I heard myself asking the (awful) coach's question: "What do you need to restore trust?". "Not possible!", they both shouted. The thought crossed my mind: end of story, assignment failed, until I feverishly managed to dredge up the term "healthy distrust" from somewhere deep in my memory. I then asked them: with what level of distrust can you still work together? This was the turning point in the conflict and now, a year and a half later, the whole team is still working together.'

xix    'A female director of a welfare institution wonders why she can't deal appropriately with a fellow member of the management team who is not functioning properly due to a depressive illness. The coachee is experienced and competent enough but, in this case, she prefers to avoid confrontation even though her colleague is underperforming. At one point I asked her, have you ever had to deal with people with depression before? She went quiet and started to twist around in her chair. I held my breath, curious to find out what was coming. After a while (you could see her literally sinking with her mood) she said, "yes, my younger brother was depressive and kept threatening suicide from the age of 11, and I tried to stop him". Ah, no wonder she felt uncomfortable having to deal with depressive people again. When this literally "came to the surface", it was a great relief to her, and to me. We didn't go into it too deeply, there was no need. After this conversation she took the time to process things herself. Then she was able to talk to her colleague, because the confusion was gone. This was a memorable moment for me, literally watching someone delving into her "subconscious". It did cost me the armrest of the chair, but that was a price I was willing to pay.'

## 6. DEEPENING BY SUMMARISING AND MIRRORING

xxiii   'When I notice a pattern in the other person's responses that is preventing him from being effective, it is exciting to see if I can put it in such a way that the other person can hear it and, indeed, if I can point him or her towards the way out.'

xxv   'An exploratory discussion session with a new coachee, a financial consultant who has been referred to me. He said on the phone that he wants to learn how to convince his clients to follow his advice. I suspect he is someone who wants to develop the relational side of consulting for himself. While getting to know this coachee it strikes me that is very evasive about his background. Usually I leave it to the coachee to decide what he wants to tell me about that, but it's taking much too long. I ask him whether all of that information is significant in terms of the aim that he wants to achieve. The coachee keeps on talking enthusiastically. I bring up the time aspect; in view of the time, could he be a bit more concise. That too has virtually no effect. I point out that he seems to be finding it difficult to rein himself in, and ask if that's also a factor in other situations. The coachee agrees, and the conversation takes a completely different turn: he recently visited a psychiatrist to investigate whether he might be manic. What do you do about this in coaching? Do you restrict the coaching programme to learning how to handle the relationship with consultancy clients better (my words), or do you aim for a more comprehensive course in which the consultant learns how to handle himself better (to contain himself) in his work (e.g. in the contact with his consultancy clients)? And who decides which choice is made? In consultation with the coachee, I decide to hold a three-way conversation with his boss (as the sponsor) to explore this further. I'm still struggling with the question of how, if the coaching becomes this comprehensive programme (which the real life cries for), I can continue to confine my facilitation to coaching alone.'

## 7. DEEPENING BY GIVING FEEDBACK

xxvi   'I am coaching a highly articulate person who acts very convinced of his own abilities. What he is saying sounds logical but I suspect it is not entirely true. I don't take to him much, although I do believe he has the best intentions in his approach to his work and is quite personable. The critical issue for me is how to confront him in such a way that I touch a chord in him that will make him open up rather than clam up. I don't experience such critical moments with people who are very senior in the organisation, but they do sometimes occur with people at lower levels.'

xxvii    'Sometimes in coaching you come across a situation where you don't know if you're broaching a topic that the coachee is willing or able to do something with. In career coaching I have confronted people with impediments that they can do relatively little about. One coachee had a pronounced droop to the corners of his mouth. As a result his facial expression was always sad and offputting. A clear handicap in communication and an obstacle in his career. In my view it was absolutely a subject for conversation. However, I always find it tricky to touch on topics like these, to give some practical examples: "Sir, you stink, you have to do something about it."; "Madam, your facial expression almost always creates distance; I can't do anything about it, neither can you, but it's holding you back enormously."; "True, you want to become a director, but I don't think you'll ever be considered for it, any more than I am likely to make prima ballerina. In my view, you lack the basic skills".'

## 8. DEEPENING BY CONTRIBUTING SOMETHING ONESELF

xxx    'If my coachee is not very forthcoming, I start talking about an experience of my own. It's exciting to see if my story will prompt the other person to step in and explore his own situation.'

xxxi    'If I offer an insight, such as the suggestion: "Would it help to look at it this way?", and the other person doesn't pick it up, I sometimes have to suppress the inclination to offer it again instead of waiting or exploring where the other person is at. That is difficult because I am pretty convinced that it will help: if I just try it one more time.'

## 9. DEEPENING BY MEANS OF TRANSPOSITION[3] (HOMEWORK, ROLE-PLAY, PSYCHODRAMA, ETC.)

xxxii    'I can think of several where I have introduced a "right-brain" approach such as a guided fantasy to explore unwanted "baggage"; a flipchart drawing to capture feelings about an issue; walking a time-line to explore difficult options; using each hand to represent opposing drives and to explore potential integration – in all I experienced a moment of breathless waiting: asking a question, seeking their response to the activity and its impact, or just waiting for them to engage with the suggestion. Each time there is a sense of "Is this a step too far for now?"; "Are they ready to engage with this issue in a deeper, more meaningful way and with this approach?"; "Will it leave them worse off or able to move forward?" Always there is a sense of asking them to move into the unknown to a degree, and of moving into the unknown with them. Often there results a deeper insight, emotional awareness, clarity – which is what I am hoping. People can get upset at times in coaching but in the incidents described they (usually) engage and become intently curious to explore. My breathless anticipation includes a fear of what may be raised to awareness and a readiness to deal with whatever materialises. The worst seems to be that occasionally the activity fizzles out, the impact seems negligible and we pass on. I don't recall any dreadful consequences. Despite this when it proves very helpful I always experience it as walking on egg shells, on a tight rope, it feels precarious.'

xxxv   'I'm reminded of some work I did last year with a coachee where she brought some poetry along to the coaching session. The session before she'd been exploring the way she presents herself in her organisation and how she holds a lot back. She had also spoken about her love of poetry and how important it had been to her during her life. I can't remember exactly how the idea emerged, but to cut a long story short, I suggested that next time she brought some poetry that in some way represented what mattered most to her, her essence, etc. She took this piece of homework very seriously and came prepared with three books of poetry, with one poem from each. I must admit I wasn't sure how the session was going to go, but I needn't have worried. The poems were beautiful and moving in their own right, but more importantly they helped my coachee get in touch with her deeper values and passions that she had been neglecting for some time at work. This opened up a whole new area of work for us and marked something of a turning point for us both. Through this experience I learned about really trusting my coachee and being prepared to go with their flow – even if it felt quite risky at the time. I wouldn't necessarily replicate this approach with others, but it was the right thing to do with this particular person. I guess the critical moment was in making the suggestion and staying with it through the process.'

## 10. DEEPENING BY BRINGING UP THE TRANSFERENCE[4] HERE AND NOW

xl   'The coachee uses long sentences and lots of words to describe the problem that he wants to work on in the coaching conversation. I summarise his issue: so, if I understand correctly, your issue for today is ... "No," says the coachee, "that's not what I mean". I am surprised because I believe I have summarised his issue well, in his own words. He explains it again. Using identical sentences, and the same words. This time I interrupt with short questions intended to clarify and occasional mini-summaries. He is constantly confused by my questions, he "didn't mean" that, and the same with my summaries, "no, you misunderstand me". I suspect I *am* on the right track but his real issue is something else, even though the coachee keeps telling me I'm on the wrong track. We try again, with the help of keywords on a sheet of paper. I intervene:

> I don't believe I can help you today, because I am obviously not able to understand what your issue is. I've spent the last fifteen minutes trying to clarify in various ways, but I'm getting nowhere. And I strongly suspect that you actually want to talk about a different issue today, but perhaps don't dare to put it into words.

This is greeted with silence. The coachee goes pale and moist-eyed and, hesitatingly, comes out with a completely different story. This often happens in conversations, coachees have to gather the courage "to pop the real question" and first spend some time "beating about the bush". But I always find these moments very exciting.'

xli    'I am asked to coach a secretary whose boss I have known for 20 years, as a friend and client. The secretary was transferred to him from another colleague, something she sees as a personal rejection. During the sessions that follow I am worn out by the torrent of words, critical, perfectionist, that flows from her. I start to discuss alternatives with her, but she doesn't take me up on them, neither does RET work, nor conversational techniques, etc. I decide to confront her: spell out the effect of her constant blaming on me and so perhaps on her surroundings as well, offer alternatives, demonstrate, suggest she watch herself on video. I work and work and work, and nothing happens. Later, I ring her boss and tell him I want to stop the coaching if he doesn't tell her that he has a problem with her performance. The next time, it doesn't appear that he's done it.'

## II. DEEPENING BY BRINGING UP THE COACHING RELATIONSHIP

xlv    'The coachee dragging her feet about getting herself out of the dysfunctional work situation she was in (which had already led to one breakdown) who finally made the choice to move on when I told her, with firm compassion, that I'd have to move on as her coach if she didn't.'

xlvii    'It is a session with a coachee who, in six meetings, has already taken a number of steps in forming a picture of her future, her strengths and the steps she can take in order to make her dreams a reality. With every meeting, I see her self-confidence grow a little. During the last two meetings she admits that she is tired, shudders to think of everything that she discovered she can do/be in the last meetings. She says she hasn't done her homework for the past few weeks, she's tired, nothing is working and she wonders if we shouldn't schedule at least another six meetings. I feel I'm not the person to supervise her now. She needs someone else's help. At the same time, I notice that she is acting dependent on me. I now have to choose. Do I keep her on or refer her to someone else?'

## 12. HANDLING SURPRISES AS A RESULT OF EXPLORING

xlix  'I was coaching someone around her career and we had used MBTI as a way of thinking about preferences etc. We'd chosen this as she wasn't sure which way to go. We were just into looking at the Extraversion/Introversion preference (she had shown a slight Extraversion preference in her profile), when she got quite emotional and upset. The conversation ensued that she felt she more of an introvert but all her life she's been encouraged to be more extroverted and scolded for being more reflective and introverted as a child. It was quite a release for her to realise it was fine to be an introvert, and as we worked on this we were able to go on and explore career options with greater confidence. So I guess for me it's often the unexpected turns in the conversation which create the "critical moment". They aren't always comfortable and I don't know if I handle them as well as I should, but I think my strategy is to listen intently, allow silence, be with the individual and let them take the direction in the conversation and take it where they want to go. I also have a belief that things will work through to a positive conclusion which helps me if I'm feeling a bit stuck or unsure.'

li  'The coachee was involved in a coaching programme designed to deliver promotion. A number of areas of behaviour were holding her back relating to influencing skills and her profile in meetings, but she had identified and worked on these progressively but no real breakthrough point had been achieved. She had always attended coaching meetings, but on one particular day had been asked to attend an all day critical business meeting, and so needed to cancel the coaching sessions to attend. This was not known to me as a coach. However she decided to attend the coaching session and negotiated that she could attend the meeting but miss part of it to attend the coaching sessions. This was a high risk behaviour requiring use of influencing skills in a very visible way. She brought this issue to the coaching session having already negotiated her opt out. She was able to reflect on what she had achieved and the skills she used. This represented a critical moment in the coaching when several elements we had been working on came together. She has dared to try, was able to apply and reflect upon her skills. She had identified her own needs and those of the business and found a way to align them.'

## 13. HANDLING SURPRISING TRANSFERENCE PHENOMENA

lii   'My coachee is a bank director. He is suspecting the head of his investment advisory group, a long-term personal friend, of theft! His question: How do I confront a close friend with such suspicion without clear evidence? We are pondering effective options on how to approach this delicate issue. We hear the ring tones of his mobile phone. His secretary can hardly speak. Her information: The suspect has committed suicide some minutes ago with a gun in his office. My coachee breaks down and starts crying. I am stunned. I stay silent, leaving him to his emotions of guilt, shame, despair now breaking forth. Haven't we lost the cause? I can feel the void, a nagging vacuum. For a long moment I feel stuck with my habitual role identity as an executive coach: to know better than my coachees how to effectively cope with difficult situations. We have a new situation. And a different question: how to effectively cope with this tragedy? To cope with the unexpected can be challenging.'

liii   'I was working with a senior civil servant. We had a contract for four two-hour sessions. The fourth session came to an early conclusion. I was concerned that as we were not using the full time allocated, I was not meeting the needs of this individual. To my utter surprise, at the end of the session he commented on how valuable the sessions had been and asked if we could continue to work together. We have now been working together for two further years. All of our sessions are very focused and relatively short as this meets his needs.'

## 14. HANDLING COUNTER-TRANSFERENCE PHENOMENA: "CAN I ACTUALLY HELP THE COACHEE?"

lvii   'I sometimes get anxious when I'm with someone who is unusually intelligent, when I wonder at first if I can keep up with this person intellectually. Fortunately, so far I have always been able to enter into the conversation with the other person from a perspective of inner peace and not one of competition.'

lviii   'I was working with a coachee who was extremely successful in his career at a relative young age. He had it all, basically. Asking him the "miracle question" he realised that he was already living his miracle. I was stumped. Where do we go from here, what is the next step in this coaching relationship? Did he need coaching at all? The coaching session was then taken up with him talking about how limited his view of his potential was. "Potential" for him he noticed was not about career success (he already had that in spades and had very good prospects too), but it was about realising his true values about life and how to live accordingly. I have been seeing this coachee once a year following monthly then quarterly sessions in 2001 and 2002. He continues to be increasingly influential and highly regarded at a global level in his organisation. Recently he turned down a top job in his organisation because it did not fit in with his view of his future. He reports that that early miracle question is one he often reflects on and helps him make decisions about the direction of his career and lifestyle now.'

## 15. HANDLING COUNTER-TRANSFERENCE PHENOMENA: "I FEEL RESPONSIBLE FOR THE COACHING"

lx   'I sometimes get anxious when I notice that I'm approaching the other person with a lot of optimism and concern, while noticing internally that I am busy playing the role of rescuer.'

Lxiii   'The coachee has been feeling for a while that she has to choose between: a) keeping her completely unassailable position as a consultant – with a lot of personal freedom, always choosing the monitor/evaluator role – or b) assuming joint responsibility for the future of the consultancy by working towards "becoming a partner", as some colleagues are suggesting. In conversations about career anchors, work/life balance, personal standards and values and the communicative strategies she has at her disposal, it has become clear to her that she has the ambition to become a partner, that she had already considered the step once before being pushed by her environment. She had considered all sorts of scenarios; from becoming extremely successful to going down, fighting bravely, in the battle against the prevailing culture. In her daydreams all of her scenarios seemed exciting and inspiring enough to warrant taking that step. Then she received the invitation from the board to discuss a partnership. At that point it is difficult (but in my view necessary) to keep the personal relationship built up between coach and coachee very businesslike. You would like to decide with her. I found the talking process whereby the coachee arrives at her decision particularly anxiety-provoking.'

## 16. HANDLING COUNTER-TRANSFERENCE PHENOMENA: "I WANT TO DROP OUT MYSELF"

lxiv    'Because of all those different people and conversations, I can't remember what exactly I discussed with a coachee the previous time. It's difficult for him to understand, I think, to my distress!'

lxv     '"Am I going on too long?", asked my coachee. I sincerely didn't think so, but my attention was diverted by something odd outside. I was able – after making my excuses – to turn things around in a positive sense: "You are more sensitive/perceptive than you described yourself before this first session!"'

## 17. HANDLING COUNTER-TRANSFERENCE PHENOMENA: THE COACH'S OWN EMOTIONS

lxix    'My most exciting coachee was a Nietzschean philosopher who surpassed my own frame of thinking and ability to put things into perspective by regarding objectives as moving panels.'

Lxx     'Male coaching client aged around 34, adept at social skills, company director. The topic love/sex/unfaithfulness. An older woman he met at a dinner is courting him. He tells me about this and interrupts himself by asking me: "Have you ever been in love with a younger man?" I reply: "Pass." Him: "Why?" Me: "Before you know it you'll start speculating about it." (I meant about the ins and outs of my love life and the inappropriateness of that topic in this setting). Him: "Speculating about what it's like to do it with you?" Me: "I didn't mean that." Him: "I've been doing that for a long time." Me – unsettled – "Back to the subject of your interaction with this woman, please." My discomfort was undoubtedly rooted in the fact that I thought I was safe hiding behind his mother transference and was suddenly being seen in a completely different capacity. A possible complication is the fact that he was a very attractive man. Just to be clear, I am 54.'

## 18. HANDLING QUESTIONS AND SUGGESTIONS FROM THE COACHEE

lxxv    'Someone else, a fast-rising manager with a lot of vision, once said after several sessions: "Oh, so I can ask something too!", although I always start openly and invite the other person just to start somewhere. But he evidently saw that as the umpteenth task in his pretty hard life, instead of feeling free to ask something. I learned from this: with melancholic people I now start by saying, would you like to say something or ask something? Anything is possible, it's your time. It can even be something very small, a tiny question, anything will do. When I said that to the manager in question he "warmed up" and proceedings suddenly moved along much faster and more smoothly.'

Lxxviii  'As a career consultant for the staff of a large organisation I have also recently been sent employees who are threatened with dismissal for, say, outplacement. With one of these coachees I had an extensive course of sessions in which I worked hard, of course, on mutual trust. On many occasions he had already expressed his appreciation for the supervision, he was even able to get criticism off his chest and we talked until it became clear to him what he wanted and how he could achieve it. Suddenly he asked if I would give him a copy of the reports that I prepare for the management of his department. He had known for a long time that I was sending them and was also made aware of their content in general terms each time. I hadn't expected this question from him and had become slightly more to-the-point in my reports. What should I do? I found that I should have been able to predict this, but I hadn't been expecting it. It was a matter of trust and we both knew that in a split second. I then told him I couldn't do it: my relationship with the principal was also at issue here. "In what way?" That turned out not to be an appropriate solution. To demonstrate that I was writing respectfully about him and the supervision, I read out passages from my last report to him. As I did so, I noticed that there was nothing in the report that I would not say to his face. In the end, I did give him a copy of my last report and the result was continuing openness and trust.'

## B.2 Overview of 48 critical moments of experienced coaches from telephone interviews

Nearly all 49 critical moments mentioned by experienced coaches during extensive telephone interviews, in the form of brief transcripts based on the interview recordings. The actual recordings contain much more detail on the background of the critical moments and their further consequences, as discussed in Chapter 3.

Working with the interviewees, we have slightly modified some descriptions to protect confidentiality. One moment is omitted due to a special request from the coach concerned that it not be brought into the public domain.

## CM1

Young woman on a course where two sessions of coaching are included: one at the end of the course and one follow-up. The end-of-course session is very emotional – the woman has been stirred up by the course – and opens up a lot of things. She says it was a very useful session.

When she arrives at the conference hotel for the follow-up session, she is closed up. When the coach pushes, she says she wasn't herself at the last session and is scathing about psychology, etc. The coach keeps pushing – she has bothered to make the two-hour journey, etc. – surely there is something, etc. (apparently a little pushing helped at the last session and caused the opening up) and the woman gets very angry. The coach also gets upset, and says there's no point in going on. The woman seems disappointed at that, though still angry. She says she feels pressurised. She leaves after 45 minutes and the post-session written feedback is dreadful.

## CM2

The last session, a couple of months ago, after the coachee and I had been meeting for two years. He is always very happy with the coaching, but I am aware of feeling a bit guilty and uncomfortable because I know it remains rather superficial work. He comes to the session but doesn't let me get near to anything difficult and keeps the conversation rather superficial. At the end of the previous session I had said something about 'we need to talk about YOU in this'. So in this last session I picked this up and pushed him gently to look at a difficult area. It went very well. The tension in my taking the risk of confronting transmitted itself to him and he really engaged with the issue. We engaged in interesting dialogues about whether his long period of not confronting was simply "laziness" as he put it, or did he sense that I wasn't ready to hear it yet.

## CM3

A new coachee – who was on the Board of Directors of a big retail firm, but behaved in a way that was difficult for peers and was effectively thrown out of the board – was being pursued by one member in particular with court cases, etc.

The coach thought, 'he is a typical retail man – he buys solutions' (and also comes across as heavy, speedy, a bit demanding). In the second session the coachee says words to the effect of 'I have told you the problems, tell me what to do'. The coach is aware that they are very different personalities in terms of style and speed, etc.

He feels stuck and avoids responding immediately. He goes away and reflects/self-supervises/makes notes to self about possible ways forward. He hasn't decided what to do.

The next session is in ten days.

## CM4

A woman sales manager wants to move on from her job. She is in a great hurry and wants it now. She can't wait to do the usual course on exploring the second half of your life, so the coach offers an afternoon workshop and six individual sessions fairly close together.

Did MBTI and discovered she was 'I' though she had always thought and been told by others that she was 'E'.

Sessions very dynamic – coachee likes stimulation and challenge – e.g. loves to be given homework assignments/things to do/plays a lot of challenging sport, etc.

She flattered the coach, saying he was really good, etc. and luring him to give her more stimulating models/homework, etc.

The coach began to worry that this was not right.

In the last session, the coachee seemed sad though she said she was fine, but on reflection said she was disappointed with herself for getting involved in diversions (exploring two internal vacancies) that had got in the way of her dream (of moving on and out, travelling round the world, starting her own business, etc.).

The coach slowed the pace down and explored with her these two diversions: the two internal jobs. What about them had involved her? They realised that one of them had enough new and stimulating aspects to satisfy her while retaining some safety and familiarity (within the same organisation, etc.) that she needed.

She went off happy and took that job.

## CM5

A coachee from a pharma company wanted coaching around her leadership style to improve her effectiveness in role. We met with her boss to discuss the learning contract. During the conversation, when asked what does he expect to change, he said 'I want her to relax'. I found it very hard. She pushed back, saying: 'it's a very tough place ... what do you mean by relaxing?'

At one level I was aware of the boss's power and authority. I was also aware that my consultancy was involved in a much larger project with this organisation.

I felt he was imposing his style, which would be very difficult for her to replicate, and making a very big request of my coachee.

I intervened – challenged him – highlighting the difficulty of his request: 'it's quite a big challenge, a big request to make of somebody'. At the same time I also made supportive comments about the beneficial impact of being less task-focused at work for my coachee.

Overall he ignored it – he felt he was right. The coachee was defensive in his view; it was left like that and we moved onto other things, it was left vague. We had a chat about it later, highlighted that she has her own style and acknowledged and appreciated what she has got and how to respond to it. 'It was helpful,' she said.

## CM6

Very senior guy in a public sector organisation, head of division. Concerned about whether he was having a mid-life crisis. He was interested in leaving his organisation and starting a new career. Was it a personal mid-life crisis ... OR ... had he had enough and needed a change / would it serve him well? I felt responsibility for him – a man in his 50s – perhaps he is making a mistake; he was looking for advice, I was careful not to give.

My dilemma... intuition on the one hand (would be a good idea to move on) versus responsibility / a safe place.

Mirrors the dilemma of the coachee. I had difficulty being directive: saying something that might be acted on by the coachee.

We explored a lot about the issue and in particular his tendency to work very hard. I allowed him to take a decision and resisted giving advice.

We explored his age, spirituality and death, links to religion, how he sees life after doing his current role, his desire to do new things, how he is facing up to his age, mortality, is his need to work neurotic, he couldn't let go of working very hard. Is he avoiding something, his tendency to work hard – is it unhealthy or pathological?

What should he do? Talking about his own needs, it emerged that he'd never taken time to explore them. It would be a big thing for him to leave his current organisation. What would it mean to say goodbye?

He left to go to a new high demanding job. I've continued to work with him. He is very happy and more aware of his patterns.

## CM7

I was working with two women new to leadership in a university. They had to modernise their departments, make them more businesslike, make things more open, participative leadership.

Both were very new; they had a sense they wanted to do it participatively but did not have the vocabulary. Often I find that I am able to give a name to something for a coachee. The coachee often used that to confirm their thinking, but I felt a lot of power in my role – especially whenever I say yes or no.

Specific example: pushing one coachee against her wishes. Whilst working on the strategy for her organisation, she was resisting the detail. Afterwards she realised how important it was. She had not previously put the new structure in writing. The Board, management and junior staff were pleased.

I went further than I normally would have done as a coach. I sat with her while she did it. I said the university recruitment process was not helpful and insisted that she use the process she wanted. She wasn't keen – a push is what she really needed.

I was thinking 'oh god am I going too far here? Am I stepping outside the boundaries of the job?' It's her choice, I wasn't doing it in a detached way; I really knew she needed to be pushed, her life pattern was not to go where she did not want to go. I never did it for her but I sat with her while she did it. At times she would say 'do we really have to do it?'

Could I persist enough to keep her going – am I prepared to suffer? Was this a parallel process?

She was delighted with the result.

The university backed off and let her do what she wanted to do. Others were coming to her saying 'how did you do it?'

## CM8

University woman wondering 'do I want to stay in this job?' Plus a very difficult personal life. It started very much about the organisation but it started to slip into personal as her relationship became more difficult – is that where she goes when she is under stress?

I supported her enough, decided that I could help her do her role but that she should take her personal life separately to therapy.

Is this the role she wants and what would she do if she stayed?

Patterns of hating to fail and of being on the outside.

Feelings of being overwhelmed – I helped her day.

## CM9

The coachee saw me as a "wicked stepmother". He saw me as critical, he would come back to sessions and hadn't done his stuff. I would say what I thought had happened, and he would get more and more closed down.

I said to him: 'I am feeling really uncomfortable here'.

I discussed with him that I was feeling uncomfortable and did not know what was going on. He said he was intellectually feeling a failure.

Supervision was really helpful. Breakthrough came when he said he did not know how to draw up an action plan – it came down to basics in assertiveness.

He also had a pattern of a critical mother – he had a deeply embedded pattern around women.

Actually critical of himself, less a dilemma more a challenge.

Helping him to understand – what does aggressiveness look like, what does assertiveness look like. He has progressed some way but he is still trying to pull me into criticising him.

## CM10

Woman in a high management position perceived by peers as authoritarian or aggressive. However, she came across as less sure. Experiences herself as a lamb. In the third session she suddenly attacks the competence of the coach. Coach felt shocked/scared but saw a parallel. Coach comments on this but she denies it. They part uncomfortably and coach asks her to reflect. Then the coach receives an email saying she is understanding more and can they have an earlier appointment.

Coach used guts and clarity to describe what she thought was going on. Coach expressed her own response of feeling attacked, defensive and a bit scared.

Coachee began to recognise her pattern and to realise that most people just withdraw or get defensive. Realised that her little girl inside did not come across.

## CM11

Female managing director, aged 45. Question: should she resign and sell her shares to directors, etc. Content got more and more personal. Her husband and parents, childhood, etc. Coach felt the contact was good. At review, coachee said it was very useful. Then one day she stopped coming – a couple of cancellations (by secretary). The coach didn't actually speak to the coachee. Coach made several attempts to contact but didn't push. At first worried, then angry. Took to supervision group. After the group, the coach sent an email saying should we have an ending session. No response from the coachee, other than 'I'll pay the bill'.

## CM12

Yesterday morning a coachee who is a senior consultant presents that the sales department are not performing (his role is acquisitions). He is usually very jolly yet superficial, so doesn't come across as very powerful. But he responds very dramatically when pushed (intelligent, etc.). Coach thinks probably his first face is not very impressive yet he becomes possibly a little over-powerful if they challenge him. Coach felt a moment of excitement and tension. How to say this helpfully, without triggering a defensive "knock down" response? A typical moment: how to invite a coachee's consciousness?

The coach asked permission to give feedback about an observation. He tried to describe what he had observed, asking if the coachee recognises the change, etc.? Coachee was surprised to hear of the difference, but interested. Coach suggests it might shed light on the problem. Coach is putting more depth to the friendly face – developing a better 'counselling approach' to deepen the relationship, therefore strengthening the coachee's social interactions. The coachee liked the idea. Coach suggested inviting the coachee to be clear about himself rather than being critical of other people's flaws in the argument. The coachee could see how it might be effective because the coach used his strength to build his weakness.

## CM13

In the last six weeks, since start of encounter, post-modern Korean, 22-year-old girl, the daughter of a colleague. Starts many studies but fails in them and abandons them. She is adopted. Very successful parents who are disappointed in her. She is keen that people find their own way. Quite happy with herself except wants more stimulation. Coach explores the meaning of her favourite films, which contain stories of lost babies. Coachee doesn't see the connection. Should the coach push the issue?

The coach consults a colleague. Should the coach make her aware? Hesitation to push it too much.

Is seeing her next week. Coach has decided to share that he has a hunch that there is a relationship between the stories and her life.

## CM14

This morning, the end of four sessions starting with an occupational personality questionnaire. The purpose was to decide whether a university student should do a PhD in science. In the third session she realised she needed a plan. Then as they were saying goodbye, the coach said 'so you chose to go on' and she replied 'did I choose?' Coach felt 'have I done or not done something?' Echoes of feeling like this before with other coachees – rushing on and not checking up. Coach said 'yes, you chose' and recapped on the last session: 'you said last time you needed a plan, etc., etc.' The coach tried to prove to her that she had chosen, and tried to get her to own it. He also said 'you have said "I must" very often, as if you never say 'I want to'. The coach wondered about her relationship with her father, the professor. He wished he'd clarified earlier in the session: 'so it sounds as if this is what you've chosen'. The coachee has said before that she doesn't make decisions. On reflection, the coach realises it was the coachee's issue and she did OK.

## CM15

In July, an employee was 'sent' to coaching for outplacement and I am not experienced at submitting a report on my work to the department so I checked it with a colleague. I shared the fact of the report with the coachee. Suddenly he asks to see all reports. I would have said yes but it is their departmental policy not to show reports. I felt very uncomfortable.

I said 'I cannot give it to you but will read everything to do with you'. I did so and indeed gave him a copy of one sheet. An HR person calls to say I urgently need the report for a university lawyer to show we have done everything necessary for this person. I was just about to go off on holiday and was overawed by the "judicial situation" so I gave a short report. I later regretted it. I shouldn't have shared it with HR. I went on holiday, then came back and saw the report was too long and also had some private reflections on his issues (e.g. he's not really trying to respond to me) so was not just factual. I regretted it, so told the coachee what I'd done and apologised. He took exception to one comment and agreed to work together on a statement to be appended to the original report. This has led to the coach feeling freer to give feedback, and be straighter about how he is in relationships.

## CM16

Worked with a programme maker and focused on delivery and being project-driven/action-oriented. When she approached the zone of feelings, etc., the coachee got uncomfortable: it was not professional, wasting the organisation's time on counselling. She questioned its validity. Coach questioned a little her own choice to go there. Is this just my interest?; I'm not qualified; we haven't got a contract; can this be useful without stirring her up and leaving, etc.? Self-doubt in the coach.

The coach encouraged her to trust that if it's come up, it's relevant. The coach discussed self-disclosed connection between own emotional life and whole life etc., and own experience of enhanced competence after exploring personal side, and wanted to make contact as an equal not as a superior expert.

It was fantastic. The coachee went deep, recognised some patterns of past in present. The coachee's awareness was raised, etc. and she left radiant.

## CM17

A woman who had taken a new role in the organisation. With my organisational development perspective, I realised they wanted something from her and she wanted to hold on to what she wanted to do. I knew they would never let her do the transformational things she wanted to do.

I kept asking what was on your job description, what was said at the interview. I felt uncomfortable about my frame, my agenda being so foreground for me. I was resisting empathising with this deluded woman.

Eventually I focused on what she wanted – how could she try and contain the situation, get support, etc.

## CM18

Omitted due to the coach's request that the material not be used publicly.

## CM19

A young high flier was working as a strategist in a modernisation programme within healthcare. Came to improve on personal impact because she was working with older, more experienced people. Did not have gravitas. She had done therapy and coaching in the past, but it had not worked. Dilemma: at the time I was really interested in using NLP. She was interested in using creative techniques. Her issues were also linked to her being very disorganised, although she produced very high quality stuff. Home was not a problem: she was single. Exciting – I think I got her to visualise something to do with her mother. Am I going where I shouldn't – would it help? Would she be able to use it? Bit of a risk; will she cooperate? By the time she got to the next session, she had dropped her baggage with her mother because of what she did in the first session. Issues from the past with her mother had gone. Finding ways for her to articulate baggage in a different way did the magic – you could read stuff in her way of being. Although risky, the heightened moment was the most intense; don't know what will happen. I can't really take it to supervision; you don't know if it will work until you have done it.

## CM20

Autumn 2005, connected with a leadership programme. The coachee was really wound up on the programme, was starting to unravel. When he had the chance to stop, so much stuff came out like a flood. He works in a high-pressure sales environment and has been promoted to senior management. However, his first requirement was to lead and manage others, where he proved quite useless. This led to negative feedback from the team: 'You are not managing us'. I was feeling full up with all this stuff, and at a bit of a loss what to do. I felt quite overwhelmed by all of this. It was difficult to hold him in one area of work. He kept going into other issues, it was difficult finding an issue to work on. This was my experience of him early in the week, on the first day. I had the feeling this was going to be very challenging. I was concerned about this unravelling – what is he going to be like at the end of the week? On Friday, he was quite euphoric – had some quite clear insights – helping more and doing less. It was sound bites. All at quite a vague, abstract level. Difficult to sit and listen and not be overruled. He is euphoric, and I don't want to burst his bubble. How to get to a more realistic level without him landing with a bump? Internally, I was thinking if we do not move to a more rational level he will quite likely leave in a euphoric state and nothing will happen – his colleagues will think he has probably gone off the rails.

How to help someone to really take it forward? Initially, just by letting it come – listen to it, let the guy talk – and I have to say I probably took more time allowing him to talk. I taped the session and reviewed it with a colleague. Colleague's observations were 'struck by how quiet you were', that I allowed the flood to take place longer than usual.

What I did do and could have done earlier was to give a good summary of his issues and what he wanted to work on, rather than just transmit he was able to receive feedback – from that part he made good progress. Since, a real surprise – he misses the usual follow-up two to three months later, and then after two or three attempts of trying to get in touch he suddenly wants a follow-up session. There was one cancellation then we got together. I was fantasising he's got back to how he was – whirling dervish – if we do get together. When we did get together, it was jaw dropping. He was looking completely different. He looked... calmer. I remembered him as someone young, something not terribly mature. Now he was much more relaxed. He told me how he had found the last session we had. I got him to think about the balance he wanted between managing and doing, and got him to do visionary alternatives: what would that look like, etc. What would you need to do it? What if he went ahead and did it? What benefits would it have for him and his family and kids? If he did change, what would be good about that? I was really surprised, to tell the truth. Probably by the fact that he learned and continued to reflect after our last coaching hour.

## CM21

The coach works in a government department. Lot of work, telephone coaching. Several coachees, often abroad. One gentleman is on his first role as head of mission. He is really aware of what he needs to work on: keeping focus on the strategic direction and not getting stuck into detail, but needs some help with defining that strategic direction and setting priorities. What went well, what I could do differently, what to follow up and any actions and any other thoughts on my mind – what was I left with. I wrote up notes in telephone coaching and initially just reviewed my notes; I jotted down key issues at the end of the session and any actions. The need was clear and I was clear about focus. I sent him an exercise with prompt questions. Posts like his are usually 3–4 year tenures, so I got him to think about his leaving do; consider his legacy, how it has changed, what he feels proud of. He really appreciated this, started communicating with his team, holding regular reviews, all was looking really good. A number of serious crises hit his division and really knocked him off course. He was getting really down on himself. In the third session he was being really negative. He was feeling he had fallen back into a pattern: too much firefighting and detail. For me in that session what I was hearing was 'there I go again'. Well actually this is necessary and you do need to get stuck in. At some point he will need to see how he gets back to strategic focus. For me it was important to stick to time. We had contracted for seven one hour coaching sessions. I kind of felt for this session that we needed to protect the time limit: I didn't want it to end on a negative session. It was a mixed ending.

What he missed was... At one point I was not sure... perhaps things were all negative – intuition was it's probably not as bad (experience) – experience greater perspective can be queried.

And one key thing came out: the coachee was a very strong thinking type, and had a perfectionist streak, thought he would think of positive things.

I made sure to ask him about progress that had been, because there were some things going on in spite of the crisis. His main difficulty or danger was negativity everywhere; had he lost perspective? I think he had; looking at what he had done right, he was able to manage; he could manage for himself when to get into that. Tension: there was too much there for catharsis and exploration; what aspects are going well (other end of tension); to appreciate what he has done well, otherwise he is thinking the coach is failing him. In fact he hadn't: my role is to help him to be aware of perspective.

## CM22

First conversation (formally, only intake) with a man somewhat younger than me. We had had several phone conversations around a programme that he wanted to partake in but which did not find enough other participants.

He needed much attention, he was extremely vulnerable: almost every question was met with tears. To do with his career, and his life.

I felt he had a need to be embraced, touched, held physically – and at the same time an attitude of 'do not touch'. At the same time I felt some aversion, some "creeps", he looked not very well kept ... I wondered, is this about me, or about him?

At the end of the conversation I decided to do something with it. I said 'I feel a need to be held, physically'. He denied it and instantly became distant.

But we did continue talking, about feelings, the need for physical exercise that he'd never responded to. The need to do more physical work. He remained with that conversation, but it was clear that he kept a huge distance, and that relationally I was done for. I think I came too close, but perhaps that was needed to take him out of his "drama".

He phoned after two weeks and requested another coach, a 'more fatherly figure'. I found such a coach for him, and they are still working well together.

## CM23

A coachee with whom I got into the same impasse several times. She is very enthusiastic and I experienced a very good chemistry between us. I did the intake, but also the coaching journey with her. She chose me and said 'I'll have to pay myself, it'll cost me dearly, and I want to work only with you'. We had a good time together, it was productive.

First impasse: we found how her relationship with her father prevented her from growing up. She was in fact able to move to a different kind of relationship, through the coaching, just before her father died.

Second impasse: she likes to initiate things but very rarely finishes anything. Much of the homework she left unfinished. At the end she was disappointed about what we had achieved for her career.

I said 'I don't know what more to do' and I felt I had let her down in some way. I said it was up to her to do the work – and finish it.

I wrote a report, as we tend to do, which we agreed was very good. But it was lying there, while she did not move on. Very unsatisfying.

As was the way our relationship ended. She turned in an anonymous evaluation (I think) but otherwise she just disappeared from the radar, as she does with others.

## CM24

The coachee is a man from Macedonia in his mid-30s. He is training with me, and is setting up a consultancy in Macedonia after having lived and worked in the UK. Very talented and passionate. Has to go back to a country that has seen war and extreme poverty. Difficult for him to reintegrate. Encounters 'non-trust energy' and 'feelings of betrayal'.

Six weeks ago he came in with 'I am in despair. Can't get enough work out there.' He'd found out that it wasn't doable; what he had to offer was too big a jump for the Macedonian culture.

I sat down and thought: I need to definitely squash the journey he is on. But: is this doable? Do I have the right?

We got a piece of paper to write down all the factors and perspectives. I got him to comment from the different places in the room. The amount of blockage made him feel relieved, empty and frightened.

Then I lent him a book on spiral dynamics and on inventing your own future. I spent the rest of the time helping him to clarify what could be done. He got a clearer sense.

He came back two weeks later. He said he had slept better, and got excited about the mystery of his own future. The session was more reciprocal, allowing him to be acted upon rather than only act himself. I did a constellation with him about Macedonia, to wipe out a whole avenue of possibilities.

### CM25

A woman successful in running a business had taken time out – she was 'treading water' – was it the wrong field? She saw others less well-trained going faster.

I asked what had been good or bad the last time she launched a business. She felt very brittle. She had a memory of how daunting it would be to stick her head out above the parapet.

I created a timeline and she walked along it. I asked her what resources she needed. She said 'I need your belief in me', and then 'more training' and then 'permission to go slowly'. Again we got this on pieces of paper on the floor. She kept on walking wobbly, until I put a paper in front of her with 'those who would benefit'. That resourced her. Her strengths became more apparent.

She went off and got started!

### CM26

The director/part-owner of a publishing company is trying to keep the company afloat. He felt too 'little' – had a longing to be a child, attached to someone bigger.

It was personal, family-systems work. He kept bringing that back. I thought "business coaching" would be more useful. His world view and relationships were predicated on this weakness, with him being rather pathetic. At a certain point I thought it was quite enough. He needed to get on to be a boss. He agreed, but found it very difficult. He was only ever an ineffective parent or a pathetic child … he had to develop mutuality. Role-play. Coaching, rehearsing ordinary leadership decisions. He felt stronger, but also sulky. Delicate balance between inner and outer work. I felt I owed it to the company that paid for me to stick to the "outer" work.

He continued with another coach and that went well.

### CM27

Female HR director: do I stay in the company or not? Dilemma for me, as the company paid.

I asked if she could involve someone from the company to contract this. I met with her manager. He was going to be okay with it, whichever way it turned out. That was fine.

Then, in another critical moment with same coachee, I was asked to do some consultancy work. I could not accept if I was their coach as well. Different outcomes in different situations. Here, I continued the coaching but did not take the other work.

## CM28

Individual coachee I have been seeing for 4–5 months, this was the third session. He professes to want to learn. If I respond by giving input or content, he says 'yes, but that's just me'. On this occasion it was about how to handle an interview. I invited him to work that out himself. He then said: 'surely there's a structure for this – can you tell me what that is?'

I explained some guidelines and he said 'that's all very well, but I have something in mind anyway'. I told him that I felt "set up" in some sense, that I felt uncertain and uncomfortable, and did not like it very much.

He says that no-one else gives him that feedback. He acknowledges that he responds like this in many circumstances. He takes it away to other people. I don't know whether he is doing things differently, but I trust that by bringing it into his awareness he has a choice to do things differently.

## CM29

Third or fourth session. The coachee has entered into this process very enthusiastically. Good rapport and relationship. In this organisation, he and his colleagues often use deflection of any emotional intensity with the help of humour.

We had a wonderful moment of intimacy, where he said he didn't feel his boss trusted him. I empathised: 'how do you feel?' Uncomfortable, disappointing ... Then there was a pause, after which he flipped into humour. I said: 'And we've just had one of those moments again, haven't we? And we've lost something into that.'

He asked: 'How did you learn not to "laugh it away"?'

I described my personal experiences with "being in a group": group therapy, group processes, etc., learning to share my emotion without humour / minimising it / brushing it aside / parodying it ... This is not easy. It takes time to learn.

We ended by him considering bringing these feelings about trust of his boss into his management team.

Our relationship shifted:

• He shared more than before.
• He took a risk because he knows I also work with that boss, so it must be difficult telling me.

## CM30

Unusual. A coachee was going through an exploration; he became very resentful, uncooperative, felt challenged.

I explained, and he became personally offensive.

It felt very uncomfortable. I became nervous of confronting.

We went to more valuable territory. I could work with him – it was more counselling than coaching.

It threw up a lot for me.

A negative feeling for both of us.

The organisation are now engaging with him, with delicacy. We are all concerned about confidentiality, as he is a very high-level manager. We are all working together.

## CM31

It was a group exploration of 360-degrees feedback. Individuals were senior managers from the same organisation. This was part of a three-day programme.

I facilitated: took care of management of feedback and division of "airtime".

It was an all-male group.

I felt threatened by one participant; someone projecting things onto me.

On the last day of the programme there was an opportunity for one-to-one closure. Participants could elect 30 minutes with me, which the same participant did.

He told me he had killed two women in his life (with no regrets), and that he had wanted to kill me.

He clearly felt incredibly offended as the 360 did not match his own ego-identification.

I said 'that must have been life-changing, thank you for sharing it with me.' I did not want to be there, so went for closure.

It was a confidential conversation, I did not want to take it any further.

I started to shake immediately after the conversation.

## CM32

Request for access to coachee notes, 5.5 years after a coaching session – to raise a grievance procedure against the employer.

I spoke with the associate that had originally contracted the work. I could not speak to the client organisation, because they were advised by their lawyers not to do so. I spoke with my supervisor, the national association for counselling professionals, my professional indemnity insurance, and raised it at supervision training.

I was told that as long as this was an informal request I wasn't required to give the notes.

Classical dilemma: my sympathy was with him, but my formal allegiance was to the organisation. Moreover, I wrote things in the notes that I would not want anyone to read.

The court case was in February and fortunately I wasn't called, but the case is still pending and there is another court case where I could become a witness.

## CM33

Boundary work. I was working with a client in private practice: career coaching. It became more psychotherapeutical than career-oriented. Did we need a tighter coaching contract – or a psychotherapeutical contract? We decided for the latter, but then, six weeks into the psychotherapeutical work, the client became uncomfortable and wanted to go back.

It was a difficult review session. The client became defensive, questioning the contract, blaming me. I could not work with the client's resistance, precisely because he was requesting a shift back. And he was "resisting resistance". He wanted solutions / outcomes / change. We got stuck.

I referred back to someone for 'making choices' and 'actions'. But I felt unhappy, exposed and had a big concern, as this client was a lawyer.

It got started, then stopped. I felt uncomfortable when I had to ask him several times to leave. I felt physically threatened, caught in a space. I had a strong internal reaction.

## CM34

An executive had been referred by his HR director. He seemed to be willing to be coached.

But when I met him, he was quite resistant and aggressive.

Almost belligerently, he asked 'So, what are your qualifications?'

I knew this would be a key moment and my response mattered.

I said: it must be quite frightening to be here. I'm not even sure if you want to be here. Let's spend a bit of time to look at why it seems to be difficult.

He kept on repeating his challenge, until he said 'I really don't want to be here'.

I think giving those professional qualifications would have been missing the point, really.

We had ten successful sessions. He was actually quite depressed. He told me later he didn't like this at all, it shocked him (the word he used was "frightening"). It was important for me to hold my own. It was critical in terms of the way we related.

Another critical moment came later in the same session, when I said: 'You find it difficult to deal with emotions'. He was shocked, but remained intellectually curious, and that was perhaps what brought him back for another session.

## CM35

She had taken over as an office manager, her first managerial role. Things went pear shaped, they ostracised her.

At the lowest point, she cried 'I've had enough. I can't take more. I have to leave.'

I said: 'Don't. Stay with me on this. You can see this through. If you leave now, it will be such a journey back.' Then for a little while (six to eight weeks) I directed her life, with very simple strategies. Teaching emotional distance, emotional resilience, to keep things in perspective.

I was very directive.

It was a decisive period for her, otherwise it would have remained a background phantom in her life.

It worked out incredibly well. There were repair jobs, particularly with her own boss, and then the team (team development).

Now she was recently headhunted for a new job, which she's just started.

### CM36

It is related to the way in which I had been introduced to the coachee by another coach who had worked with this person in both individual and group settings. The coachee worked for an organisation which was new to me. I met with the coachee's manager, and she outlined her and the organisation's reasons for this person being coached. I was "accepted" by the manager and arranged my first meeting with the coachee. My concern or challenge was about the different levels of information I had received about the coachee from the previous coach and the coachee's manager. My dilemma was about to what extent I should share this information with the coachee? The information differed from and contradicted what the coachee shared with me first hand.

I took it to both individual and group supervision.

After supervision (in the next meeting) I suggested we explore via an "empty chair" to talk openly and objectively within the coaching relationship "with" his manager about the issues. He was not open to this, but we did have an open conversation addressing his feelings about his manager. We identified that something had "shifted", and the manager was now more reflective and appreciative of him and what he was doing. We recognised that he was stylistically different from his manager and that the manager, at least in part, wanted him to be like her.

I offered, as always, the option of a 360 or other psychometric input, to which he was reluctant. I felt he was resistant. My way of doing 360 would be phoning up his nominated colleagues and exploring with them on the phone his strengths and development needs as they saw them. Instead we re-visited an "old" 360 instrument that was built round a set competency framework, with little if any qualitative comments. It proved a little useful at best.

### CM37

In May. It was a further education context; she was a head of department, facing challenges with reorganisation. She came from a black minority ethnic and was coping with quite difficult personal issues, abuse in her past. The contract was for a set number of hours. Though this was not part of the contract, it was having an effect on her as an individual and her ability to cope with change. Difficult work context and personal context. I could deal with it because of my background but it was not congruent with the contract. It was not practical for me to take her on as a private coachee. She chose me because she saw I was a qualified psychotherapist. I am still helping her manage in her context. Because I work as a psychotherapist, for me there was not a dilemma. I could have said I would take on the therapy; I have done in the past. My dilemma seems obvious ... Would I say yes to someone in great need? Momentarily I may have done but it was not appropriate because of the contract. I suggested where she might go, given where she lives. I helped her manage the effect of this revelation on her private life, as her team helped her manage herself as a person.

### CM38

June 2006. Woman, a very senior European manager in a FTSE 100 company. I had worked there, she came back, I had done some work with her early in the year. I am working with the individual and she is confident I will often ask the management or organisation to set successful criteria for the coaching. She wanted to know if I would work with someone else and with her. Someone who worked with her regularly and was fighting with an ex-husband who was appearing in her dreams. I had done quite a lot of work on personal development and feelings of shame. She sees guardian angels and guides. I said I would work with her. 'I think you will be able to keep your boundaries,' said the first coachee.

Five to six weeks before my first appointment with the second coachee, I took the issue to two forms of supervision. I was warned that she was becoming psychotic. She wasn't.

In supervision, I asked for any thoughts on how they might approach it. They suggested co-coaching and monthly supervision. How to include guides and guardian angels in the work? I was thinking this was a very interesting situation (but some of my co-coaching people thought I was mad to consider working with her). I suppose it was a bit of a challenge – I had not worked with guides and guardian angels before. Very odd situation. Not a usual situation. Not something I've met before; how to work with someone inside their beliefs and view of the world.

The outcome was that I did work with her. She chose to work with the dreams about the ex-husband and asked advice from guides, while I did something but not through them. I gave her the choice of how we might do it – what did she think the test was? She gave me another dream to work with – it was a very metaphorical way of working. But what we have done worked.

## CM39

I was asked by my Associate organisation to provide "coaching support" for a senior manager. The Associate organisation had "no input agenda", which was very unusual for them. They said the coachee had 'personal issues'. This rang alarm bells for me. When I met the coachee and began to explore potential ways to work together and boundaries, we found that there were four main areas. These were 1) phobias, which had not yet been addressed, 2) a health issue, 3) a relationship issue and 4) a work-life issue. She worked long hours and said 'there is nothing I can do about it' and 'I have no choice'. I was left with a concern for the coachee's overall health.

This was as far as we reached in the first two hours I allowed her to tell her story.

Post-supervision, we explored boundaries and agenda. I gave her pen and paper and asked her to draw a picture of the areas we had described in the first meeting. We explored each in turn. With the phobias, we explored together the different therapies available so that she could make an informed choice. The relationship issue we decided was "off-limits" for our work. We decided to work on the work-life issue and explore her "self-defeating patterns" which would in turn, we felt, address her health issue in a kind of cascading fashion.

We are still working together, meeting every two months or so, until March next year.

## CM40

Similar brief from the same Associate organisation as before (asked by my Associate organisation to provide "coaching support" for a senior manager). The Associate organisation had "no input agenda", which was again very unusual for them. They said the coachee had 'personal issues'. This was a very senior manager with a terrible work-life balance. He told his story for two hours, and mentioned the suicide of a close relative and the pressures this had brought. I thought to myself 'has he thought about suicide in his present circumstances?' This came from the "Suicide and Sudden Death in the Workplace" workshop. In the end, I asked him 'What sort of thoughts are you having?' and then explored if he had thought about suicide. He said no, as he was married with two children. I was reassured and yet I did still had some lingering doubts.

As a result of the workshop, I had courage to explore the suicide question.

The coaching is ongoing; we are meeting once a fortnight for another four months.

## CM41

Traumatic incident outside the organisation. Significantly affected the coachee and the organisation. Coachee didn't express emotions in the session, but the coach cried. Only then did the coachee cry. Coach was angry with herself for crying in the session in front of the coachee.

Took it to supervision.

Carrying on with the coachee, even as she changes organisation and her role.

## CM42

From a personal and organisational basis, and from my psychotherapeutic background, I always take a personal history and inventory of the coachee's life. This can feel invasive, especially if they are not expecting it. This is something around contracting and boundaries. With this coachee, we got into his stuff, which was about work challenges over the last ten years and his level of confidence. The critical moment was how quickly this became the focus. It seems he always wanted to talk about it, and here was a forum where he could talk about it.

I simply "minded" and allowed him to talk.

Post-supervision and in the second session, I explored and challenged the physicality of his confidence issue, namely his stooping as a person and his sloped shoulders. The positive nature of the first meeting helped me express this in a powerful way.

He wanted a global job in this extroverted, USA entertainment organisation, and he needed to believe in himself, 'stand up tall' and project himself in a positive way.

We are still in an ongoing coaching relationship.

## CM43

The coachee's goal was around promotion and her needing to articulate and take ownership of her part in the promotion process. Her organisation required people to 'blow their own trumpet' as they went for interviews, and she needed to articulate herself more effectively if she was to make progress. In taking the history, I identified the critical incident: giving positive strokes about what and how she had progressed in her career. She left school at 15, and only achieved modest qualifications late in her life. She would say 'I think other people think I am not qualified' as she recognised that the other contenders had MBAs or similar. We explored how she had achieved so much without those things (MBAs, etc.) and as such that may not be important to the role. She has value and worth as she is.

In the second session, we looked at the job description and saw that it had an MBA as a minimum requirement, which she did not have. We reflected together on the fact that she doesn't need one, and explored the question: Does she really believe she has enough to go forward?

It is now our seventh session, and we always refer back to that fundamental belief in herself. She subsequently secured the role and also lobbied for a higher salary based on her new sense of self-respect, value and worth.

### CM44

The coachee was avoiding strategic issues around his own personal development. He took refuge in the complex details of daily work. I found myself "angling" him to-wards his personal strategic development. His diversion was around encouraging his team to take a strategic objective. It got to the point where he would explain this team need very explicitly. I played this back to him and there was an "Oh, I see" moment. I had allowed him to 'talk about what he wanted to talk about' and had seen a parallel in his story which I played back. It was an 'incident' because of the 'economy' of it.

I let things run with the energy the coachee had for the work, and then made an increased connection.

### CM45

The coachee had come with an agenda from elsewhere (Business Health Check via Business Link who had 'prescribed' coaching and awarded a grant to pay for it). The issue was around his personality and preferences, and I saw him over a period of six months. He had a 'determined avoidance' to face his issues, spending time behind his desk, on the phone, on his computer, etc. His argument was: if coaching is right for me, then it will work; if it is not right for me, then it won't work.

In the first meeting, I was at a loss and 'felt bad' about what was happening be-tween us and in me. In the post-supervision session, I saw it as part of the issue and not (just) how he dealt with me. I reflected to him how he was operating, and gave him specific requests he should follow through on.

In the end, he decided not to proceed with 'our' strategy. He was looking for a specific strategy which wasn't happening. I felt that this was 'par for the course' and, upon reflection, the signs were there at the beginning. I can now see structurally how it all came about.

### CM46

A director of an organisation who had received 360-degree feedback and had had an appraisal interview. As an outcome, development needs were identified and he received some personal coaching around his management style, people management and how he managed himself. In relationship to supporting individuals and the way he obtained work and gave feedback to his staff and peers. This was critical because, as things developed, the issue was about approval. We had an hour-and-a-half "chemistry meeting" to explore whether we could work or not work together. I was left thinking I could work with him together, but he was withholding a critical piece of information. So the question was would he disclose or not and would I need to assist him? What told me this? We had checked out the issues of confidentiality, trust and rapport and, in response, he had asked questions around 'would I work with the whole of him or just the business part?'. He went out for a cigarette twice in 20 minutes and asked detailed critical questions around my website pointing to the 'personal part'. He disclosed that he wanted to speak about something he had not told anyone else; his body language showed that something was worrying him. We started off negotiating a contract for 12 sessions in the year, but he was a little resistant and in the end we agreed six sessions. He immediately put the six sessions in his diary, which was encouraging for me.

I took it to the next supervision session.

We have now finished the sixth session and have agreed to re-contact in January to explore potential ways forward.

## CM47

I was asked by an organisation to coach a senior leader. In the "chemistry meeting" with the individual, we identified his issues as cultural identity, race and the ability to be seen by his colleagues and his difficulties in communicating his own messages. It went well and we contracted for six sessions. Just before the first session, his boss, who was supportive of the coaching, moved on and the new boss saw no need and no funds in the budget for coaching. This left us with a move to 'personal coaching', i.e. with the coachee paying from his own finances. This meant we reduced both the planned time together and the number of sessions, and I offered a different rate for the coaching. I was now delivering the invoices to the individual and then chasing payment as he was regularly later than the 14 days. This created a different relationship. There was a different professional element: I am used to working with the individual and not dealing with the financial arrangements (like the Psychotherapy model), but now I am invoicing the individual at each session with cancellation charges, and at what location will we work together? Sessions were delayed as he felt 'not ready for a session yet', with the result that three months of coaching became nine months of coaching and eight sessions became five sessions. This was critical because he was questioning and talking about the value of coaching, I was challenging myself about my value as a person and as a coach, and all this was happening in the midst of a chaos where he wasn't paying his bills with me and he had some other outstanding petty cash issues that were two years old.

We explored issues of trust and (dis)honesty by my 'mirroring' to him what was going on between us in our coaching relationship as a small picture of some of his wider life challenges. He was very much task-driven and not people-driven.

He forgot about a session, which I read as part of his "visibility" issue that he had raised earlier. He cancelled a session and queried the coaching as 'value for money', when I explained our agreement on cancellation fees. He got angry and accused me of being unreasonable – we ended up having a short coaching session on the phone and he paid half the cancellation fee. He then chose to end our contract because of his 'budget'. In our last session last week, he said he had received a number of 'golden nuggets' from me in the form of scripts and other 'gifts', and now needed time to integrate these ideas into his life. He suggested 'meeting for lunch' which I saw as signifying the end of our coaching relationship. I aim to work with clear boundaries

## CM48

At the beginning of the summer, HR woman in Africa. We have some face to face but mainly telephone contact. She has difficulty with work relationships. In the session she is full of ambivalence about what she wanted help with; she also makes odd mixed-message comments like 'I don't want to say anything I will regret'. I ended feeling de-skilled and failing. I wondered, is this a one-off or is this how she makes everyone feel?

I didn't want to talk on the phone so sent an email saying how the coachee had made me feel and suggesting that she find out from her colleagues if that's how she makes them feel. At first the woman was very angry. Then she went and checked with her colleagues and got the feedback that yes, others felt the same. Ultimately the coachee found it very useful.

## CM49

About 12 months ago, a woman coachee had decided to leave her firm (later it emerged she was fired) and wanted coaching for next steps. During the session, she mentioned a friend who might help her find a job in her own firm; the friend's baby had died and the coachee had been supportive and said she thought the friend would remember her because she had been nice. The coach was shocked at the apparent calculating use of others, especially after a deceased child. She did nothing and said nothing. She felt too shocked; anxious about how to say something so accusing. Wondered if she was being too judgemental. The coach thinks the coachee picked up on her sense of disapproval, as she left and didn't return.

# Appendix C: Critical moments of coachees

## Overview with a selection of coachee moments

### Examples of the 59 critical moments of coaching clients

1 'Realisation that my future career progression was in my own hands, and that I have the ability to influence its direction and also the ability to say "no" if my aspirations don't match those of the company.'

2 'The realisation at the beginning of my coaching that I was more than capable of writing plans and strategies which in turn helped me realise I was very capable of being successful in the new position I had been promoted to. It was critical because it gave me the confidence and belief in myself and my strategies, which in turn made the presentation of the strategies to my team very powerful.'

3 'I had a tense moment which was both significant and exciting when after a lengthy communication with my coach I came to the realisation I had to make a significant change to the structure of my team, which would entail having to make a very difficult decision which would negatively affect one person but positively affect the rest of my team and the company as a whole.'

4 'A telephone coaching session close to a bereavement in which the coach took me into a visualisation to look into the future as to how I saw myself in say 5–10 years time. It was a tense and distressing experience as all I could see was coloured by the powerful experience of sitting in the home of the person who had just died and seeing myself in the same position – living and dying alone. Now there is nothing bad about either as the individual led a creative, independent life, but the session brought me to tears such that it was difficult to continue. The coach was unsure where to take this and soon after I decided not to pursue further sessions with the coach. This was a critical moment because it brought into question the experience of the coach and clearly my emotional readiness for that type of exercise.'

5 'It was related to my confronting a very challenging issue and both being very concerned about my ability to deal with it and also the sense of liberation I felt to be able to navigate my way to a resolution. It was very charged and quite emotional as I had to face up to an issue that in the past I have chosen to avoid, but the process of expressing it verbally helped enormously, coupled with the positive and supportive environment created by my coach.'

6 'Something that had been holding me back suddenly seemed such an easy thing to overcome. My fear, of several things, was stopping me.'

7 'The moment was the realisation that there is a point that a person will not step or move beyond. My particular case centred on the lack of support of my line manager taking specific action to report inappropriate behaviour of a project partner. From then on I realised the limits to my line manager.'

8 'I would describe the critical moment as "significant" in that it was a moment that really enabled me to clearly visualise the situation I was in (by relating it to disembarking from a small rowing boat!), and through the visualisation, to understand the issue I was creating by not focusing 100% on my goal (but instead hesitating between two options).'

9  'Very briefly there was a glimpse into how other people view me as a business person – and of course they see a quite different view than one sees of oneself. Knowing what they see allows a very different interaction with them, of course, and it made be behave (in certain circumstances) in a completely different way.'

10 'Simply the recognition (realisation) that I had successfully evolved to a competent (not necessarily expert) manager. It was at a time when I had been asking quite challenging questions of myself in terms of career and life decisions and my coach (a retired business director) encouraged me to look at what I had achieved and what that meant in terms of potential for the future. Through the conversation it became clear that while I might not have recognised it consciously, I had accrued a significant amount of management experience and competence through quite varied and broad activities and could therefore justifiably call myself (generically) a manager.'

11 'When asked by my coach to consider what would happen to my newly created unit if key people left and what effect that would have on me. It had never occurred to me before that this team I had spent time putting together would want to do anything other than stay! The same day one of my staff told me they have been approached by someone else about a job. I have now started to look at the current unit structure as less of a "sacred cow" and to think about options for different, more flexible models and about how I would fill short term gaps.'

12 'In solving a problem that was causing some doubt in my ability. A breakthrough in understanding that my approach to this situation was based on previous experience and that an alternative was out there which could stretch me as an individual and achieve better long-term results. This gave greater confidence in tackling other issues without a preset agenda.'

13 'When working with a "new ventures development" organisation I worked closely with a very experienced businessman who had been assigned as a mentor. In putting together a business plan for a new product my company wished to launch I would spend some time reviewing objectives and progress with him. In this particular case the "critical moment" was the understanding of what would work as a business venture. What works is an idea; a service or an offering which has value must be simple to communicate if it is going to succeed. If it cannot be simply expressed, if the venture takes a lot of time and thought to write down in an executive summary, then it is likely to fail. In this case my particular idea was just taking me too long to express in the business plan and therefore was doomed to failure unless there was another way of packaging the product or bundling it with other services.'

14 'A critical moment for me was in my second coaching relationship. My coach had done a note of our discussions including some things which I did not want shared with a third party. He sent the notes of the discussions to me and copied in his own coach. He did not know I rather had not shared that issue, so did not ask my permission ahead of time. I considered ending the relationship after this, but later relented.'

15 Through an awareness exercise looking at plusses and minuses of my current role I became aware of critical factors that I had taken for granted about my role. Once I became aware of them and discussed their importance I realised that the decision I was just about to take was the wrong one.'

16 'The most recent of these was this week. It was like a kind of "chiropractic click". I had been struggling with having meaningful "value" conversations with my coachees. Through the coaching I had realised that I had been "unhelpfully" focusing on getting the business rather than helping the coachee. The "click" came about when I was really challenged on my primary intention when I said it was to help the coachee. Bringing this into my consciousness allowed my rational brain to see that this will build trust with the coachee and business will more naturally flow as a strong relationship develops. Also, if it doesn't, it is more likely to be because they do not need my help rather than my not being able to help if things were different. That's fine with me too as I only want to work on work that needs to be done. This insight is foundational to many aspects of my work at present and I have a sense of relief now.'

17 'Sorting why I was finding it hard to think about and plan for an event in a positive way, even though it was one I would normally look forward to. What made the moment significant was that through the use of metaphor I was able to recognise an unhelpful pattern to my experience which was connected to previous events and people in my life. As a consequence I was able to go on and "de-couple" these for the future. And the event was great!'

18 'Following a discussion on my response to an individual that I was having extreme difficulties managing, it became clear to me that my response was one that I had been repeating throughout my career. Changing that one response has changed my entire management style over time. The results have been very tangible.'

19 'Whenever the coach asked questions which touched issues, which were critical, unpleasant or pleasant to me and were relative near to the core of my personality.'

20 'It was when my coach directly challenged me to be bolder and give more of myself as a management team member. "I'm sure you have more to give to xxx." I had been reflecting on this for a while and his challenge was what was needed. The timing was right.'

21 'Another one was when I was wrestling with how to end a relationship, and my coach asked a very pertinent question that I had not thought to ask myself, and it made me go deep into myself and reflect. She asked "what do endings mean to you?" I may have been hiding it through my recent bereavement.'

22 'Facing up to moments of truth, realisation that I could have handled situations differently. One time I was being badly treated (verging on bullying?) by a senior peer and it was exciting to be able to explore with an impartial and trusted 'other' options available. I executed the planned course of action and gained help to mastermind each of the next steps – an exhilarating opportunity to "not feel alone" and have guidance to step outside of this situation (unemotionally) to consider the risk/options. Being able to speak with my coach over the phone for 10 minutes just to gather my thoughts and gain perspective has been a critical aspect of my development.'

23 Years later another coach really "gave me a piece of her mind". I was close to a heavy burn-out and had not realised it myself then, but still identified with being very busy and important. After trying many things and ways of getting to the point with me she spoke more than frankly and engaged. During that session we

also made a list covering seven areas of (my) life which indicated the focus and attention that went (or did not go) into the special areas. This list underlined her words quite impressively and the results of our session kind of shocked me. After the session I really changed many things in my life and until today several findings of this session have become part of my everyday life. Still the "critical" thing about it was not the list or visualisation, but her very clear words and her absolutely unvarnished opinion.

24  'I listened to myself describe a reason why I hadn't done something and realised that there was no factual basis for it at all and in fact it was a deeply flawed way of thinking. It was critical because it made me understand that in fact I can be very good at making excuses for inaction and that in turn made me realise that that has always been the case for me. I suppose though that it will only be truly critical if I use it to make changes to my approach. It felt strange and almost as though time had slowed down while I thought this through, although actually it probably was just a moment!'

25  'Yes, I have had that "critical moment" as described above, although I referred to it as the moment "I saw the path clear". It was so profound; I wanted to end the session immediately so I could take action. I specifically remember that the issue I wanted to deal with appeared not to have any solution, and even to the point of me being unable to imagine a beginning to resolve the issue. When questioned about advice I might offer to someone in a similar situation, or what advice I would give to a colleague who had posed a similar question to me, it was after a moment or two completely obvious, and according to my coach I then spoke freely for 20 minutes, offering up multiple suggestions. This moment was critical, as from then onwards I was able to put a plan together which I later used to re- solve the issue.'

26  I can recall two such moments. One involved making a connection between an aspect of my professional behaviour as a manager and my personal emotional profile, i.e. recognising how a cause of my personal anxiety was prompting a specific (unhelpful) approach to people I managed.'

27  'The second was recognising the significance of a simple analysis of how I spent my time which helped me understand why I was making limited progress on im- portant objectives.'

28  'Probably the moment of naming my constant conflict with my boss and the real- isation of my repetitive nature of dealing with it by reinforcement and substanti- ating my opinion rather than finding a way to deal with it.'

## Examples of "no" responses

29  'No, more of a feeling of being generally comfortable with the concepts, and an understanding of the position at the time. Not a *eureka* moment but a steady gradual realisation.'

30  'No, that is why I stopped the process after four sessions. I felt that through the coaching (and the little "tasks" I was given by the coach) the pressure was rather increasing than decreasing ...'.

31  'No, I have never felt exhilarated by anything that happened in a coaching ses- sion, it was more a sense of support. I certainly haven't crossed any critical barri- ers in such sessions, although I have only had a few.'

32  'Ah, how I was looking for those critical moments! If they did happen, they have alas now escaped my consciousness. On reflection, for all my coaching, I think any benefits stemmed from the amalgamation of the various talks, discussions and training I undertook.'

33  'I cannot say that I have had a critical moment. There have been occasions when there is a gradual realisation which when further observed, has contributed to making a change. These can be inside or outside of a coaching experience, or through mentoring, peer mentoring or timely, clear, appropriate feedback.'

34  'No, all my coaching experiences have been vague and not very fulfilling.'

The phone interviews gave more background detail for some of the critical moments, and more understanding for the absence of critical moments in other submissions. Each of the three interviewees who had experienced no critical moments reported positive experiences of coaching. They all felt that their coaching had been useful in helping them tackle issues and problems in their work roles. They did not experience an "abrupt" or "sudden" moment of insight or learning. Instead, they each reported that they experienced a gradual process of insight relating to their issues during the coaching process. They each felt that upon reflection they had learned something about themselves as a result of the coaching experience. See examples 29, 31 and 33, above.

# Appendix D: Comparing critical moments of coaches and coachees

## D.1 Overview with examples of coach-coachee moments from shared sessions

### Examples of the 86 critical moments from coachee and coach interviews

To help the reader gain a better connection with the full dataset we have chosen 15 vignettes from the 86 critical-moment descriptions. We have chosen this dataset purposefully, to give an indication of the range of data and also to show two occasions where coach and coachee comment on the same moment in the session (the pairs 3co9-3cl10 and 14co51-14cl52). Rather than showing a random selection here, we have deliberately chosen a more meaningful and engaging range of vignettes. The numbering of these vignettes follows the chronological order of the interviews, i.e. conversation number, 'co' for 'coach moment' and 'cl' for 'client moment', and then critical moment number. We have not edited these fragments. These are just 1,166 words; the full dataset is over 27,000 words long.

[1cl2] 'I suppose really for me it's through the process of discussion it's the realisation on my part that there's something that I have to do. So it's the sort of the processes of opening my eyes to you know, ooh hang on there's something I need to do here that you know wouldn't otherwise. So the you know it's the what helps me realise is the point that I get the light bulbs going off to like, hey hang on why haven't I thought about this?'

[1cl4] 'So the feeling for me is really say its sort of a… it's a point that I recognise that there's something that's needed. It's sort of highlighting it. So it's almost a feeling of surprise and realisation around there's something there that I'm able to see it's just that I haven't previously been able to.'

[3co9] 'And that was the tipping point I think, when he recognised that he could use one thing to do the other, he thinks in a very linear way. And he was thinking about I've got to do the projects, I've got to be more approachable but really by linking the two together he was able to see that … I think he recognised that actually I can do both of these together and one will help the other. And that was the… that was the… the key I think. It was partly his erm… he was clearly doing some visualising sitting there in thought, looking up at the ceiling. So erm… And a period of silence after when he said "erm yeah I hadn't thought of looking at it like that." Erm what else did he say? "I think I've crossed a bridge," that's what he said.'

[3cl10] 'I'd written it down as an action to do, which is kind of respective of my style. It's because it's… I describe it as opening my eyes to a blind spot really it's easy with hindsight to say that's a good way of approaching it but prior to the conversation or prior to today I would not have thought of trying to do the project in that particular direction. So it's a change in direction to what I would have done otherwise.'

[4co13] 'He was asking me to raise an issue outside of the coaching relationship. Erm you know to show I was sort of agreeing with him a form of words that he was…

that he would be happy with, for me to sort of try and get something fed back into the organisation that he thought was important. So that was quite an important... err an interesting part of the conversation. Erm well this was an issue about the person's boss... erm and the person's boss is being coached by erm one of my colleagues... so is it was a sort of a "can you use your influence with the other coach?"'

[5co17] 'Er, he started to make notes... actually he started to make notes and started to get more animated in how he was talking about it.'

[5co19] 'That he began drawing on my pad. And the adult to adult was his meeting. The meetings that he controlled. That was his meeting. The big circle was his meeting.'

[6co23] 'He sat back and thought about it rather than being accused by it.'

[8cl30] 'I think the key moment might have been that I asked him what he felt about the work we'd been doing and he said that he was pleased that the report he'd done had led to substantial change and efficiencies and he seemed to take some pleasure in it. (...) I think it was good to hear that he'd taken some pleasure from it himself and felt that... taken some pleasure out of the fact that he'd been effective.'

[9cl32] 'It's basically stating the obvious, but I didn't see it, it was staring me right in the face.'

[14co51] 'It was a bit odd the way that we started off because he thought that he'd sent me some information and I... I'm perfect you see... I knew that I was thinking, I did check all of my emails but I don't recollect what you've sent me you know and I looked through I'm sure I printed everything off that folk had sent me. So we had a kind of a twenty-minute forage around whether we could find this information. So it's kind of like erm, it felt like a weird start to the session and I did say to him given that we haven't got the information can you talk to me about what was important to you and what you'd written through and we can cover it here and now. (...) So it's really important to him about appearances and again being professional, doing the right thing, you know doing what he says he's going to do. So it was a real... I was really noticing how I was getting hooked into, well I haven't got the information you know we're looking on computers, I was searching my Blackberry thinking this is bizarre really because we don't need it. So it was this bizarre start to him (...) It really linked into how he wants to get things done and wants to get things right and look good to other people. That's really, really important to him. Erm, so links from that.'

[14cl52] 'It's important that we got sorted today, the mix up we had at the beginning so we knew where we were going. That was important and I must say within two or three minutes we had it sorted. We realised there'd been a mistake and agreed appropriate action and it got resolved very easily. It wasn't confrontational in any way, don't think that, just a mix up but a few negotiation skills on both our parts we could resolve it, so we didn't lose anything out of those five minutes of the hour and a half session, so it was very important that we could speak our way round it to recover the situation.'

[21cl83] 'It was really the characterisation. It was just kind of that makes perfect sense to me. I've been thinking, reflecting about this at various levels for a long time. Occasionally you have those moments of realisation, you forget them and then when you're reminded it not only provides clarity it provides comfort to the person who's being coached.'

[21co84] 'My hunch is it's probably more important to my coachee than it was to me. He can tell you for himself but my hunch was that was new and interesting information that he was quite intrigued by.'

[21co86] 'I was surprised. So I suppose I was monitoring my own reactions and my own reactions were well that feels like something important and new so I guess it felt like it meant something. Whether it's just because I was worried I missed it I don't know but it was something about this is new and feels significant. My coachee was very animated in talking about it.'

## D.2 Overview of critical moments from the coachee/coach case study

In this section we will give the full case study in the words of coachee and coach, copied verbatim from the original critical-moment descriptions, with only a few identifying details changed or omitted in the text.

| Session 1: Coachee critical moments | Session 1: Coach critical moments |
|---|---|
| There were two critical moments for me in this session:<br>The first critical moment for me was introducing the topics that could be discussed in the coaching as a whole and this session in particular. I was very unsure of what was expected of me in the situation, and since there was hardly any reaction from the coach's side, I felt very insecure if these were the "right" topics. I also felt like they were a bit "unimportant" compared to what the coach probably usually talked about in his sessions with other coachees. It turned out that one of the topics I introduced was not really useful for coaching at that moment, which was a good insight already. Furthermore, it felt extremely strange to me to introduce such personal issues to someone who is pretty much a stranger to me.<br>The second critical moment was something the coach reflected to me. I had been talking about career options quite a bit at that point, and the coach then reflected to me that he felt like I really knew what I was striving for and what goals I wanted to and didn't want to achieve. This wasn't at all what was going on inside of me, because I felt like I was ruminating quite a bit about the options I had. It was very insightful to get the feedback that I didn't make this impression on someone else, but actually the opposite. | I am struck by how easy it is for me in going back to coaching sessions thinking about what was critical, to focus on the consequences of what I have just said: the *response* of the coachee, or even, if I am brutally honest, the quality of my own intervention. To put it more succinctly: I think my memory of sessions is very biased towards what *I* said and what *I* thought during the session. I should try to practise more "trial identification" (Casement, 2002) in registering what the coachee is saying or doing when things are critical.<br>The critical moments in this first session were around moments that I almost "come too close". I experienced a professional, ambitious, reflective "persona" in front of me. This Christiane would like to receive reflections on her thesis and her career. Underneath I experience more anxiety, particularly around "will you not come too close?" Once I felt provoked to comment on this, and then I said "the face you pull" which is an uncharacteristically strong expression which I immediately regretted. |

**Phenomenological analysis of the critical-moment descriptions**: Coach and coachee are clearly still finding their feet with the new arrangement. The coachee is thinking about what is expected of her, the coach seems self-aware in his focus on how he is biased in writing up his critical moments. The coach is using some jargon (e.g. "trial identification"). The coachee has two critical moments, the coach mentions one. For the coachee there seems to be some anxiety around beginning in the coaching, for the coach around coming too close. The coachee achieves insight through feedback on how she comes across.

| Session 2: Coachee critical moments | Session 2: Coach critical moments |
|---|---|
| The beginning of the session was a critical moment for me. Neither the coach nor I started the conversation at first, so I felt under pressure to set the agenda for the session. I would have liked to avoid deciding what we were going to talk about, because I trusted the coach to decide which topics we had discussed in the previous session were worth continue talking about. Although I know it's probably the better approach to let the coachee decide on the agenda, the silence still made me feel uncomfortable and insecure whether I would raise the right topics. Another critical moment for me occurred when the coach reflected back and interpreted something I had said: I mentioned that I was considering applying at a consultancy because I would feel like it would be a good reference in my CV and thus help my career in the longer run. He replied that I thus wanted to be a "Big Player" in business (or a similar expression). I had never seen myself striving to be a "Big Player" anywhere, so I felt almost offended by the comment. However, I was glad that he reflected back to me what impression my words had made on him, although I hadn't intended to do so. It made me self-reflect on the question why I would say that, and if maybe it wasn't all that far away from the truth after all. | I think there were two or three times in this session when Christiane said "that is a good question" so I suppose those are indications of something critical happening. I cannot remember any longer when these moments occurred, exactly. Also when I checked where we were, saying "it is now halfway through the session, how is it going", she said "insightful" and I think that was genuinely meant. I was intrigued by a few paradoxes we discovered. Christiane seems at the same time very successful – in her peer group of MSc students – and young, i.e. inexperienced, so she feels she has to be bold and modest at the same time. There was another paradox about "being a loyal team player" (as in basketball) and "wanting to be different / distinct" (as in having other occupations from fellow students and highlighting her difference in that choice). We may be getting closer to where the ambivalence is. |

**Phenomenological analysis of the critical-moment descriptions**: The two moments from the coachee seem similar to those in the first session: the first suggesting some anxiety about what is expected of her or how she can lead this coaching relationship, the second showing some insight through feedback (or in this case a summary plus interpretation of the critical-moment descriptions) from the coach. The coachee also writes about the emotional (somewhat painful) impact of this learning process

("I felt almost offended… however, I was glad"). In this the coachee wrote about her ambivalence and it is striking that the coach mentions ambivalence as well.

Also in the comments of the coach there are some similarities with the first session. Again, the coach couches some of his language in jargon (e.g. "getting where the ambivalence is"). Following his own realisation after the first session that he is overly central to his own critical moments, he now tries to find something critical in the responses of his coachee, responses like "good question" and "insightful". There seems to be no identified critical moment for the coach.

| Session 3: Coachee critical moments | Session 3: Coach critical moments |
|---|---|
| I started out the session introducing a topic that we hadn't talked about in the previous session. It had to do with me finishing one stage of my life to go back to what I had previously done. When I started talking about it, I noticed how I became nervous, started blushing, my voice became shaky, and tears came to my eyes. I was surprised to notice those symptoms, because I hadn't been aware of the fact that the topic was an emotional one to me. This was definitely a critical moment for me. Talking to the coach about why this evoked such strong emotions inside me definitely made me realise that it had a more underlying reason that I hadn't been aware of. The initial emotional reactions just lead to a more rational understanding of the topic, which helped me to work through it with the coach. | I thought there were a lot of emotions around particularly at the beginning of the session. I saw red colour on your face. I thought you were just very grateful for the time you had had at one research project, very satisfied about what it gave you. I felt very moved at the beginning of the session. I may have misread the emotion. I regret I didn't ask you what it was about. I probably didn't dare asking and felt protective of the "bubble" or "bubbly feeling". I did not want to burst the bubble. |

**Phenomenological analysis of the critical-moment descriptions**: Both coachee and coach descriptions are much shorter than those for the previous two sessions. And they both point to exactly the same moment a few minutes into the session, an emotional moment that remained unexpressed verbally, but that had clearly touched both coach and coachee. Following the felt emotions, the coachee reports a critical moment that is of a different nature as in the previous sessions, a moment of "working through" with the help of reflection.

| Session 4: Coachee critical moments | Session 4: Coach critical moments |
|---|---|
| The critical moment of this session was a change in my perception of the relationship to the coach. While we were discussing, we proposed to me an interpretation of a situation which was less favourable to me, namely that I had felt some kind of jealousy. While I was first reluctant to discuss this option openly, | A session about competition and ambition, as related to the tasks you are engaged in and the layers of relationships that you need to manage. Very tough for you and I hope I haven't been too tough as a response. In fact, I felt very caring, careful and "parental". |

| | |
|---|---|
| I noticed that I had indeed built enough trust in my coach over the past few sessions that I was able to consider his idea and admit that he was right. I felt like this took the conversation a lot further and deepened the conversation as well as the relationship to the coach. It was a very honest conversation, and I was thankful that the coach had not been holding back, reluctant to express his interpretation of the situation. | Critical moments: (1) I did once feel the competition flaring up between the two of us as well. A difficult moment. It was in the beginning of the session when you related how you had mentioned some prominent consultancies that you are involved with. I then laughed rather loudly and you said "What? What? rather anxiously – upon which I said "Big Names. You dropped some 'Big Names' with them." I think you were again sensitive in the here and now, this time about my response to you. (2) I think it was a relief for you to hear from me that "yes you might be projecting out ambition and competition while you are also quite competitive yourself – and there is nothing wrong with that". You had pondered on how competitive you were and how much you were suppressing this. I think it was somehow better for you to acknowledge yourself as competitive, envious, desiring to impress, etc., rather than placing that in other people. Hopefully it will help you to take a bit of detachment (relax, smile) from this as a next step. I am wondering why I am writing in the second person to "you". I think it is because I am making these notes still within the session time, i.e. straight after the session ended prematurely after your phone ran out of battery. |

**Phenomenological analysis of the critical-moment descriptions:** This time the length of the writing of coachee and coach is dissimilar, with the coach writing a much longer piece. The coachee's critical moment is again of a different order, as it is more related to the relationship she experiences with the coach, which has enabled her to hear feedback. As before, open and frank feedback appears to lead to insight, or at least to a new perspective. Similarities are that both coachee and coach report a deepening of the relationship, which the coach seems to underline by continuing to write in the second person; and that coach and coachee apparently write about one critical moment that they both experienced: the acknowledging of competition and jealousy/envy. Again, there are hints of an emotional learning process for the coachee.

| Session 5: Coachee critical moments | Session 5: Coach critical moments |
|---|---|
| For me this coaching session involved two critical moments. The first moment occurred somewhere in the middle of the session. We had been talking about career options in the previous sessions, exploring what I was able to apply for after finishing my studies. I had been holding the assumption that I could do pretty much anything I wanted. However, prior to this session, I had been turned down for a workshop I had applied for. While I saw this as a "one-timer", something that had never happened to me and wouldn't happen again, the coach offered a different interpretation. He made me aware of the fact that by choosing a Research Master programme, I had limited my career opportunities. This was also an explanation of me procrastinating on my application for another position. I highly valued this new view on the matter, as it opened my eyes to something I probably simply didn't want to see before. The other critical moment occurred at the very end of the session. The coach had been a bit late for the session, and at the end of it he suggested that maybe there was a subconscious reason for him being late. This idea was a bit in line with what we had talked about during the session, that sometimes it is not obvious what underlying reasons for our actions are. Although I appreciated the coach's honesty in this particular moment, it also made me feel a bit uncomfortable. Was I a difficult coachee? Was I boring him during the sessions? I think hadn't this moment occurred at the very end of the session, it would have influenced the course of the session in a negative way, because it would have made me a bit more hesitant. | In spite of my being late I thought this was a really rich session, particularly thanks to your openness and willingness to hear quite challenging feedback. The first critical moment was obviously my being late, in particularly the moment when I discovered I was not simply going to be two minutes late (as I let you know), but I was going to be fifteen minutes late. I felt guilt, I also immediately asked myself why I was permitting myself such an infringement, a breaking of boundaries, when I would never allow myself to do that with a "real", i.e. "full fee paying" coachee. The second critical moment was obviously when I shared that with you at the end of our session, and I was vulnerable and questioned my own motives just like I had questioned yours. I wondered what you were making of that. There was another critical moment for me when I checked with you "how I can help" with regard to the two issues you introduced at the very beginning of the session. You said with regard to the first one, "I feel already helped a great deal, by recognising some of my own ambition and drive". That was such positive feedback, I felt the session was already a success even if it was still relatively early into the session. I did check towards the end whether we had really taken enough time for the first issue, and you reassured me again. |

**Phenomenological analysis of the critical-moment descriptions**: The session is clearly heavily influenced by a boundary infringement at the very beginning, even if a small one: "the coach was a bit late" in the words of the coachee. It shows us never to underestimate the effects of boundary issues in coaching. This one turns out to have major repercussions in the next two sessions as well (see below). Both coachee and coach critical moments refer to the lateness of the coach, although the coachee seems unaffected until the coach raises it later in the session. Again, in the first coachee critical moment a new perspective (a frank view from the coach) leads to insight. The second coachee critical moment builds on the theme of the deepening relationship from the previous session, showing how a coaching relationship is never a given, a fact, but that it is always evolving and changing, and that ruptures are never far off even in well-established coaching relationships. We see both coachee and coach wondering how they are coming across to the other, and we see the coach still affected by self-doubt even when receiving very positive feedback (his third critical moment).

| Session 6: Coachee critical moments | Session 6: Coach critical moments |
|---|---|
| The critical moment of the session occurred somewhere in the end of our session. Not much had happened on the topics that we had been discussing in previous sessions, so I didn't really "bring much" to the conversation. The coach noticed this as well and mentioned it to me. What followed was a very honest but difficult conversation. As mentioned in the critical-moment description of the last session, there had been a comment that made me quite conscious of my inferior role in the relationship. I had however not decided to address this. The coach offered the suggestion that this feeling of me being inferior, unimportant, or boring, probably was something that I experienced in other relationships as well. Unfortunately we weren't able to discuss this further, because we had reached the end of the session. However, I felt like it was a very honest moment. It made me realise that the coach noticed such underlying things as well. Although I found his interpretation a bit hurtful, I appreciated him noticing and mentioning it to me. I think it will probably help to discuss this in the following sessions. | This was a really tough session I think for both of us, certainly for me. The first really critical moment occurred when you said "I am just... unimportant. My work is... unimportant. I must be different from your other coachees, as I am 'just' a student. Coaching with me must be quite boring for you". You said these thoughts were triggered by me saying there may have been an unconscious reason on my part for my being late at our previous session. And you added that it felt like a rupture, then. Then for me there was a second critical moment when you said "I cannot pay you for the work" and in the same breath "This coaching is only for your research", implying the coaching was not really for you but rather for me and you wouldn't be able to afford it anyway. It felt like you were really angry with me, and like you were accusing me of being disinterested, or rather of being self-interested, and of not being able to keep you in mind or be interested in you. I remember I was so taken aback that I said things like "you are doing just fine", "this is not boring to me", and "it is wonderful that you are paying a charity for this work" (in other words, I was arguing back: "you *are* paying for this"). I got so wrapped up in defending the coaching that I wasn't coaching any more. I am really curious as to where this will take us next time. Hopefully you will learn something about your desperation and your anger. At the moment you will probably not feel you have learned anything. Another rupture. If I think back again I notice lots of other critical moments as well, before these two which occurred towards the end of the session. So these are earlier in the session: (1) How I gave you a tough challenge when I said you hadn't been very proactive regarding this session and perhaps you could be more proactive as well regarding the dependencies you are experiencing in your MSc-work. (2) How I felt self-doubt when contemplating if I should suggest finding rooms with a commercial assessment centre provider (which in the end I did – and it made little difference). I felt this would be too advisory to be coaching. |

**Phenomenological analysis of the critical-moment descriptions**: The session is still highly influenced by the boundary problems identified in the previous session, and by the various ways of mentally dealing with the "issue", independently by coach and coachee, to the point that we can infer that there was a rupture or a near-rupture in their work together during this session, with feelings of humiliation and anger on the side of the coachee, and of panic and embarrassment on the side of the coach. Both coachee and coach write this theme up as one big critical moment, to which the coach adds two others from earlier in the session. One is a hunch of some possible further "insight through feedback", and the other is a fairly common doubting process around whether or not to offer advice as a coach. Fairly typically, the advice when offered (as is also usually the case when not offered) makes very little difference.

| Session 7: Coachee critical moments | Session 7: Coach critical moments |
|---|---|
| The critical moment of this coaching session for me occurred when the coach decided to bring up the topic we had not been able to fully discuss in the previous session. The present session was going pretty well, there was a lot to discuss and I felt I was making progress. The coach could have decided to leave it to that, but he brought up what we had talked about in the end of our previous session, namely how I felt I was in an inferior role. We discussed how this might also translate to some of my other (working) relationships. I felt like this was probably the first time the coach had actually brought up a topic. I probably would not have done it myself because I didn't feel it was still relevant at that point, but I was thankful for him doing it. That way, I could reflect on what had happened in the previous session in a bit of a hindsight, which allowed me to see some parallels to other aspects of my life. | The session started very neutral but with slight misunderstandings between us and interruptions in both directions. I thought strong emotions would still be there. You chose to talk about some new challenges and successes in the areas of work and study.<br>One major critical moment for me was when I brought back the talk of "rupture" – and my experience of "rupture" – from the previous session. You said your notes were that it would be good to raise that again this time. The relief was palpable, both for you and for me, and I think you were genuinely grateful for having a fuller conversation touching on both developments in your work and our relationship. |

**Phenomenological analysis of the critical-moment descriptions**: The one critical moment mentioned by both is exactly the same for coach and coachee, and harks back to the boundary infringement identified two sessions previously, to the near-ruptures of the previous session. Both coachee and coach comment on how the decision of the coach to bring up the issue and their relationship again, makes a difference within the relationship and leads to new insight on parallel processes in other areas. Gratitude is mentioned by both coachee and coach.

| Session 8: Coachee critical moments | Session 8: Coach critical moments |
|---|---|
| Since the previous session, both topics in our coaching contract had developed quite a bit and to an extent resolved themselves. The coach and I talked about what this meant for me, just like in the previous session. The critical moment of this session to me was then to admit to the coach that I felt there was not much else to talk about in the following sessions. I felt guilty about that because I felt like it was my responsibility to "come up" with a new topic. I especially had this feeling because of one of the previous sessions, where I didn't have much to talk about and the session was very difficult for both of us. I worded those concerns towards the coach, who pointed out that the session I had in mind had indeed been a difficult one, but that it also was one of the sessions that helped me take a step further. He assured me that I didn't have to come up with a new topic to talk about, but that sometimes the sessions where you feel like you really do not have anything to talk about are the best. It made me feel really relieved to know that the coach had this opinion because it took some pressure off of me. He then started talking a little bit about one of the topics that had emerged out of our previous sessions, which could be used as a basis for our following sessions. | The most critical moment was when the coachee suggested that "as there were no more objectives left perhaps we can think again about the next two sessions". I took this as an "ending phenomenon", a response to the impending end of our coaching journey. Retrospectively, I feel I did not listen or ask enough about her suggestion and what she intended to do about the sequel. So I held firm about the boundary, and suggested we'd work with whatever would come up in those sessions – but I did not really listen to a possible "alternative plan" that the coachee might have suggested. |

**Phenomenological analysis of the critical-moment descriptions**: Once again the single critical moment mentioned by coach and coachee is clearly the same: the discussion about running out of steam and the sense of having completed the contract already. Both coach and coachee seem to feel slightly guilty about the handling of this moment

| Session 9: Coachee critical moments | Session 9: Coach critical moments |
|---|---|
| To me it felt like there was not one distinct critical moment in this session. Rather, I felt like there were several, similar moments that felt critical to me. In all of those moments, the coach gave me some kind of an insight that I could have seen as threatening to my ego. There are two reasons why this made those moments critical to me. First, it showed that the coach felt comfortable sharing his insights with me, although they could have meant a rupture for our relationship. Second, I noticed that his comments did not offend me, although they were quite strong. | What was critical about this session was that Christiane reminded us at the beginning of the session that we were now strictly "outside of the contract" as the two areas that we embarked on "were now resolved" or had now moved on. There was less of a sense of urgency about this session than about some of the other sessions. This is a general sense, not a specific moment. In retrospect I feel I should have offered more space, more listening and silences in order for other things to emerge. |

| | |
|---|---|
| Coming from any other person, I would have probably been hurt and would have walked away from the conversation. In this case, I however tried to explore together with the coach where his comments were coming from and whether there was some truth in them for me. These two reasons together made the moments critical to me, as they showed that our relationship was trustful enough to both make and receive honest remarks like that. | My most critical action during the session was for me the challenging move from "treating us like children" (which is what Christiane reported) to "a childish response to others" (which I alleged Christiane may have, pointing to her own possible share in the "treating us like children"). I did this as gently as possible, but fear I may have bruised or lost her in the process – and I also wonder if there would have been more mileage in exploring more deeply the "treating us like children" bit, staying with what Christiane actually brought to the session. |

<u>Phenomenological analysis of the critical-moment descriptions</u>: Interestingly, both coach and coachee mention for the first time that there were no critical moments in the session as, according to the coachee, there were "several similar moments", and according to the coach, "more of a general sense less of a critical moment". Both coachee and coach write about the coach feeling confident to honestly share his "insights" (coachee) / "challenges" (coach), even though they "could have led to a rupture" (coachee) / "may have bruised or lost the coachee" (coach). This is taken, at least by the coachee, as evidence for a strengthening coaching relationship (or perhaps as a full recovery of the coaching relationship after the major rupture in sessions 5, 6 and 7).

| *Session 10: Coachee critical moments* | *Session 10: Coach critical moments* |
|---|---|
| There were two moments in the session that I experienced as critical. The first moment was actually more of a time-span quite early in the session. I had introduced a topic that we had only discussed very briefly in a preceding session. Once I had explained the situation to the coach, it seemed to me like he paraphrased and interpreted what I had said and then gave me advice on how to deal with this issue. This was quite a new feeling for me, because I felt like in the previous sessions, he had been more reluctant to provide me with any kind of expert opinion. I didn't feel like it was out of line at all, rather I was thankful for his advice. I did however notice it as some sort of change in the coach's role. The second moment occurred when we had finished talking about the first, new topic that I had introduced. The coach then asked me about some of the other topics we had talked about in the previous sessions. What was critical to me was that he seemed to remember so many details of what I had told him, such as names of people involved. This made me feel very honoured and as if the coaching, or the coaching relationship, really was something important not only for me, but also for the coach. | It was fascinating that the first "topic" was all about becoming a practising occupational psychologist and what that means for how people will see Christiane, and about "setting up practice" as an organisational psychologist. Although Christiane said she hadn't realised this was an ending session, this topic seemed appropriate as it was related to "going out into the wider world". The only critical moment I experienced was when I found myself talking so much, when we had returned to the theme of being "junior" and slowly moving up the ranks, the theme of dependence on and perceived inferiority to more senior people. I found myself unable to stop talking or associating with that theme, and wondered if it was more my theme than Christiane's. |

**Phenomenological analysis of the critical-moment descriptions**: An ending session where coach and coachee really part ways: for the first time in eight sessions the critical moments appear unrelated and the perspectives are different. The coachee's critical moment is different from earlier ones, as it is related to "getting advice from the coach". There is some overlap still as both coachee and coach notice that that the coach has been more forward and directive during this session, by e.g. "giving advice" (coachee) and "being unable to stop talking" (coach).

Shortly after the tenth and last session, the notes of coachee and coach were emailed across and shared, and on the same day both coach and coachee formulated a first response to reading the other person's critical-moment descriptions. We give those initial responses here in full, for completeness and also because they provide a good initial summary of relational themes in this coaching journey. However, it is good to point out that in this case the coach's response was written after reading the coachee's response, so here the right-hand column is not independent and partly a response to the left-hand column:

| Coachee's response to coach's notes | Coach's response to coachee's notes |
|---|---|
| The first overall impression that struck me was that there are so many doubts expressed in your descriptions. I guess I should have expected that, considering your previous research, but somehow I didn't. You write a lot about whether something that you said or did was right or wondering whether you could have done something differently. To be quite honest, I actually did notice some of those moments as well, but I was under the impression that you actually consciously and deliberately initiated those. For example, the critical moment you describe in the very first session, you write that you said something about "the face I pulled". I did notice that phrase as something critical as well, but I actually thought you deliberately tried to provoke me with that. I find it very interesting that you change the style of writing in between, changing from third to second person narrative and back. I wonder why that is the case, but don't really have any assumptions or ideas about it. You raise it as a question as well though. Another thing I noticed was that you seemed to have some idea of where we were heading from the very beginning. You write something about ambivalence, which is sort of what we ended up talking about a bit more. I wonder whether those impressions you had in that second session were true, so that we ended up talking about them, or whether it guided you to lead our conversations in that direction. | When I look at your critical moments descriptions, I am struck by the following: The range of your experience of me as a coach, all the way from "abstinent" in session 1 to "advisory" in session 10. For me there was probably less of a range as I tried to facilitate your own development all along. I feel more confident now than I did when we were working together, that we were mostly working on relevant and important themes. I take that e.g. from your statements "I felt they were a bit unimportant" and "one of my topics was not really useful" in your very first session note – which are already hints towards bigger themes such as "feeling unimportant" in later sessions. Your notes made me think again of the importance of coaching for "learning about the impressions one makes", in other words for "getting feedback" or "participating in a self-reflective relationship" – aspects of coaching that are often considered secondary but strikingly important from some of your notes. I love your slip when you write "we proposed to me" (in session 4), which I take as a very concise description of some of our best work together. I think some of our work must have been quite challenging for you (and for us both) and I admire your courage of staying with it and staying with this reflection on it as well. |

| | |
|---|---|
| I find it striking how similar some of our descriptions are, for example the third session, sixth session, and the eighth session, the latter having almost no critical moments.<br><br>It feels like the moments that refer to a "meta-level" are especially interesting. If you look at the fifth session, for example, we both describe a moment that is *about* the coaching itself, and didn't occur *within* the coaching. It seems like we both felt it was critical to consider this meta-level, and we both describe that it was important to do so. I see similar patterns in both our descriptions of the seventh session. | My hypothesis about a possible unconscious reason for my coming late for two sessions is not a reflection on you or the material (as you suggest), more on the multiple bonds that existed between us, which have perhaps made me feel more confident that both of us would stick to the coaching contract even if there were going to be difficulties, because we both had ulterior motives to do with the research work we were doing together. In other words, I think I was just more confident that you would wait for me than I would have been with other coachees. |

# Appendix E: Overview with examples of the critical moments of coachees, coaches and sponsors

Below are 51 examples of the critical-moment descriptions, line by line, relating to the same coaching process, so 17 are from coachees, 17 from coaches and 17 from their sponsors. The examples are ordered in such a way that towards the bottom of the table one can observe the degree of "congruence" between the three parties increasing.

| | Coachees' critical moments | Coaches' critical moments | Sponsors' critical moments |
|---|---|---|---|
| 1 | I had a lightbulb moment in session 3 when I realised that my future may not be in public health and I should consider other avenues. I realised that the things I am really good at are not necessarily those valued in public health terms. | It was significant when S realised that her inner script was dictating how she saw her world and how her critical voice was stopping her moving forward and dealing with anxiety about career moves. | Prioritising her work. Being clearer with others on expectations and deadlines. Confidence in discussing with me her workload and when the workload is getting too much. |
| 2 | Significant moment when I realised, through input from my coach, how a helping conviction can improve your confidence and behaviour. | Challenging was the fact that I didn't know if I was the right coach for her. I didn't feel comfortable. I called HR to reflect. That helped to make a fresh start. | Due to the coaching my direct report has made a good step towards the next role in her career, which is being a senior on audit engagements. In general during interaction with other team members and the client, where my direct report was much more open and engaged in the discussions. |
| 3 | Realising that my anxiety in groups was created by me most of the time by negative thought patterns and hence I also had the capacity to change that thinking (and hence the feelings). | When she tackled a long-standing area of concern with her partner and had a positive outcome. She had been avoiding it – literally for years – as she was afraid of how he would react. Her fears were groundless in reality. | Increased confidence in conversing at multi-professional meetings where there are strong dominating personalities. |

| 4 | There was a session when the coach let me talk to myself in a role playing game. | My coachee told me about a clash between her and a colleague of hers about her sub-assertive behaviour. She got emotional about being unable to gather the courage to stand up to her. She says to me 'I'm doing all I can'. I ask her where she got that sentence and to whom she actually says it. She realises that she tells it herself and afterwards to her parents. We continued on her childhood, the expectations of her parents on her as an intelligent daughter and the expectations of her as a woman. At the end of our session she decides to take a new look at the rules and values; she addressed herself as an adult woman. She made decisions of her own and readjusted herself to whom she truly is and who she wants to be. | More responsibility in her work, placed as leader of the doctors. Colleague is more self-confident, is open about what she has learned by coaching. She has made progress, especially in situations with a colleague who can be quite snappy. Before coaching F was swiped off her feet or intimidated, after coaching she stands by her opinion, doesn't let herself get blown away or intimidated. She takes time to reflect on what is happening and, if necessary, talks about it at another moment. At the same time she stays who she is, her friendly and natural way of communication has not changed. |
| 5 | In one session we acted out several ego positions with physical positions on different chairs. This was very heavy (and I had quite a headache afterwards), but also very helpful in the following sessions. | The session in which my coachee plays out her internal dialogue between the managing and normative part, the worker, the inner child. She discovered she missed a sort of conductor. This helped her in developing this part and becoming stronger in self-management. | Choosing priorities. We had an appointment with a client and privately she had a funeral at the same time, which her parents wanted her to attend. Before the coaching she would have tried to do both things. Now she did one thing and afterwards she was very pleased with herself. |
| 6 | Role-playing improved my confidence. | The session when my coachee did an "embodiment" exercise and experienced for herself how to behave in a physically confident way, created a significant shift for her, as she realised what she was capable of and how she could apply that in her working life. I created a safe space which pushed her out of her comfort zone and she used it incredibly well. It was wonderful to see her learning so profoundly through this. | I have seen a tremendous increase in confidence, in particular around the complex business function of the organisation. |

(Continued)

| 7 | [The coach was] asking me to use my body to describe how I facilitate in different places where I am comfortable and where I am not. | One goal of my coachee was to "be more powerful". In most of our calls she characterised her colleagues on the board of her company as all lawyers and accountants, except for her. The only ones she spoke about were men. After session 7 her new daily practice was to explore the position of openness (a body position associated with love) as well as resolution (a body position associated with determination). At session 8 she told me the practice didn't work because she is already naturally open and loving. We found that rather than her promise to do it daily, she did it once and stopped. That was tense. She resisted seeing this. She retracted that it didn't work and saw that she didn't do it. We chose to let that be and continue with coaching. She emailed me after our call and said 'OH! The point was to combine openness (what I am good at) with resolution. I can be both. Wow – that's going to make a difference. I get it!' She went on to have a call with her prospective junior executive (a male lawyer) and designed how they would work together and support each other given their different strengths. The point, by the way, was to explore – I didn't know what she would see or get from it. But it was clear to me that she saw the male lawyers etc. as powerful and herself as needing to be like them and not "herself". | Change in approach and confidence. Level of participation in team meetings has increased as well as the level of confidence. No longer avoiding or making excuses as to why she is not selling. Has developed a much more direct approach to speaking with potential clients which has seemed to really work. She has set up more meetings with potential clients in one week than she had in over six months in the previous year. |

| | | | |
|---|---|---|---|
| 8 | The appreciation that I had many strengths and that I should focus more on these than areas that I felt I needed to develop. This was a significant shift in my self-awareness. | The first time we met, I was introduced to him by a former coachee (who was his boss). In the first few minutes of our initial conversation, I made it very clear that ours was a separate piece of coaching work and that there would be absolutely no feedback to his boss about the content or direction of our discussions. We did, however, have a brief three-way conversation, in which his boss gave his clear support for this development and that he would be glad to offer feedback and any development opportunities that would support his coaching and leadership development. It was clear that their relationship was a strong and affirming one that would help and not hinder. This enabled us both to enter the coaching relationship with greater confidence. | S has become bolder – he has taken some (well considered) business risks and is creating a faster pace as a result. He is bolder. A specific example relates to the use of a key space at the property he is responsible for and it has been a bit of a "totem" for his resolve to challenge inherited thoughts. S has responded to this and put the space to a new business use in autumn 2012. |
| 9 | The coach K was engaged by my employer to work with me regarding my career. During our first session she identified that it wasn't my career that was the problem, it was my personal circumstances, lifestyle and goals. She explained to me that if I had my personal life in order then my professional life would fall into place, so we changed the scope of the coaching ... and she was right! She changed my life significantly by helping me recognise what was keeping me in a rut and gave me practical solutions for making changes. My life has changed for the better in the past 12 months and a big part of this was K's coaching. | I think it was in the second session when E realised the impact that her personal life was having on her ability to perform at work. This helped her (and me) to gain clarity about where her focus should lie in order to achieve the goals she had set herself at work. | More self awareness and less self focus |

*(Continued)*

| 10 | Working through an unpleasant situation where colleagues had been extremely critical and unpleasant to me. I thought I had not performed in an optimal way and was beating myself up about it. Coach reframed my feelings of having performed badly and gave me confidence that actually I had done the right and only thing I could have done in the circumstances. | Working with my coachee on a particularly difficult meeting she was preparing for and helping her develop her capacity to challenge and confront bullying behaviour – and then hearing how successful she had been afterwards. | My colleague is planning to apply for a new role at Director level. She is more prepared to negotiate a deal with others (win/win) rather than one view prevailing. |
| --- | --- | --- | --- |
| 11 | The moment that I realised I don't have to be different than I am. The moment I became aware that it's ok for everyone to work in the way that suits them, was an eye-opener to me. From that moment on I got more relaxed in my work. | The point that she told me that it is her choice to stay or leave the job, not the decision of her manager. | My employee got a steady job contract afterwards. When I first met her, she was almost invisible. During the coaching she became stronger and stronger and "took her place at the table" to say what she had to say. |
| 12 | I was close to a burn-out, and taking measures as advised by my coach to adapt the structure of my division to my needs and improve work flows and work delegation allowed me to get my act together … I now have a full-time assistant, this was a must for me to be more organised in times of great pressure and crises in the Middle East. I also took better care of my health, by doing more sports and massages and trying to unwind from time to time with my family. | When my coachee told me that she was expecting their second child … she felt so much more confident, at ease and "together" in her – no longer new role, in her ability to find a harmony in the complexity and in her own feminine side… | My colleague was much better able to handle tense situations around staffing or budgeting issues in management team meetings. There was a notable difference in capacity to plan, put forward positions and then to step back and regroup when things didn't go as planned, without this becoming antagonistic. |

| 13 | Some of the advice was eye-opening for me. For example: when a customer is angry on the phone, this doesn't have to be taken personally. | Coachee said she had a switched a button (between the fourth and fifth session), she didn't know how. Before, these things were easily problematic to her, after this she could more easily relax about things. | She is now more open for critical notes. She now knows that if she choose a different attitude she can make her own happiness in her work. / She has learned to recognise when she begins to stress. |
|---|---|---|---|
| 14 | At one point during a coaching session I felt I was being pushed to confront a situation I wasn't ready to confront and I started to feel particularly uncomfortable. However my interpretation of the situation was incorrect and I was relieved to be assured all decisions were mine to take and to decide. | After four sessions where the coachee had skirted around the real issue of what was creating the biggest problem for her, she finally had an epiphany that her own perception of her line manager was negatively impacting their relationship and her future career. This was a particularly tense moment, where I had been challenging her on an ongoing basis and constantly checking goals and issues for the session. Suddenly, in one session, it all made sense to her and we could both see the physical and emotional changes in her as a result. She was able to park her hurt and resentment, using EQ tools, reflection and "mirror" work, to improve the relationship and allow her to focus on her new job and leave her old one behind. | The coaching was to support a development role. The success of the coaching is reflective of the individual. I have had other members of staff receive coaching and seen very positive results. The coachee has shown more willingness to use her initiative and "have a go" when requirements aren't fully defined. |
| 15 | The moment I recognised, through my coaching, that all my brothers and sisters I was the one who organised; that we ought to be together and solve "the problem" when there was one in the family. Through the years I had got better and better at this. At the same time it had become a larger problem in my work. Not everything can be solved by this method. | I experienced a significant moment when this coachee realised that his behaviour as adult was still influenced by limiting beliefs from his youth. Specially in a voice dialogue where he made contact with his vulnerability. For me a challenge to help him see where and when he tried to go away from his vulnerable position and or be to critical towards himself. | In my management team we concluded that a team of my colleagues had worked out a project in the wrong direction. Before the coaching my colleague usually had a big problem in dealing with a situation like this and put all his energy into defending the approach of his people. It was remarkable that he took his time to listen, ask and analyse and immediately could go for the solution! |

*(Continued)*

| 16 | In one of the sessions I realised that I had the know-how in dealing with a confrontational situation, I just had to remain calm and deal with it in a calm manner. This has really helped in difficult situations recently. | At the end of the second session I felt a marked shift in her attitude and confidence in moving forward effectively. She suddenly appeared in control and not just reacting emotionally. | I would say my colleague's attitude to her work (management role) is more positive as a result of the coaching. My colleague appears to be more patient with those she manages and appears to be more approachable. There appears to be less conflict situations in the office. I must also stress that other colleagues are also engaged in coaching and this may be as a result of everyone being involved in it. Everyone is now more positive about their work. There is better collaboration. |
|----|----|----|----|
| 17 | The first day of coaching I was in a situation in my job that was overwhelming me. I had a new position that was a great challenge and I wasn't getting any help from my organisation. I felt like almost giving up. The first session with my coach made me totally change my attitude to a "Can do" attitude, or a "Go for it" attitude. It significantly changed the situation thanks to the coach. | The critical moment happened in the first session when she told me that she did not know whether to continue in her function and I challenged her, saying that if she had doubts she was going to go back. I invited her to decide if she wanted to continue with coaching sessions. She was in survival mode and she had had a previous coaching experience that I thought was not very helpful for her. | She changed her category in the company. Nevertheless, it is difficult to say that was only due to coaching, since she was doing other actions at the same time. A specific example was: I was in the airport and hadn't seen her for some time. Then I saw a woman, looking quite professional, smart and mature. I didn't recognise her. When she started to speak, I realised who she was. I remember I thought: 'I cannot believe the positive change in appearance and how self-assured she looks'. I still think the same each time I see her photo and CV in our IT system. |

## Notes

1 Counter-transference is the phenomenon whereby the coach's own "baggage" or previously learned modes of interaction play a role and enter the coaching situation itself. The term is especially used where this phenomenon makes the coach's coaching actions more difficult. The concept of "counter-transference" was introduced by Freud.

2 All coaching contracts are (implicitly or explicitly) triangular, because they take place between at least three parties: the coachee, the coach and other parties involved within the coachee's organisation. This triangular aspect is often only noticed when the coachee and others within the organisation have different views on the coaching, for example on its objectives or the themes that need to be addressed.

3 Transposition is a collective term for a broad range of interventions by the coach, in which the context of or approach to a coaching question is changed by the coach, for example by suggesting a different manner of expression, or by practising and experimenting in the coaching relationship.

4 Transference is the phenomenon whereby the coachee's own "baggage" or previously learned modes of interaction play a role and enter the coaching situation itself. The concept was introduced by Freud.

# References

Alvey, S., & Barclay, K. (2007). The characteristics of dyadic trust in executive coaching. *Journal of Leadership Studies, 1*(1), 18–27.

Anderson, J. P. (2002). Executive coaching and REBT: Some comments from the field. *Journal of Rational-Emotive & Cognitive-Behavior Therapy, 20*(3–4), 223–233.

Argyris, C. (1991). Teaching smart people how to learn. *Harvard Business Review*, May–June 1991, 99–109.

Aristotle (4th century BC). (1984). Physics book III. In J. Barnes (Ed.), *The complete works of Aristotle – the revised Oxford translation*. Princeton, NJ: Princeton University Press.

Athanasopoulou, A., & Dopson, S. (2018). A systematic review of executive coaching outcomes: Is it the journey or the destination that matters the most? *Leadership Quarterly, 29*(1): 70–88.

Audet, J., & Couteret, P. (2012). Coaching the entrepreneur: Features and success factors. August 2012. *Journal of Small Business and Enterprise Development, 19*(3), 515–531.

Bachelard, G. (1938). *La Formation de l'esprit scientifique: Contribution à une psychanalyse de la connaissance objective*. Paris: Vrin.

Bachkirova, T., Arthur, L., & Reading, E. (2015). Evaluating a coaching and mentoring programme: Challenges and solutions. *International Coaching Psychology Review, 10*(2) 175–189.

Baron, L., & Morin, L. (2010). The impact of executive coaching on self-efficacy related to management soft-skills. *Leadership & Organization Development Journal, 31*(1), 18–38.

Ben-Hador, B. (2016). Coaching executives as tacit performance evaluation: A multiple case study. *Journal of Management Development, 35*(1), 75–88.

Berglas, S. (2002). The very real dangers of executive coaching. *Harvard Business Review, 80*(6), 86–92.

Berne, E. (1972). *What do you say after you say hello?* New York: Grove Press.

Bickerich, K., Michel, A., & O'Shea, D. (2018). Executive coaching during organisational change: A qualitative study of executives and coaches perspectives, *Coaching: An International Journal of Theory, Research and Practice, 11*(2), 117–143.

Bion, W. R. (1963). *Elements of psychoanalysis*. London: William Heinemann.

Bion, W. R. (1970). *Attention and interpretation*. London: Tavistock Publications Ltd.

Blackman, A. (2006). Factors that contribute to the effectiveness of business coaching: The coachees perspective. *Business Review, Cambridge, 5*(1), 98–104.

Blattner, J. (2005). Coaching: The successful adventure of a downwardly mobile executive. *Consulting Psychology Journal: Practice and Research, 57*(1), 3–13.

Bloch, S., Reibstein, J., Crouch, E., Holroyd, P., & Themen, J. (1979). A method for the study of therapeutic factors in group psychotherapy. *British Journal of Psychiatry, 134*, 257–263.

Boyce, L. A., Jackson, R. J., & Neal, L. J. (2010). Building successful leadership coaching relationships: Examining impact of matching criteria in a leadership coaching program.

*Journal of Management Development* [Special Issue on Coaching and the Relationship], 29(10), 914–931.

Brauer, Y. (2005). Wie Zielvereinbarungen im Coaching helfen. *Wirtschaftspsychologie aktuell, 1*, 40–43.

Breuer, J., & Freud, S. (1895). *Studien über Hysterie.* Leipzig: Verlag Franz Deuticke. Translated as *Studies on Hysteria* by James Strachey in collaboration with Anna Freud in *The Standard Edition of the Complete Psychological Works of Sigmund Freud,* vol. II, Hogarth, London (1960).

Brunning, H. (2006). *Executive coaching: Systems-psychodynamic perspective.* London: Karnac.

Buckle, T. (2012). "It can be life-changing"; an interpretative phenomenological analysis of the coach and coachee's experience of psychometrics in coaching. *International Journal of Evidence Based Coaching and Mentoring, 6,* 102–118.

Burger, Y. (2013). *Spiegel aan de top; over de praktijk van executive coaching.* Amsterdam, Mediawerf.

Bush, M. W. (2005). Client perceptions of effectiveness in executive coaching. *Dissertation Abstracts International Section A: Humanities and Social Sciences, 66(4-A),* 1417.

Carlberg, G. (1997). Laughter opens the door: Turning points in child psychotherapy. *Journal of child psychotherapy, 23(3),* 331–349.

Casement, P. (2002). *Learning from our mistakes.* London: Routledge.

Caskey, N., Barker, C., & Elliott, R. (1984). Dual perspectives: Clients' and therapists' perceptions of therapist responses. *British Journal of Clinical Psychology, 23,* 281–290.

Clutterbuck, D. (1985). *Everyone needs a mentor: Fostering talent in your organisation.* London: CIPD.

Clutterbuck, D., de Haan, E., Wels, I., Lucas, B., & Winter, J. (2009). *Development at the top: Who really cares? A survey of executive teams.* Ashridge Research Report, ISBN 978-0-903542-81-4.

Cohen J. (1960). A coefficient of agreement for nominal scales. *Educational and Psychological Measurement, 70,* 213–220.

Corbin, J., & Strauss A. J. (1990). Grounded theory research: Procedures, canons and evaluative criteria. *Zeitschrift für Soziologie, 19,* 418–427.

Cox, J. (2012). Do we understand each other? An inquiry into the coaching relationship when working in different languages. In E. de Haan & C. Sills (Eds.), *Coaching relationships* (pp. 171–182). Faringdon: Libri.

David, S., Clutterbuck, D., & Megginson, D. (2014). Goal orientation in coaching differs according to region, experience and education. *International Journal of Evidence Based Coaching and Mentoring, 12(2),* 134–145.

Day, A. (2010). Coaching at relational depth: A case study. *Journal of Management Development, 29(10),* 864–876.

Day, A., De Haan, E., Sills, C., Bertie, C, & Blass, E. (2008). Coaches' experience of critical moments in the coaching. *International Coaching Psychology Review, 3(3),* 207–218.

De Haan, E. (2006). *Fearless consulting: Temptations, risks and limits of the profession.* Chichester: Wiley.

De Haan, E. (2008a). *Relational coaching: Journeys towards mastering one-to-one learning.* Chichester: Wiley.

De Haan, E. (2008b). Becoming simultaneously thicker and thinner skinned: The inherent conflicts arising in the professional development of coaches. *Personnel Review, 37(5),* 526–542.

De Haan, E. (2008c). I doubt therefore I coach – critical moments in coaching practice. *Consulting Psychology Journal: Practice and Research, 60(1),* 91–105.

De Haan, E. (2008d). I struggle and emerge – critical moments of experienced coaches. *Consulting Psychology Journal: Practice and Research, 60(1),* 106–131.

De Haan, E., & Burger, Y. (2005; 2nd ed. 2013). *Coaching with colleagues: An action guide to one-to-one learning.* Basingstoke: Palgrave Macmillan.

De Haan, E., & Duckworth, A. (2013). Signaling a new trend in coaching outcome research. *International Coaching Psychology Review, 8*(1), 6–20.

De Haan, E., & Kasozi, A. (2014). *The leadership shadow: How to recognise and avoid derailment, hubris and overdrive.* London: Kogan Page.

De Haan, E., & Nieß, C. (2012). Critical moments in a coaching case study: Illustration of a process research model. *Consulting Psychology Journal: Practice and Research, 64*(3), 198–224.

De Haan, E., & Nieß, C. (2015). Differences between critical moments for clients, coaches, and sponsors of coaching. *International Coaching Psychology Review, 10*(1), 38–61.

De Haan, E., & Nilsson, V. O. (2017). Evaluating coaching behavior in managers, consultants and coaches: A model, questionnaire, and initial findings. *Consulting Psychology Journal, 69*(4), 315–333.

De Haan, E., Bertie, C., Day, A., & Sills, C. (2010a). Critical moments of clients of coaching: Towards a 'client model' of executive coaching. *Academy of Management Learning and Education, 5*(2), 109–128.

De Haan, E., Bertie, C., Day, A., & Sills, C. (2010b). Critical moments of clients and coaches: A direct-comparison study. *International Coaching Psychology Review, 5*(2), 109–128.

De Haan, E., Culpin, V., & Curd, J. (2011). Executive coaching in practice: What determines helpfulness for clients of coaching? *Personnel Review, 40*(1), 24–44.

De Haan, E., Grant, A., Burger, Y., & Eriksson, P.-O. (2016). A large-scale study of executive coaching outcome: The relative contributions of working relationship, personality match, and self-efficacy. *Consulting Psychology Journal: Practice and Research, 68*(3), 189–207.

De Haan, E., Baldwin, A., Carew, N., Conway, S., Elliman, J., Hazell, J., … Wanke, C. (Eds., 2013; expanded 2nd ed. 2016 with A. Craig, R. Evers-Cacciapaglia, I. Duit, & M. Grant). *Behind closed doors: Stories from the coaching room.* Faringdon: Libri.

Denzin, N. K. (1989). *Interpretive interactionism.* Newbury Park, CA: Sage.

Diedrich, R. C. (1996). An interactive approach to executive coaching. *Consulting Psychology Journal: Practice & Research, 48*(2), 61–66.

Dollard, J., & Auld Jr., F. (1959). *Scoring human motives: A manual.* New Haven, CT: Yale University Press.

Downey, M. (1999). *Effective coaching.* New York: Thomson Texere.

Dumont, F. (1991). Expertise in psychotherapy: Inherent liabilities of becoming experienced. *Psychotherapy, 28,* 422–428.

Elliott, R. (1983). "That is in your hands" – A comprehensive process analysis of a significant event in psychotherapy. *Psychiatry, 46,* 113–129.

Elliott, R. (1985). Helpful and nonhelpful events in brief counseling interviews: An empirical taxonomy. *Journal of Counselling Psychology, 32,* 307–322.

Elliott, R., James, E., Reimschuessel, C., Cislo, D., & Sack, N. (1985). Significant events and the analysis of immediate impacts in psychotherapy. *Psychotherapy, 22,* 620–630.

Elliott, R. K., & Shapiro, D. A. (1992). Client and therapist as analysts of significant events. In S. G. Toukmanian & D. L. Rennie (Eds.), *Psychotherapeutic change: Theory-guided and descriptive research strategies* (pp. 163–186). Newbury Park, CA: Sage.

Elton Wilson, J., & Syme, G. (2006). *Objectives and outcomes: Questioning the practice of therapy.* Maidenhead: Open University Press.

Evers, W. J. G., Brouwers, A., & Tomic, W. (2006). A quasi-experimental study on management coaching effectiveness. *Consulting Psychology Journal: Practice and Research, 58*(3), 174–182.

Fahy, T. P. (2007). Executive coaching as an accelerator for whole system organizational change. *Dissertation Abstracts International Section A: Humanities and Social Sciences, 68*(3-A), 1066–1067.

Farrelly, F., & Brandsma, J. (1974). *Provocative therapy.* Cupertino, CA: Meta Publishing.

Fatien-Diochon, P., & Nizet, J. (2015). Ethical codes and executive coaches: One size does not fit all. *The Journal of Applied Behavioral Science, 51*(2), 277–301.

Feifel, H., & Eells, J. (1964). Patients and therapists assess the same psychotherapy. *Journal of Consulting Psychology, 27,* 310–318.

Feldman, D. C., & Lankau, M. J. (2005). Executive coaching: A review and agenda for future research. *Journal of Management, 31,* 829–848.

Flanagan, J. C. (1954). The critical incident technique. *Psychological Bulletin, 51,* 327–358.

Fleiss, J. L. (1971). Measuring nominal scale agreement among many raters. *Psychological Bulletin, 76*(5), 378–382.

Foster, S., & Lendl, J. (1996). Eye movement desensitization and reprocessing: Four case studies of a new tool for executive coaching and restoring employee performance after setbacks. *Consulting Psychology Journal: Practice and Research, 48*(3), 155–161.

Freedman, A. M., & Perry, J. A. (2010). Executive consulting under pressure: A case study. *Consulting Psychology Journal: Practice & Research, 62*(3), 189–202.

Freud, S. (1905). Bruchstück einer Hysterie-Analyse. *Monatsschrift für Psychiatrie und Neurologie.* Vol. XXVIII.4. Translated as "Fragment of an analysis of a case of hysteria", by James Strachey in collaboration with Anna Freud, in *The standard edition of the complete psychological works of Sigmund Freud,* Volume VII, pp. 3–125, Hogarth, London (1960).

Freud, S. (1912). *Ratschläge für den Arzt bei der psychoanalytischen Behandlung. In: Zentralblatt für Psychoanalyse,* Band II. Translation: "Recommendations to Physicians Practicing Psycho-analysis", by James Strachey in collaboration with Anna Freud, in *The Standard Edition of the Complete Psychological Works of Sigmund Freud,* Volume XII, pp. 109–120, Hogarth: London (1960).

Gallo, F. T. (2015). *The enlightened leader: Lessons from China on the art of executive coaching.* Bingley: Emerald.

Gessnitzer, S., & Kauffeld, S. (2015). The working alliance in coaching: Why behavior is the key to success. *Journal of Applied Behavioral Science, 51*(2), 177–197.

Giddens, A. (1991). *Modernity and self identity: Self and society in the late modern age.* Cambridge: Polity.

Glaser, B. G. (1992). *Basics of grounded theory analysis.* Mill Valley, CA: Sociological Press.

Goodman, G., Magnussen, S., Andersson, J., Endestad, T., Løkke, C., & Mostue, C. (2006). Memory illusions and false memories in real life. In S. Magnussen & T. Helstrup (Eds.), *Everyday memory.* London: Psychology Press.

Graf, E. (2012). Narratives of illness and emotional distress in executive coaching: An initial analysis into their forms and functions. *Poznań Studies in Contemporary Linguistics, 48*(1), 23–54.

Grant, A. M. (2003). The impact of life coaching on goal attainment, metacognition and mental health. *Social Behaviour and Personality, 31*(3), 253–264.

Grant, A. M. (2014). The efficacy of executive coaching in times of organisational change. *Journal of Change Management, 14,* 258–280.

Gray, D., Burls, A., & Kogan, M. (2014). Salutogenisis and coaching: Testing a proof of concept to develop a model for practitioners. *International Journal of Evidence Based Coaching and Mentoring, 12*(2), 41–58.

Gray, D. E., & Goregoakar, H. (2010). Choosing an executive coach: The influence of gender on the coach-coachee matching process. *Management Learning, 41*(5), 525–544.

Gray, D. E., Ekinci, Y., & Goregaokar, H. (2011). Coaching SME managers: Business development or personal therapy? A mixed methods study. *The International Journal of Human Resource Management, 22*(4), 863–882.

Gray, D. E., Gabriel, Y., & Goregaokar, H. (2015). Coaching unemployed managers and professionals through the trauma of unemployment: Derailed or undaunted? *Management Learning, 46*(3), 299–316.

Greenson, R. R. (1965). The working alliance and the transference neuroses. *Psychoanalysis Quarterly, 34*, 155–181.

Greif, S. (2007). Advances in research on coaching outcomes. *International Coaching Psychology Review, 2*(3), 222–249.

Greif, S. (2010). A new frontier of research and practice: Observation of coaching behaviour. *The Coaching Psychologist, 6*(2), 21–29.

Gyllensten, K., & Palmer, S. (2007). The coaching relationship: An interpretative phenomenological analysis. *International Coaching Psychology Review, 2*(2), 168–177.

Hall, D. T., Otazo, K. L., & Hollenbeck, G. P. (1999). Behind closed doors: What really happens in executive coaching. *Organizational Dynamics, 29*, 39–53.

Harrison, R. (1963). Defenses and the need to know. *Human Relations Training News, 6*(4), 1–3.

Hawkins, P., & Smith, N. (2006). *Coaching, mentoring and organizational consultancy: Supervision and development.* Maidenhead: Open University Press.

Heimann, P. (1950). On counter-transference. *International Journal of Psychoanalysis, 31*, 81–84.

Heron, J. (1975). *Helping the client.* London: Sage Publications.

Horvath, A. O., & Marx, R. W. (1990). The development and decay of the working alliance during time-limited counselling. *Canadian Journal of Counselling, 24*, 240–259.

Howard, K. I., Kopta, S. M., Krause, M. S., & Orlinski, D. E. (1986). The dose-effect relationship in psychotherapy. *American Psychologist, 41*(2), 159–164.

Huggler, L. A. A. (2007). *CEOs on the couch: Building the therapeutic coaching alliance in psychoanalytically informed executive coaching.* Thesis. Fielding Graduate University, California.

Humphrey, R. (1993). Life stories and social careers: Ageing and social life in an ex-mining town. *Sociology, 27*, 166–178.

Hurd, J. J. (2009). Development coaching: Helping scientific and technical professionals make the leap into leadership. *Global Business & Organizational Excellence, 28*(5), 39–51.

Ianiro, P. M., & Kauffeld, S. (2014). Take care what you bring with you: How coaches' mood and interpersonal behavior affect coaching success. *Consulting Psychology Journal: Practice and Research, 66*, 231–257.

Ianiro, P. M., Lehmann-Willenbrock, N., & Kauffeld, S. (2015). Coaches and clients in action: A sequential analysis of interpersonal coach and cliënt behavior. *Journal of Business and Psychology, 30*(3), 435–456.

Ianiro, P. M., Schermuly, C. C., & Kauffeld, S. (2012). Why interpersonal dominance and affiliation matter: An interaction analysis of the coach-client relationship. *Coaching: An International Journal of Theory, Research and Practice, 6*(1), 1–22.

Jones, R., Woods, S., & Guillaume, Y. (2015). The effectiveness of workplace coaching: A meta-analysis of learning and performance outcomes from coaching. *Journal of Occupational and Organizational Psychology, 89*(2), 249–277.

Jung, C. G. (1921). *Psychologische Typen.* Olten: Walter-Verlag AG.

Jung, C. G. (1946). *Die Psychologie der Übertragung.* Zurich: Rascher.

Kampa-Kokesch, S., & Anderson, M. Z. (2001). Executive coaching: A comprehensive review of the literature. *Consulting Psychology Journal: Practice and Research, 53*, 205–228.

Kauffman, C., & Hodgetts W. H. (2016). Model agility: Coaching effectiveness and four perspectives on a case study. *Consulting Psychology Journal: Practice & Research, 68*(2), 157–176.

Kets de Vries, M. F. R. (2013). Coaching's 'Good Hour': Creating tipping points. *Coaching: An International Journal of Theory: Research & Practice, 6*(2), 152–175.

Kiel, F., Rimmer, E., Williams, K., & Doyle, M. (1996). Coaching at the top. *Consulting Psychology Journal: Practice & Research, 48*(2), 67–77.

Kilburg, R. (2000). *Executive coaching: Developing managerial wisdom in a world of chaos.* Washington, DC: American Psychological Association.

Kolb, D. A. (1984). *Experiential learning – Experience as the source of learning and development.* Englewood Cliffs, NJ: Prentice Hall.

Kombarakan, F. A., Yang, J. A., Baker, M. N., & Fernandes, P. B. (2008). Executive coaching: It works! *Consulting Psychology Journal: Practice and Research, 60,* 78–90.

Lakoff, G. (1993). The contemporary theory of metaphor. In A. Ortony (Ed.), *Metaphor and thought* (2nd ed.). Cambridge: Cambridge University Press.

Landis, J. R., & Koch, G. G. (1977). The measurement of observer agreement for categorical data. *Biometrics, 33*(1), 159–174.

Lapworth, P., Sills, C., & Fish, S. (2001). *Integration in counselling and psychotherapy: Developing a personal approach.* London: Sage.

Lawrence, P. (2015). Building a coaching culture in a small Australian multinational organisation. *Coaching: An International Journal of Theory: Research and Practice, 8*(1), 53–60.

Lawton, B. (2000). 'A very exposing affair': Explorations in counsellors' supervisory relationships. In B. Lawton & C. Feltham (Eds.), *Taking supervision forward: Enquiries and trends in counselling and psychotherapy.* London: Sage.

Leary, T. (1957). *Interpersonal diagnosis of personality.* New York: The Ronald Press.

Levenson, A. (2009). Measuring and maximizing the business impact of executive coaching. *Consulting Psychology Journal: Practice and Research, 61,* 103–121.

Liljenstrand, A. M., & Nebeker, D. M. (2008). Coaching services: A look at coaches, clients, and practices. *Consulting Psychology Journal: Practice and Research, 60*(1), 57–77.

Llewelyn, S. (1988). Psychological therapy as viewed by clients and therapists. *British Journal of Clinical Psychology, 27,* 223–237.

Llewelyn, S. P., Elliott, R. K., Shapiro, D. A., Hardy, G. E., & Firth-Cozens, J. A. (1988). Client perceptions of significant events in prescriptive and exploratory periods of individual therapy. *British Journal of Clinical Psychology, 27,* 105–114.

Machin, S. (2010). The nature of the internal coaching relationship. *International Journal of Evidence Based Coaching and Mentoring, Special Issue, 4,* 37–52.

MacKenzie, H. (2007). Stepping off the treadmill: A study of coaching on the RCN clinical leadership programme. *International Journal of Evidence Based Coaching and Mentoring, 5*(2), 22–33.

Machrill, T. (2011). The case of "Jane and Joe": A diary-based, cross-contextual case study. *Pragmatic Case Studies in Psychotherapy, 7*(1), 187–229.

Mahrer, A. R., & Nadler, W. P. (1986). Good moments in psychotherapy: A preliminary review, a list, and some promising research avenues. *Journal of Consulting and Clinical Psychology, 54,* 10–15.

Mandelbaum, D. G. (1973). The study of life history: Gandhi. *Current Anthropology, 14,* 177–193.

Mansi, A. (2007). Executive coaching and psychometrics: A case study evaluating the use of the Hogan Personality Inventory (HPI) and the Hogan Development Survey (HDS) in senior management coaching. *The Coaching Psychologist, 3*(2), 53–58.

Maroda, K. J. (1998). *Seduction, surrender and transformation: Emotional engagement in the analytic process.* Hillsdale, MI: The Analytic Press.

Martin, D. J., Garske, J. P., & Davis, M. K. (2000). Relation of the therapeutic alliance with outcome and other variables: A meta-analytic review. *Journal of Consulting and Clinical Psychology, 68,* 438–450.

Martin, J., & Stelmaczonek, K. (1988). Participants' identification and recall of important events in counseling. *Journal of Counseling Psychology, 35,* 385–390.

McGovern, J., Lindemann, M., Vergara, M., Murphy, S., Barker, L., & Warrenfeltz, R. (2001). Maximizing the impact of executive coaching: Behavioural change, organizational outcomes, and return on investment. *The Manchester Review, 6*, 1–9.

Merton, R. K., & Barber, E. G. (2003). *The travels and adventures of serendipity: A study in sociological semantics and the sociology of science.* Princeton, NJ: Princeton University Press.

Metselaar, C., & De Haan, E. (2015). A critique of the use of diagnostic instruments in executive coaching. *Coaching Today, July,* 16–17.

Miller, A. (1979). *Das Drama des begabten Kindes und die Suche nach dem wahren Selbst.* Frankfurt am Main: Suhrkamp.

Mintz, J., Auerbach, A. H., Luborsky, L., & Johnson, M. (1973). Patients', therapists' and observers' views of psychotherapy: A 'Rashomon' experience or a reasonable consensus? *British Journal of Medical Psychology, 47,* 319–334.

Motsoaledi, L., & Cilliers, F. (2012). Executive coaching in diversity from the systems psychodynamic perspective. *A Journal of Industrial Psychology, 38*(2), 1–11.

Myers, A. C. (2014). *A multiple perspective analysis of a coaching session.* PhD Thesis, Oxford Brookes University.

Myers, A. C., & Bachkirova, T. (2018). Towards a process-based typology of workplace coaching: An empirical investigation. *Consulting Psychology Journal: Practice and Research, 70*(4), 297–317.

Nanduri, V. (2018). How the participants experienced a coaching intervention conducted during company restructure and retrenchment: A qualitative research study using interpretative phenomenological analysis. *Coaching: An International Journal of Theory, Research and Practice, 11*(2), 144–154.

O'Broin, A., & Palmer, S. (2010). Exploring key aspects in the formation of coaching relationships: Initial indicators from the perspective of the coachee and the coach. *Coaching: An International Journal of Theory, Research and Practice, 3*(2), 124–143.

O'Neill, M.-B. (2000). *Executive coaching with backbone and heart – A systems approach to engaging leaders with their challenges.* San Francisco, CA: Jossey-Bass.

Olivero, G., Bane, K. D., & Kopelman, R. E. (1997). Executive coaching as a transfer of training tool: Effects on productivity in a public agency. *Public Personnel Management, 26,* 461–469.

Orenstein, R. L. (2002). Executive coaching: It's not just about the executive. *The Journal of Applied Behavioral Science, 38*(3), 355–374.

Orlinsky, D. E., & Howard, K. I. (1975). *Varieties of psychotherapeutic experience.* New York: Teachers College Press.

Parrott, W. (2001). *Emotions in social psychology.* Philadelphia, PA: Psychology Press.

Parsloe, E., & Wray, M. (2000). *Coaching and mentoring.* London: Kogan Page.

Peel, D. (2008). What factors affect coaching and mentoring in small and medium sized enterprises. *International Journal of Evidence Based Coaching and Mentoring, 6*(2), 27–44.

Perkins, R. D. (2009). How executive coaching can change leader behaviour and improve meeting effectiveness: An exploratory study. *Consulting Psychology Journal: Practice and Research, 61*(4), 298–318.

Peterson, D. B. (1993). *Measuring change: A psychometric approach to evaluating individual coaching outcomes.* Presented at the conference of the Society for Industrial and Organizational Psychology, San Francisco.

Peterson, D. B., & Millier, J. (2005). The Alchemy of Coaching: "You're Good, Jennifer, But You Could Be Really Good". *Consulting Psychology Journal: Practice and Research, 57*(1), 14–40.

Present, J., Crits-Christoph, P., Connolly Gibbons, M. B., Hearon, B., Ring-Kurtz, S., Worley, M., … Gallop, R. (2008). Sudden gains in the treatment of generalized anxiety disorder. *Journal of Clinical Psychology, 64*(1), 119–126.

Racker, H. (1968). *Transference and countertransference.* New York: International Universities Press.

Ragins, B. R., Cotton, J. L., & Miller, J. S. (2000). Marginal mentoring: The effects of type of mentor, quality of relationship, and program design on work and career attitudes. *Academy of Management Journal, 43*(6), 1177–1194.

Reason, P. (1994). *Participation in human inquiry.* London: Sage.

Reason, P., & Bradbury, H., (Eds.), (2001). *Handbook of action research: Participative inquiry and practice.* London: Sage.

Rekalde, I., Landeta, J., & Albizu, E. (2015). Determining factors in the effectiveness of executive coaching as a Management Development Tool. *Management Decision, 53,* 1677–1697.

Rennie, D. L. (1990). Towards a representation of the clients' experience of the psychotherapy hour. In G. Lietaer, J. Rombauts, & R. Van Balen (Eds.), *Client-centred and experiential psychotherapy in the nineties.* Leuven: Leuven University Press.

Rice, L. N., & Greenberg, L. S. (Eds.). (1984). *Patterns of change: Intensive analysis of psychotherapeutic process.* New York: Guilford.

Rogers, C. R. (1961). *On becoming a person – A therapist's view of psychotherapy.* London: Constable.

Rohmert, E., & Schmid, E. W. (2003). Coaching ist messbar. Ist corporate coaching eine sinnvolle investition in führungskräfte? *New Management, 1–2,* 46–53.

Safran, J. D., Crocker, P., McMain, S., & Murray, P. (1990). Therapeutic alliance rupture as a therapy event for empirical investigation. *Psychotherapy, 27,* 154–165.

Safran, J. D., Muran, C. J., & Wallner Samstag, L. (1993). Resolving therapeutic ruptures: A task analytic investigation. In A. O. Horvath & L. S. Greenberg (Eds.), *The working alliance: Theory, research, and practice.* New York: Wiley.

Salomaa, R. (2017). Coaching of international managers: Organizational and individual perspectives. *Acta Wasaensia 372, Business Administration (Diss.).* University of Vasaa.

Schein, E. H. (1985). *Organizational culture and leadership.* San Francisco, CA: Jossey-Bass.

Schlosser, B., Steinbrenner, D., Kumata, E., & Hunt, J. (2006). The coaching impact study: Measuring the value of executive coaching. *International Journal of Coaching in Organizations, 4*(3), 8–26.

Schnell, E. R. (2005). A case study of executive coaching as a support mechanism during organisational growth and evolution. *Consulting Psychology Journal: Practice and Research, 57*(1), 41–56.

Searles, H. F. (1955). The informational value of the supervisor's emotional experience. *Psychiatry, 18,* 135–146.

Sherman, S., & Freas, A. (2004). The wild west of executive coaching. *Harvard Business Review,* November, 1–8.

Sieler, A. (2003). *Coaching to the human soul: Ontological coaching and deep change.* Australia: Newfield.

Sills, C. (2012). The coaching contract: A mutual commitment. In E. de Haan & C. Sills (Eds.), *Coaching relationships: The relational coaching field book* (pp. 76–88). Faringdon: Libri Publishing.

Skinner, D. (2012). Outside forces in the coaching room: How to work with multiparty contracts. In E. de Haan & C. Sills (Eds.), *Coaching relationships* (pp. 111–125). Faringdon: Libri.

Skinner, S. (2014). Understanding the importance of gender and leader identity formation in executive coaching for senior women. *Coaching: An International Journal of Theory, Research and Practice, 7*(2) 102–114.

Smith, J. A. (2003). *Qualitative psychology: A practical guide to research methods.* Sage: London.

Smith, I. M., & Brummel, B. J. (2013). Investigating the role of the active ingredients in executive coaching. *Coaching: An International Journal of Theory, Research and Practice, 6*(1), 57–71.

Smither, J. W., London, M., Flautt, R., Vargas, Y, & Kucine, I. (2003). Can working with an executive coach improve multisource feedback ratings over time? A quasi-experimental field study. *Personnel Psychology, 56*, 23–44.

Spence, G. B., & Grant, A. M. (2005). Individual and group life-coaching: Initial findings from a randomised, controlled trial. In M. Cavanagh, A. M. Grant, & T. Kemp (Eds.), *Evidence-based coaching Vol. 1: Theory, research and practice from the behavioural sciences* (pp. 143–158). Bowen Hills Queensland: Australian Academic Press.

Spinelli, E. (2008). Coaching and therapy: Similarities and divergencies. *International Coaching Psychology Review, 3*(3), 241–249.

Starr, J. (2003). *The coaching manual: A definitive guide to the process, principles & skills of Personal Coaching.* Harlow: Pearson.

Stern, D. N. (2004). *The present moment in psychotherapy and everyday life.* New York: Norton.

Stern, D. N., Sander, L. W., Nahum, J. P., Harrison, A. M., Lyons-Ruth, K., Morgan, A. C., ... Tronick, E. Z. (1998). Non-interpretive mechanisms in psychoanalytic therapy: The 'something more' than interpretation. *International Journal of Psycho-Analysis, 79*, 903–921.

Stevens Jr., J. H. (2005). Executive coaching from the executive's perspective. *Consulting Psychology Journal: Practice and Research, 57*(4), 274–285.

Stiles, W. B. (1980). Measurement of the impact of psychotherapy sessions. *Journal of Consulting and Clinical Psychology, 48*, 176–185.

Strauss, A., & Corbin, J. (1990). *Basics of qualitative research: Grounded theory procedures and techniques.* Newbury Park: CA: Sage.

Styhre, A. (2008). Coaching as second-order observations: Learning from site managers in the construction industry. *Leadership & Organization Development Journal, 29*(3), 275–290.

Sue-Chan, S., & Latham, G. P. (2004). The relative effectiveness of external, peer and self-coaches. *Applied Psychology: An International Review, 53*(2), 260–278.

Tallman, K., & Bohart, A. C. (1999). The client as a common factor: Clients as self-healers. In M. A. Hubble, B. L. Duncan, & S. D. Miller (Eds.), *The heart and soul of change: What works in therapy.* Washington, DC: APA Press.

Tang, T. Z., & DeRubeis, R. J. (1999). Sudden gains and critical sessions in cognitive-behavioral therapy for depression. *Journal of Consulting and Clinical Psychology, 67*, 894–904.

Tang, T. Z., DeRubeis, R. J., Hollon, S. D., Amsterdam, J. A., & Shelton, R. C. (2007). Sudden gains in cognitive therapy of depression and depression relapse/recurrence. *Journal of Consulting and Clinical Psychology, 75*, 404–408.

Terblanche, N., Albertyn, R. M., & Coller-Peter, S. (2017). Designing a coaching intervention to support leaders promoted into senior positions. *SA Journal of Human Resource Management, 15*(1), 1–10.

Thach, E. C. (2002). The impact of executive coaching and 360 feedback on leadership effectiveness. *Leadership and Organization Development Journal, 23*, 205–214.

Thomson, R., Bell, R., Holland, J. Henderson, S., McGrellis, S., & Sharpe, S. (2002). Critical moments: Choice, chance and opportunity in young peoples' narratives of transition to adulthood. *Sociology, 36*, 335–354.

Timson, S. (2015). Exploring what clients find helpful in a brief resilience coaching programme: A qualitative study. *The Coaching Psychologist, 11*(2), 81–88.

Timulak, L., & Keogh, D. (2017). The client's perspective on (experiences of) psychotherapy: A practice friendly review. *Journal of Clinical Psychology, 73*(11), 1556–1567.

Tobias, L. L. (1996). Coaching executives. *Consulting Psychology Journal: Practice & Research, 48*(2), 87–95.

Turner, C., & McCarthy, G. (2015). Coachable moments: Identifying factors that influence managers to take advantage of coachable moments in day-to-day management. *International Journal of Evidence Based Coaching and Mentoring, 13*(1), 1–13.

Van Nieuwerburgh, C. (Ed.). (2012). *Coaching in education: Getting better results for students, educators, and parents*. London: Karnac.

Waldman, D. A. (2003). Does working with an executive coach enhance the value of multi-source performance feedback? *Academy of Management Executive, 17*(3), 146–148.

Wampold, B. E. (2001). *The great psychotherapy debate – models, methods, and findings*. Mahwah, NJ: Lawrence Erlbaum Associates.

Wasylyshyn, K. M. (2003). Executive coaching: An outcome study. *Consulting Psychology Journal: Practice and Research, 55*, 94–106.

Wasylyshyn, K. M., Gronsky, B., & Haas, W. (2006). Tigers, stripes, and behavior change: Survey results of a commissioned coaching program. *Consulting Psychology Journal: Practice and Research, 58*, 65–81.

Watling, R. (2012). Learning and relearning: Putting relationships at the centre of executive coaching. In E. de Haan & C. Sills (Eds.), *Coaching Relationships* (pp. 41–52). Faringdon: Libri.

Weiss, I., Rabinowitz, J. & Spiro, S. (1996). Agreement between therapists and clients in evaluating therapy and its outcomes: Literature review. *Administration and Policy in Mental Health, 23*(6), 493–511.

Whitmore, J. (1992). *Coaching for performance – GROWing people, performance and purpose*. London: Nicholas Brealey Publishing.

Will, T., Gessnitzer, S., & Kauffeld, S. (2016). You think you are an empathic coach? Maybe you should think again. The difference between perceptions of empathy vs. empathic behavior after a person-centred coaching training. *Coaching: An International Journal of Theory, Research and Practice, 9*(1), 53–68.

Winum, P. 1995. Anatomy of an executive consultation: Three perspectives. *Consulting Psychology Journal: Practice and Research, 47*(2), 114–121.

Yalom, I. D. (1970). *The theory and practice of group psychotherapy*. New York: Basic Books.

Yalom, I. D., & Elkin, G. (1974). *Every day gets a little closer: A twice-told therapy*. New York: Basic Books.

Yedreshteyn, S. (2009). A qualitative investigation of the implementation of an internal executive coaching program in a global corporation, grounded in organizational psychology theory. *Dissertation Abstracts International, 69*(7), 4471B.

Yin, R. K. 1994. *Case study research: Design and methods*. Thousand Oaks, CA: Sage.

Zeus, P., & Skiffington, S. (2002). *The complete guide to coaching at work*. New York: McGraw-Hill.

# Index

Printed in Great Britain
by Amazon

33142321R00139